How to Build and Manage an

Entertainment Law Practice

by Gary Greenberg

ABA

LAW PRACTICE MANAGEMENT SECTION

Commitment to Quality: The Law Practice Management Section is committed to quality in our publications. Our authors are experienced practitioners in their fields. Prior to publication, the contents of all our books are rigorously reviewed by experts to ensure the highest quality product and presentation. Because we are committed to serving our readers' needs, we welcome your feedback on how we can improve future editions of this book. We invite you to fill out and return the comment card at the back of this book.

Cover design by Gail Patejunas.

Printed in the United States of America.

Library of Congress Catalog Card Number 00-135868
ISBN 1-57073-904-8

05 04 03 02 01 5 4 3 2 1

Discounts are available for books ordered in bulk. Special consideration is given to state bars, CLE programs, and other bar-related organizations. Inquire at Book Publishing, American Bar Association, 750 N. Lake Shore Drive, Chicago, Illinois 60611.

Contents

CHAPTER 5
Getting Set Up and Creating the Right Image 37

CHAPTER 6
Getting Paid (Setting and Collecting Fees) 47

CHAPTER 7
Marketing Your Entertainment Law Practice 57

CHAPTER 8
Keeping the Entertainment Client Happy 63

CHAPTER 9
Keeping the Entertainment Lawyer Happy (General Tips for Managing Stress) 75

CHAPTER 10
Pitfalls of an Entertainment Law Practice 87

Chapter 11
Managing the Workload (Getting the Work Out) 93

CHAPTER 12
Managing the Workload (Information Gathering and Fact Investigation) 113

CHAPTER 13
Managing the Workload (Working with Other Professionals) 121

APPENDIXES

Foreword

A funny thing happened while I was writing this book. I learned a lot about my practice. I can handle the work. However, I realized that I was not as expert at running my business. As respected members of the bar, it is easy for lawyers to lose sight of the fact that we sell services. If we want to be good at it, we should constantly be on the lookout for ways to improve our salesmanship.

The first rule of sales is never to apologize for your product. I am going to break that rule by starting this book with a few disclaimers. First, this is not intended to be a comprehensive manual on how to set up and run a law office. It is specifically about entertainment law. If you are starting a practice for the first time, I recommend reading other material in conjunction with this book. For good nuts-and-bolts advice on everything from how to save money on postage to how to finance your practice with credit cards, consult Jay Foonberg's book *How to Start and Build a Law Practice,* Fourth Edition (American Bar Association, 1999). For that matter, each of the publications in the ABA's "How to Build and Manage" series contains insights useful to the development of any law practice.

Second, any book that purports to characterize an entire field of law must include generalizations. The reality is that every entertainment law practice is unique. More than anything else, what makes entertainment law special is the personalities of those involved, and I don't mean just the clients, but executives and other lawyers as well. This book will give you a first-hand glimpse of what a day in the life of an entertainment lawyer is like. Along the way, I will offer practical suggestions on how to get your foot in the door, get properly set up, network and market yourself to prospective clients, keep your clients happy, avoid mistakes, and manage your time effectively. But beyond the information contained in this book, I hope you enjoy reading it. After all, it's entertainment.

To give you a sense of how I put this book together, the following briefly describes each chapter.

1. *How I Got Started*—Summarizes my career.
2. *Getting Ready (Preparing a Business Plan)*—Gets you thinking about the basic business issues involved in starting your practice.
3. *What Is Entertainment Law?*—Gives you an overview of the field, including who the clients and key players are.
4. *Getting Your Foot in the Door*—Gives you tips on how to break into the business, get clients, and gain experience.
5. *Getting Set Up and Creating the Right Image*—Gives you ideas on how to set up your office and maintain the right image.
6. *Getting Paid (Setting and Collecting Fees)*—Walks you through the pros and cons of different fee arrangements.
7. *Marketing Your Entertainment Law Practice*—Offers suggestions on how to get good clients.
8. *Keeping the Entertainment Client Happy*—Alerts you to typical client concerns and how to address them.
9. *Keeping the Entertainment Lawyer Happy (General Tips for Managing Stress)*—Makes you aware of the unique stresses that an entertainment lawyer faces and how to deal with them.
10. *Pitfalls of an Entertainment Law Practice*—Warns you of the problems you may encounter in building your practice.
11. *Managing the Workload (Getting the Work Out)*—Offers practical suggestions on how to maximize the efficiency of your work habits.
12. *Managing the Workload (Information Gathering and Fact Investigation)*—Gives you nuts-and-bolts advice on how to conduct a client interview.

13. *Managing the Workload (Working with Other Professionals)*—Discusses how you can ease your workload by working with other professionals and lawyers.

At the end of the book, you will find several appendixes. They include samples of retainer and fee letters, a conflict-of-interest waiver, office and computer configurations, and form contracts, as well as articles on the role of the entertainment lawyer and conflicts of interest. Because networking is so fundamental to the development of an entertainment practice, pay particular attention to the detailed resource materials in Appendixes C, E, F, G, and H, which are designed to help you research and network within the entertainment industries. Note that these appendixes are also on the accompanying diskette.

Acknowledgments

I would like to thank the following people: Bill Henslee for recommending me for this project and keeping me on track; Beverly Loder, Tim Johnson, Linda Ravdin, Neal Cox, and the rest of the ABA Law Practice Management Publishing Board; Kimberly DaSilva, Richard Greenstone, Rick Paszkiet, and the Forum on the Entertainment & Sports Industries for their guidance and information; Lachina Publishing Services for their meticulous editing; Mark Litwak for sharing his library with me; Ed McPherson and Owen Sloane for permitting me to reprint their articles on conflicts of interest; Mark Halloran for his insights on "packaging"; Marc Diener for sharing "war stories"; Gary Stiffelman for his sage perspective; every mentor who tutored me along the way, including Allen Leonard, Mario Gonzalez, Jay Cooper, Jeff Light, Chuck Hurewitz, Christine Cuddy, John Flock, Rick Finkelstein, Howard Behar, and Don Engel; my assistant, Tara, for fitting the preparation of this manuscript into her hectic workday and keeping me going; my wife, Kerry, for preparing the office plan and for putting up with my late-night writing sessions (or obsessions); my sister, Sheri, for her help in putting together the business plan chapter; and last, but not least, my parents for convincing me I should go to law school in the first place.

Acknowledgments

About the Author

Gary Greenberg received his B.A. from Brown University in 1979 and earned his J.D. from Boalt Hall and was admitted to the California bar in 1985. From 1986 to 1987, he was an associate in the entertainment department of Finley, Kumble, Wagner, et al. For the next two years, he was an associate in the music department of Cooper, Epstein & Hurewitz before starting his own practice in 1989. His current clients include Sergio Mendes, Jimmy Cliff, The Rippingtons, David Benoit, Larry Carlton, Ramsey Lewis, Spyro Gyra, Craig Chaquico, The Whispers, Shai, Howard Hewett, The '69 Boyz, E-40, MC Ren, Yukmouth, Reel Big Fish, and several independent record companies, industry executives, producers, managers, and writers.

Mr. Greenberg has published the following articles concerning entertainment law:

"The Plight of the Personal Manager in California: A Legislative Solution," *Comm/Ent Law Journal*, Hastings College of Law, Volume 6, Number 4, Summer 1984.

"The Plight of the American Musician: A Study of Comparative Copyright Law and a Proposed Performers' Protection Act," *Loyola Entertainment Law Journal,* Volume 6, 1986.

"Seven Years to Life: The Fight for Free Agency in the Record Business," *Entertainment and Sports Lawyer* (Publication of the American Bar Association), Volume 12, Number 3, Fall 1994.

"Crossing the Thin Line between Manager and Attorney in the Entertainment Industry," *Entertainment and Sports Lawyer* (Publication of the American Bar Association), Volume 14, Number 3, Fall 1996.

He also co-authored with Kashif Michael Jones the popular music industry book *Everything You'd Better Know About the Record Industry,* Brooklyn Boy Books, 1996.

Mr. Greenberg has lectured at music industry seminars and to graduate students. He has also appeared on local radio and television talk shows in Los Angeles.

Mr. Greenberg welcomes inquiries about the book at

garygreenberg@earthlink.net

1 How I Got Started

SO YOU WANT TO BE an entertainment lawyer? Having practiced in the field for fifteen years, I can recommend it to you highly. Although I get burned out from time to time, I still look forward to going into work, which is saying a lot in this day and age. In this book, I will give you a sense of what this specialty is all about and offer practical suggestions on how to build and manage an entertainment law practice.

My journey began before law school. I started singing and playing drums as a child and continue to do so today. After graduating from college, I pursued music full-time for almost three years. Although this was a glorious time for me, I realized that I was not prepared to make music my lifelong profession. As a client, I had dealt with entertainment lawyers and was fascinated by their work, so I went to law school with the sole intention of becoming an entertainment lawyer.

As a rule, firms specializing in entertainment law do not interview at law schools. Therefore, I became one of the few members of my class who did not have a job upon graduation. Instead, after I passed the bar I set about finding a position on my own. My lucky break came from a family friend who was practicing film finance law. He arranged an interview for me at a firm he knew was shorthanded. He warned me that the prospects of employment were dim, since most firms are not anxious to train new associates. As it turned out, however, I was in the right place at the right time. Two junior associates had unexpectedly left and the firm was having difficulty replacing them. I convinced the partners that because of my experience in the entertainment business and my willingness to work twenty-four hours a day, I could relieve some of their workload.

That was my foot in the door. Once inside, I worked tirelessly, which not only endeared me to the partners but accelerated my learning curve. After two years, I was recruited by a smaller, boutique firm that offered me more money and required fewer billable hours. By this point, I knew that to be successful, I needed to get my own clients. I targeted musicians, hoping that, because of my background, I could make them feel comfortable with me and earn their trust. After networking extensively for about two years, I built up a small but profitable client base. When the career of one of my clients suddenly skyrocketed, I set out on my own.

At the time, I was living with two friends who allowed me to use the guest bedroom of the house as a makeshift office. With my half-dozen loyal clients in tow, I used most of my savings to purchase basic equipment—phones, computer, copier, and fax.

At first, I operated on my own, answering my own phones and typing my own letters. By working out of the house and keeping my equipment and support costs to a minimum, I was able to offer services at a lower hourly rate than the firm was charging for my level of experience.

I also supplemented my income by personally managing a few of my clients. As I became busier, I hired a young lawyer who was looking to gain experience in entertainment law. She performed secretarial services in addition to associate work at a modest salary.

As my practice grew, I moved to a larger house with a separate wing of rooms that I converted into an office. I hired a receptionist/secretary and gradually raised my rates.

When my associate left to accept an offer for more money than I could afford to pay her, I began to search for a replacement but quickly realized that doing the work myself made my practice more profitable. I became more selective in accepting new clients and withdrew my representation of clients who were chronic nonpayers or overly demanding of my time. Eventually, I moved to a conventional office and continued to upgrade my client base. And the rest, as they say in Hollywood, is history.

Now, before you sell your house and move to Manhattan to start practicing entertainment law, I should caution you that my experience is not typical. I was lucky. Most aspiring entertainment lawyers spend years trying to get a foot in the door. One colleague of mine spent over six years doing everything from real estate brokerage to litigation to struggling with his own fledgling entertainment practice before finally landing the position he always wanted in business affairs at a prominent record company.

On the other hand, I believe that this is an excellent time to consider starting your own entertainment practice, primarily because of two factors:

1. The trend toward the re-emergence of large entertainment law firms is leaving many small but potentially valuable clients searching for representation.
2. The dynamic technological changes currently reshaping the way entertainment product is produced and activated are creating new areas of specialty for entertainment lawyers.

Both of these topics are discussed in more detail in Chapter 3, What Is Entertainment Law?

As you build your entertainment practice, keep in mind these basic rules:

1. *There Is No Substitute for Experience*—without it, you cannot be successful, but once you get it, you can write your own ticket.
2. *Expect the Unexpected*—entertainment clients, lawyers, and professionals can be eccentric and require special handling.

3. *Build Relationships*—because the golden rule in the entertainment business is that who you know is more important than what you know.
4. *Network As Much As Possible*—it is the best way to get clients.
5. *Protect Your Reputation*—it is the most important asset you possess.
6. *Manage Your Time Effectively*—it is the only way to reduce the stress of a crushing workload.
7. *Image Is Everything*—always act and look like a winner.

In this era of growing disenchantment with traditional areas of legal practice, entertainment law stands out as an exciting and dynamic specialty. One friend of mine from law school who decided to leave the law told me that of all of our school friends, I seem to be the happiest with my work, but to her mind, it was still like having the best stall in the bathroom. Entertainment law is certainly not nirvana, nor is it necessarily right for everyone. But if you are committed to making a go of it, fasten your seatbelt and hold on for the ride of your life.

2 Getting Ready (Preparing a Business Plan)

Dialing for Dollars

I assume that one of the reasons you became a lawyer was for financial security. Unfortunately, law school does not teach how to turn a degree into dollars. Since starting your own practice is like opening a small business, you should have a business plan—not necessarily in a formal sense, but at least a mental blueprint of the kind of practice you envision for yourself. This will force you to come to grips with your strengths, weaknesses, and goals. It will also serve as a road map to keep you on track as your practice develops.

If you do not have business training or experience, do some homework. There is no shortage of good material on how to start a new business. One particularly interesting new book is *The Real World Entrepreneur Field Guide* by David H. Bangs and Linda Pinson (Upstart Publishing Company, 1999). Appendix B contains other recommended literature on the subject.

I Have a Dream

The first step in formulating your plan is to identify your specific interests. Start by breaking down the field of entertainment law into separate areas—for example, music, film, and television. Next, identify the distinctive skills you possess—in other words, what sets you apart from other lawyers. Based on your skills, interests, and contacts, decide in which area you are most likely to succeed. As a practicing musician, I set my sights on music law. You may be a movie buff and want to target clients in film. Or you may have a background in finance that you can use to specialize in film financing.

Going My Way

Once you decide which area of entertainment law you want to target, describe for yourself the type of practice you want. Ask yourself the following questions:

1. Do you enjoy working on your own or with other lawyers? If the latter, do you think you would be more comfortable in a small firm or a large firm? Large firms allow you to offer broad-based services to your clients. On the other hand, the firm's managing committee may not always agree with you that taking chances on up-and-coming entertainment clients is worth the risk. Large firms are often more permissive in footing the bill for seminars and conventions, which can help you network, but they may not appreciate the value of other expenses, such as for client lunches.
2. Are you a wheeler-dealer or a behind-the-scenes type? If you intend to make it on your own, you need entrepreneurial inclinations. Otherwise, you will be better off at a large firm or company where you do not necessarily need to be a rainmaker.
3. Would you rather interact with creative people or with business people? Working with talent can be exciting but unstable. Business clients tend to be more reliable but do not typically request advice on creative issues.
4. Do you want to experiment with nonlegal work, either part-time or eventually full-time? At the outset, supplementing

your income by working as a manager or agent can be an effective way to survive. You may find the combination rewarding and stick with it. You can also use entertainment law as a springboard to develop your own entertainment business.

5. Do you want to combine entertainment work with other legal work, such as litigation? Entertainment litigators are among the most powerful figures in the industry.

At the outset of your career, of course, you may not know exactly where you want to go. Even if you do, you need to be open to change. Opportunities and obstacles will come up that may force you to rethink your plans.

But no matter where you are going, following the basic rules discussed in this book can help you get there. It may seem that if you aspire to an in-house position, as opposed to private practice, you would not need a plan. The truth, however, is that company work and private practice are more similar than different. Maintaining efficient work habits and building relationships are needed for success in both.

Float Like a Butterfly, Sting Like a Bee

Once you have a clear vision of the kind of entertainment practice you want for yourself, put together a game plan for implementing it. Make sure your plan is realistic and can withstand setbacks.

The first step is to identify prospective clients and figure out how to get them. Once clients are on board, the next step is to make sure you can keep them. This means finding out what clients want, and discerning what problems they have that you can solve. These topics are discussed in more detail in Chapter 7, Marketing Your Entertainment Law Practice, and Chapter 8, Keeping the Entertainment Client Happy.

My Practice Is Better Than Your Practice

Next, size up your competition. Start by learning how other entertainment lawyers do business. You can do this not only by reading articles on the subject and attending entertainment law seminars, but by asking entertainment executives and artists what they like and don't like about their lawyers. This will help you determine what you can offer that other lawyers cannot.

In making this assessment, be realistic. At the beginning of your practice, you cannot expect to offer more expertise than established entertainment lawyers. Nor can you claim to have the same contacts. However, you can promise prospective clients that you will be cheaper, faster, and more personally involved in their business affairs. Here's how:

1. Keep your overhead down, so you can offer lower rates than more-established lawyers and be more flexible with fee arrangements. You may find a client who is uncomfortable with paying his lawyer 10 percent of everything he makes, and may be willing to give you a chance if you are willing to charge less. If a client has enough work, offer volume discounts or monthly flat fees. Refer to Chapter 6, Getting Paid (Setting and Collecting Fees), for more information on fee arrangements.
2. Take the time to get to know each client's needs and give them extra attention. Established lawyers are often too busy to pay attention to smaller clients. A prospective client may like the idea of being a big fish in your small pond. Point out that you will handle the work personally, not turn it over to a junior associate as often happens in larger firms.
3. Offer to custom-make agreements for clients to speed up their transactions and save them money.

Looking for Work in All the Wrong Places

In sizing up your competition, don't look solely at other entertainment lawyers. Personal managers, agents, business managers, and other nonlawyers may be negotiating deals for prospective clients, especially in situations where legal fees are an issue. You may convince a client in this position that he would be better off hiring you to handle his business affairs.

Lawyers specializing in other fields, such as litigation, may also be representing clients who would be better served by a full-time entertainment lawyer. I had one prospective client call me who was being offered a recording contract, but was hesitant to accept it because of a prior contract. A friend introduced him to a litigator who recommended that he file a claim for declaratory relief regarding the prior contract before negotiating the new deal. In going over the prior contract with the client, I concluded it was not worth the paper it was written on and had been materially breached by the prior record company. I know from experience that unless artists pursue offers while they are hot, they tend to disappear. Without discrediting the advice the prospective client had received from litigation counsel, I suggested that he disclose the prior contract to the new company and see if they felt inhibited by it. They weren't, and the old company never pursued the matter. In this instance, my understanding of the way the music industry works set me apart from my competition.

Doctor, Lawyer, Indian Chief

A fundamental decision for every new practice is to choose the best organizational structure—sole proprietorship, professional corporation, limited liability corporation, or partnership. A sole proprietorship is the easiest and least expensive way to get started. All you need is a business license and stationery. A partnership is also easy if you are going in with other lawyers. Corporations and limited liability partnerships can offer tax advantages and protection from liability, but add administrative expenses and obligations.

Cash Flow

The next, and perhaps most important, decision is forecasting how much money you will need. Appendix D contains a checklist of expenses for a typical start-up entertainment practice. Beyond the obvious line items for staff, rent, and outside services, don't forget to include your networking and personal expenses.

Obviously, you hope to start generating fees right away. However, your collections may not be sufficient to cover your start-up costs and overhead at first. Prepare a cash flow analysis to give you an idea of how long it will take you to become profitable.

Remember that receivables in an entertainment practice are rarely steady, and you need to account for bad debts.

Brother, Can You Spare a Dime?

Just because you may project a deficit cash flow at the outset of your practice, don't throw in the towel. The following are some short-term financing options to help you get through the early lean months:

1. Personal savings
2. Liquidation of or borrowing against your assets
3. Loans from friends, family, and colleagues
4. Bank or government small business loans
5. Lines of credit and credit cards
6. Income from other work, such as nonentertainment legal work and nonlegal consulting.

In addition to arranging short-term financing, you can minimize early cash flow problems by:

1. Working off retainers. See Chapter 6, Getting Paid (Setting and Collecting Fees), for specifics on retainers.
2. Forming strategic alliances with other professionals, such as in the case of office sharing. Perhaps you know a law firm with overflow work with which you can barter services for rent and access to staff and equipment.
3. Paying bills over time. Many vendors have plans that allow you to postpone payment for a year or so. You can also lease equipment or buy used equipment. You can always upgrade as your cash flow improves.

One Small Step for You, One Giant Leap for Your Practice

Once you figure out how to get up and running, map out a plan for the growth and expansion of your practice. This means targeting new and better clients. It also entails developing new marketing techniques and incurring additional costs. For example, if you start your practice with creative clients but want to add corporate clients, you need to network at different events.

Every thriving practice eventually faces the question whether to hire associates, contract work out, and/or take on partners. This issue is discussed in Chapter 13, Managing the Workload (Working with Other Professionals).

As you read the rest of this book, revisit the issues raised in this chapter. I also recommend Bill Henslee's book *Entertainment Law Careers,* 2d ed. (American Bar Association, 1998), for a candid discussion of the pros and cons of a career in entertainment law.

3 What Is Entertainment Law?

So Misunderstood

Defining entertainment law is more complex than you might think. Generally, it involves the representation of clients who are involved in the business of providing amusement to the public. This can include virtually any endeavor in which intellectual property is created and exploited. The five areas traditionally regarded as entertainment law specialties are film, television, music, book publishing, and live theater. However, since the largest number of entertainment lawyers today make their living servicing the music, film, and television industries, this book will concentrate on those three. Radio, fine art, and advertising are among other significant industries in which entertainment lawyers are used.

Sports law, often grouped with entertainment law, is actually a distinct specialty with its own issues and politics. An interesting trend in sports law is the increasing use of lawyers rather than agents to negotiate athletic contracts. It should be noted that many sports agents are lawyers.

Despite its growing popularity, entertainment law remains largely misunderstood. Florida is the only state whose bar officially recognizes the specialty, and few outside of the entertainment industries know what entertainment lawyers actually do.

So Special

Although the entertainment industries share many legal concepts, each has its own customs and practices. Primarily because of the time required to maintain industry relationships, it is not feasible to be a general practitioner in all areas of entertainment law. As a result, most entertainment lawyers specialize in one field. It is also common to concentrate on areas within a field. For example, a film lawyer may subspecialize in film financing, or "packaging" as it is sometimes called. The advantages of specialization are discussed at the end of Chapter 7, Marketing Your Entertainment Law Practice.

Despite the tendency toward specialization, a practitioner is well advised to have a working knowledge of related areas. This is because they often overlap—not just on a working level, say in the case of an actor recording an album, but on a corporate level. Most of today's major film, television, and record companies have affiliated entities functioning in other entertainment areas under the same corporate umbrella.

Some firms employ specialists in different areas to offer clients a spectrum of representation. In addition, there are lawyers in other fields, such as tax, corporations, and litigation, that gear their practices to service entertainment clients. Although not entertainment lawyers per se, they may advise clients about entertainment contracts.

Going Where No Lawyer Has Gone Before

Generally, entertainment lawyers negotiate and prepare contracts for rights and services, resolve disputes, orchestrate mergers and acquisitions, and counsel clients about the customs and practices of the entertainment industries. However, most entertainment lawyers do much more, often venturing into nontraditional legal territory. Therein lies the primary allure of the specialty—as well as the pitfalls. It is also what distinguishes entertainment law from most other areas. On a normal day, I may reassure a client about the merits of an artistic endeavor or investigate the background of a potential employer for an entertainment executive.

Accomplished entertainment lawyers are not just negotiators and dispute resolvers, but power brokers. In this role, entertainment lawyers often function more as business consultants than as legal advisers. One noted commentator succinctly defined the specialty as follows: "The business realities of the entertainment industry give flesh to skeletal legal principles, thereby creating a body of law referred to as entertainment law" (*Entertainment Law,* 2d ed., by T. Selz, M. Simensky, P. Acton, and R. Lind, West Group, 1998). To make the point another way, one prominent entertainment lawyer I interviewed explained that he views his role as that of chief executive officer of his clients' businesses in that he makes virtually every business decision for them.

Since the survival of any business depends upon the creation of money-making opportunities, it often falls to the entertainment lawyer to solicit and consummate deals for clients. For most entertainment lawyers, expertise in contracts and intellectual property law is simply not as fundamental to success as skill at deal making. To be sure, clients will seek your advice on the enforceability of agreements, but they will also expect you to know the going rate for their services. This knowledge cannot be obtained in school, but only on the battlefield. Ergo, the first basic rule of entertainment law is that *there is no substitute for experience.* Get it however you can.

Deal of the Century

The art of deal making is a combination of persuasion, intuition, and knowledge. The first two are determined in large part by your personality. The third derives from an understanding of how the entertainment industry works. As an overview, most entertainment product goes through three stages of evolution: creation, production, and distribution. To be an effective deal maker, you need to understand how each part of the process affects the others. In Appendixes C and G, you will find lists of informative entertainment industry publications, seminars, and conventions that you can use to educate yourself. For an interesting discussion on the dynamics of deal making, I also recommend *Getting to Yes* by R. Fischer (Penguin Books, 1991) and *Deal Power* by Marc Diener (Owl Books/Henry Holt, 1998).

One manager client of mine defines show business as part "show" and part "business." Many share his view that the line between the two is uncrossable. Simply put, creative people create, producers produce, and lawyers transact. If you aspire to be a difference maker, don't limit yourself to this narrow perspective. You will be a more impassioned advocate if you take the time to appreciate the value of an original screenplay, and your ability to sell that creative product will be enhanced if you understand what goes into marketing and promoting it.

The Wild, Wild West

If you are accustomed to working in other business areas, you may be surprised by the wide-open nature of the entertainment industry. Although it has become increasingly corporate in the 1990s, powerful figures continue to emerge out of nowhere, creating a "street" environment in which the participants seem free to make their own rules.

There are few codified regulations governing entertainment transactions. For a discussion of the two best-known entertainment-related statutes—the so-called seven-year rule and the guaranteed annual compensation provision—see my article "Seven Years to Life: The Fight for Free Agency in the Record Business" in Appendix A-2. This lack of regulation allows lawyers to be creative in structuring deals and resolving disputes. Entertainment lawyers are often empowered by their clients to make final and immediate decisions.

Strength in Numbers

Particularly in film and television, the financial burden of production and the influence of unions and agents limit the lawyer's influence somewhat. In these areas, unions wield considerable influence and act as a counterbalance to the bargaining power of distributors. In the golden age of film, entertainment "contracts" were little more than contracts of adhesion that were not subject to meaningful negotiation. Today, the demand for name actors and directors and the perceived value they bring to film and television projects has shifted much of the bargaining power away from the studios.

The most influential unions are the Writers Guild of America (WGA), the Directors Guild of America (DGA), the Screen Actors Guild (SAG), and the American Federation of Television and Radio Artists (AFTRA). Their policies are widely used to determine minimum compensation and credit issues, even for nonunion projects. There are also unions for non-talent, or "below the line," workers, such as make-up and wardrobe artists, who are governed by the International Alliance of Theatrical and Stage Employees (IATSE). The American Federation of Musicians (AFM) governs musical performers.

Familiarizing yourself with these collective bargaining agreements is a good way to learn the customs and practices of the entertainment industries. Appendix G gives contact information on them.

Part of the Team

An unusual feature of entertainment law is the lack of clearly defined duties for lawyers. To put the role of the entertainment lawyer in context, the typical team representing an artist consists of a personal manager, a talent agent, a business manager, a publicist, and a lawyer. A personal manager is charged with coordinating the client's daily activities and overseeing the client's career, while a talent agent is responsible for procuring employment. Managers and agents may assume different roles depending on the type of client and the area of entertainment. For example, a film composer's agent may perform all career duties for a client, whereas a record composer may rely exclusively on a manager for the same tasks. A business manager handles the client's finances and a publicist is responsible for molding the client's image.

Personal managers typically commission 15 to 20 percent of a client's aggregate earnings, subject to specifically negotiated exclusions. Talent agents commission 10 percent of personal appearance income, package fees, and other agency-generated earnings. Business managers work either on an hourly basis (typically $100 to $300 an hour), for a monthly flat fee, or on a percentage basis (generally 5 percent of aggregate earnings). Publicists work on retainers (usually $2000 to $5000 a month).

In music, the manager typically occupies the most influential position, although some music clients prefer to handle their own careers. In film and television, the agent is the power player—in many cases there is no personal manager. Recently, many powerful television and film agents have left their agencies to become managers instead. This is because licensed talent agents must comply with the California Labor and Professions Code and with union regulations. Managers are not currently regulated. The absence of regulation enables managers to charge whatever the client will accept and to engage in business practices that agents are not allowed to, such as signing clients to their own business ventures.

The only position on the team that is not discretionary is that of the lawyer. In many circumstances, lawyers, knowingly or unknowingly, act as managers and agents themselves. This is particularly common in music and film packaging where the lawyer can have a hand in virtually every aspect of the client's career. The extent of the lawyer's involvement in providing career guidance for clients will depend on whether the client has a manager and/or an agent, the sophistication of those representatives, and the client's confidence in the lawyer's ability to handle those responsibilities. For a discussion of the pros and cons of crossing the line between lawyer and manager, see my article "Crossing the Thin Line between Manager and Attorney in the Entertainment Industry" in Appendix A-1.

Entertainment lawyers are so interwoven into the fabric of the entertainment industries that many forsake the practice of law to become clients themselves, and many prominent industry figures are former lawyers.

Law and Order

Since creative people are often unsophisticated and insecure, they are easy prey for the many unscrupulous opportunists looking to feed on their success. The lawyer can be the one safe harbor in this sea of troubles. As professionals who are governed by codes of conduct and regulated by state bars, it is felt we can be trusted. In addition, as professionals trained in the art of negotiation and educated in the complicated issues surrounding intellectual property rights, lawyers are uniquely qualified to oversee complex entertainment transactions. Finally, the opportunity for a client to share information that will remain confidential is prized in an arena where secrets are sacred.

In the House

Entertainment law is practiced in a number of ways. The primary distinction is between private practice and in-house employment. Every major record, film, and television company employs its own full-time in-house lawyers to implement the company's policies. Although the basic policies of many entertainment companies are similar, there are important differences, and lawyers in private practice must have a working knowledge of these differences to advise clients choosing between them. In-house lawyers must also be familiar with the policies of their competitors to argue the merits of their practices on a comparative basis.

Most entertainment companies have separate "business affairs" and "legal" departments. Generally, the business affairs department handles deal making. This involves negotiating the basic terms of agreements and trouble-shooting disputes. Like lawyers in private practice, they may be given virtual autonomy over negotiations. The legal department prepares the contracts and drafts provisions negotiated by business affairs. Sometimes these duties overlap and in smaller entertainment companies frequently are combined. In addition, many companies have general counsel to oversee internal corporate issues, as well as to supervise litigation and other noncontractual matters. Finally, some entertainment companies have separate copyright departments with lawyers and paralegals to handle the licensing of rights.

Not all business affairs executives are lawyers, although most are, and even those who are not can usually hold their own in negotiations with accomplished entertainment lawyers. Business affairs executives may also take an active role in the production process, often evaluating the viability of projects and supervising them to completion. Along the way, the business affairs executive may be called upon to make creative decisions and may also recommend new projects for production. That is one of the main reasons business affairs lawyers frequently ascend to top-level management positions.

Smaller entertainment companies usually employ private lawyers until they can afford to staff their own legal departments. Many companies also employ private lawyers to handle specific deals or overflow work.

The Many Faces of Private Practice

There are many different types of private entertainment practice—solo practitioners, small firms (generally consisting of two to seven lawyers), medium-sized or "boutique" firms (generally consisting of seven to fifteen lawyers), and larger firms. Since the practice of entertainment law is so unlike other areas of legal practice, especially in terms of nontraditional billing arrangements and the need for extensive networking, the entertainment departments within larger firms often function like firms within firms. The recent trend is for solo practitioners and small firms to join larger firms, mirroring in some ways the trend in the entertainment industry in general toward centralization of power. This trend is discussed in more detail later in this chapter.

Finally, there are a number of lawyers who practice entertainment law part-time, some in connection with other areas of legal practice and some in conjunction with nonlegal work, such as personal management.

No Such Thing As a Typical Client

It is impossible to describe the typical entertainment client. Musicians, songwriters, producers (of film, television, and music), directors, actors, executive producers, screenwriters, television writers, novelists, executives, composers, agents, managers, record companies, film distributors, television production companies, engineers, editors, models, radio stations, fine artists, advertising companies, and athletes are just some of the clients who may require the services of an entertainment lawyer. Entertainers can range from children who are under the supervision and control of their parents/legal guardians to seasoned performers. Some entertainment clients are highly educated and formally trained. Others are unsophisticated and untrained. Some are responsible, stable people. Others seem to be in a constant state of disorganization. This is why my second rule of entertainment law is *expect the unexpected.*

You Don't Have to Be a Star

Entertainment clients are no different from other legal clients in expecting competent representation. However, many people in entertainment also expect their lawyer to give their matters top priority, dropping everything at a moment's notice to attend to their concerns.

Entertainment clients expect more than just attention. They want the best and the brightest representing them. This not only assuages their insecurities, but validates their worth to their peers. In a business where image is everything, having a well-known lawyer is an important part of the package.

The Name Game

The by-product of this is the name-dropping game. If not the first, then certainly the most important, question a prospective client will ask you is, "Who do you represent?" The obvious paradox is that prospective clients expect you to have other notable clients, but none as impressive as they are.

If you are not familiar with opposing counsel, you may find yourself playing the same question-and-answer game every time you enter a new negotiation. Not surprisingly, your client list is the yardstick by which your success in entertainment law is measured. The quality of your work is not as important as who you represent, and being a good lawyer does not guarantee you good clients. For techniques on attracting and keeping quality entertainment clients, refer to Chapter 7, Marketing Your Entertainment Law Practice, and Chapter 8, Keeping the Entertainment Client Happy.

Tell Me You Love Me

Entertainment clients expect loyalty. Because the entertainment industries are so closely knit, you are likely to represent competitors. These may not be direct competitors in any formal sense, but merely other companies, composers, artists, producers, directors, or writers in the same field. Whether a particular client is right for a particular project or not, he will expect you to recommend him for it, even if you represent more-qualified clients. For a discussion of conflict-of-interest issues unique to entertainment law, refer to Chapter 10, Pitfalls of an Entertainment Law Practice.

Most clients want you to appreciate their work. As a result, although you may be tempted at times, never criticize your client's endeavors. Even the most innocent comment can be taken as a vote of no confidence. Having learned this lesson well, the approach of one experienced manager I represent is "I don't smell 'em, I sell 'em."

R-E-S-P-E-C-T

Finally, entertainment clients deserve respect. This should be obvious, but I have known entertainment lawyers who view clients as nothing more than spoiled brats incapable of making their own decisions. I was told by several experienced lawyers on my way up that clients should be kept in the dark to maintain control over them.

In my experience, most entertainment clients are intelligent. If you encourage clients to read their agreements, you may be surprised when a client raises an issue you may have overlooked or makes a helpful suggestion.

You Oughta Be in Pictures

One of the more rewarding aspects of an entertainment law practice is the opportunity to see and hear the tangible results of your behind-the-scenes work. The arts are a favorite pastime, and everyone has memories of their favorite songs, movies, and television shows. Many entertainment lawyers are (or were) creative themselves and for them, involvement in the process has added meaning.

You've Got a Friend in Me

Another attractive aspect of the area is the opportunity to become a "counselor" in the truest sense of the word. My clients rely upon my judgment for many day-to-day decisions. As a result, I forge relationships that are more than just attorney/client and continue long after a case is resolved. I am proud to count among my friends many clients who are sensitive and caring people—and, of course, always entertaining.

Never a Dull Moment

Whatever else can be said about entertainment law, it is certainly not boring. Although many of the contractual tasks are repetitive, every day brings new challenges. Intellectual property and the uses that can be made of it are myriad and ever-changing. For example, when a song is written, rights may be negotiated for the recording of that song in a phonorecord, the synchronization of that song in a motion picture or television soundtrack, the use of the title of that song as the title of a new work, the public performance of that song on radio, television, and in clubs, and the adaptation of that song by different performers. Each of these transactions requires input from an entertainment lawyer.

The representation of entertainment clients can also segue into other areas of legal practice. Entertainment clients have tax issues, they marry and divorce, they set up corporations, they buy and sell homes, and yes, they find themselves in lawsuits, both civil and criminal. This creates the opportunity for meaningful referrals, or if your heart desires, for you to develop other expertise.

One prominent entertainment lawyer built his entertainment practice from a criminal defense practice. After successfully defending some high-profile criminal prosecutions for artists, he obtained their trust and started to handle their business affairs.

Poor, Broke, and Lonely

The negative aspects of most entertainment law practices are not unlike those in other professions—namely, long hours, stressful working conditions, and sometimes tedious work. One of the negatives unique to an entertainment practice is dealing with the temperamental nature of artists, their representatives, and executives. Because success for an entertainer can be difficult to achieve and fleeting once achieved, entertainment clients can be insecure. The pressure to produce art that the public will embrace is enormous and can cause moodiness. I often remark to aspiring entertainment lawyers that the work is not nearly as difficult as managing the clients.

As an example, one short-lived client of mine who was having trouble finding meaningful production assignments barged into my office one day when I was at lunch angrily demanding his files from my assistant. When I returned, he told me that he was leaving because he could not tolerate my not returning his phone calls immediately and accused all lawyers of being arrogant. This was the same client who earlier that day had told me how pleased he was that I had resolved a complicated dispute for him and that he was coming in to pay his bill.

The difficulty in maintaining consistent receivables is perhaps the most serious problem entertainment lawyers encounter. Since entertainment clients may come into money for the first time in their lives, they can experience difficulty assuming financial responsibility. It is not uncommon for a young client to receive a substantial advance on a new deal one month and call me the next month claiming to be broke, without having paid taxes or set aside any savings. As a result, legal fees can be a burden for entertainment clients and may go unpaid during difficult times in their careers. Possible solutions to this problem are offered in Chapter 6, Getting Paid (Setting and Collecting Fees).

Show Me the Money

Although this is a bit of a generalization, many entertainment clients think short-term when it comes to their contracts, and may not always allow you to be as thorough as you might like. Since the flow of income for most entertainment clients is irregular, when a lucrative deal is on the table, they want it closed immediately. Clients in this position, particularly if they are unsophisticated, are less likely to be concerned with the ramifications of contractual provisions than they are with how quickly they can get to work. See Chapter 11, Managing the Workload (Getting the Work Out), for tips on how to conclude transactions efficiently.

Trend Setting

Entertainment law is a relatively new specialty. The first entertainment lawyers literally fell into the field in the 1960s when the use of sophisticated contracts became commonplace. Before that time film studios monopolized the market and dictated terms. With the popularization of television and records, the business of entertainment came of age.

It took several decades for entertainment lawyers to catch up. The early practitioners were primarily business attorneys who were handed entertainment contracts to negotiate. In contrast, the new generation of entertainment lawyers have been weaned on the specialty and are not afraid to flex their creative muscle.

New Media

Perhaps the most startling new developments affecting the entertainment industry and the practice of entertainment law involve new technology. The information highway has taken the efficiency of research and communication to previously unimagined levels. These developments have also opened up new areas of specialty like multimedia law, which encompasses the exploitation of entertainment product through multiple media, such as interactive audiovisual devices. For a detailed discussion of the subject, I recommend Mark Litwak's book *MULTIMEDIA Producer's Handbook: A Legal and Distribution Guide* (Silman-James Press, 1998).

The technology revolution has also created new areas of controversy for entertainment lawyers. Every segment of the entertainment industry is grappling with ways to adapt its traditional business practices to the ever-changing technological landscape. Proprietary issues have become paramount. Not surprisingly, entertainment lawyers are at the forefront of the Internet game.

Lean and Mean

Another interesting trend throughout the entertainment industries has been the corporatization of what used to be a culture driven by charismatic individuals. In the free-spending 1980s, entertainment lawyers worked out of high-rent suites decorated with opulent art and dined in expensive restaurants, just like their executive counterparts. For an entertaining account of executive excess in the entertainment industry, I recommend *Hit and Run* by Nancy Griffin and Kim Masters (Simon & Schuster, 1997). Although the spirit of this excess lives on, more attention has been paid to the bottom line since the mid-1990s.

Most entertainment companies have adopted the same bottom-line attitude. Inside the major record companies, television networks, and film studios, oversight committees have been instructed to cut fat. Many observers have bemoaned this shift as a departure from the days when artistic integrity was more important than commercial success. They argue that with more emphasis placed on economically viable projects that will produce immediate results, less patience is available for the development of cutting-edge art. Company executives disagree, arguing that the streamlining of their operations allows them more resources to devote to truly deserving projects. The bottom line for aspiring entertainment lawyers is that there are fewer legal positions available at most companies and fewer new projects in production. Layoffs and consolidation of legal departments have forced many in-house lawyers to put in longer hours and take on more responsibility.

Declaration of Independents

In many instances, smaller, independent companies have picked up the slack. For evidence of this, you need only watch the industry awards shows (the Academy Awards in film, the Emmy Awards in television, and the Grammy Awards in music) to see how many independents are taking home the bacon these days.

Until recently, large film studios, television networks, and major record companies maintained virtual strangleholds on their respective industries. That is not to say that the so-called majors have relinquished control of the market, especially if you take into account their financial interests in many independents.

In film, the current major studios are generally considered to be Walt Disney, Warner Bros., Sony, Universal, and Paramount. In television, the Columbia Broadcasting System (CBS), the National Broadcasting Company (NBC), and the American Broadcasting Companies (ABC) remain the big three, but have been challenged by the Fox Broadcasting Company, the United-Paramount Network, and the Warner Bros. Television Network. In music, Sony, Warner/Elektra/Asylum (WEA), the Universal Music Group (UMG), EMI Music Distribution (EMD), and the Bertlesman Music Group (BMG) are on top.

Four of the larger film independents are MGM, Dreamworks, New Line Cinema, and Miramax. Some of the better-known cable operators (many of whom are owned by Time-Warner) are Home Box Office (HBO), USA Network, ESPN, Music Television (MTV), Turner Broadcasting System (TBS), and Cable News Network (CNN). In music, RED, Koch, TVT, and Navarre are some of the more active independent distributors.

The power of the major entertainment companies extends beyond their ability to sell product. They set the parameters of agreements and establish industry custom and practice. In most cases, smaller companies follow their lead. On the other hand, some independents have developed creative deal structures to compete for product. For example, an independent company may be more willing than a major to enter into a joint-venture arrangement with an artist or producer who is prepared to share the financial risk of a project in exchange for co-ownership and control. Industry commentators have also theorized that the inability of the majors to adapt to the changing technological landscape will create new opportunities for independents.

At the same time, many of the major companies have consolidated into even larger conglomerates, absorbing smaller companies and merging with other majors. An example is Seagram's acquisition of MCA/Universal and then Polygram, creating the largest record company in history. Another example is Viacom's acquisitions of Paramount Pictures, MTV, Black Entertainment Television

(BET), and Blockbuster Entertainment and then its subsequent merger with CBS Corp. What this means for entertainment lawyers is that executives are now answerable to boards of directors and shareholders, and many deals that would have been made in a single telephone call must now be put through multilevel approvals.

Interestingly, the same trend can be seen in the reemergence of large entertainment law firms. In the wake of the demise of several prominent entertainment firms in the 1980s, powerful boutique practices emerged. Recently, many of these entertainment law boutiques have added solo practitioners, acquired smaller entertainment firms, and/or merged with larger firms to take advantage of lawyers in other areas, such as corporation, tax, and patent law. In some ways, this is making it harder for lawyers on their own or practicing in small firms to compete for big clients. On the other hand, it is making it easier for them to attract smaller clients who may not be able to afford a big firm retainer.

One effective way to keep up with trends in the entertainment industry is to subscribe to industry trade publications and entertainment law periodicals. You can also subscribe to an e-mail clipping service to locate articles about your specific areas of interest. Refer to Appendixes C, E, G, and H for lists of resource materials.

4 Getting Your Foot in the Door

Catch-22

Every successful entertainment lawyer has his or her own story of how he or she achieved success, but the common denominators are getting a foot in the door and building a client base once you do so. If you are not lucky enough to have entertainment clients fall in your lap, you need to learn by working on someone else's. The catch-22 is that established entertainment lawyers are hesitant to hire associates without experience. So how do you gain experience unless someone gives you a chance? Certainly, you can become educated by attending seminars and reading entertainment law materials. However, education is not a substitute for experience.

The frustrating dilemma that confronts many aspiring entertainment lawyers is that prospective employers often insist on extraordinary academic credentials and/or prior experience in a name firm as a prerequisite to employment. Because the competition for entertainment law positions is so intense, prospective employers may not take the time to look beyond your class ranking as an indication of your potential value to their firm. The bottom line is that if you are not from a top-ten law school, or near the top of your class, you may need to work harder at landing a position in entertainment law. If that position eludes you despite your best efforts, start your own practice.

Breaking and Entering

Any discussion of how to get your foot in the door must begin with the golden rule of the entertainment industry: *Who you know is more important than what you know.* Getting in touch with working entertainment lawyers and executives by whatever means necessary is the best way to break in. During the course of negotiations, I frequently learn of new positions. Most entry-level jobs can be found at major entertainment companies. This is because companies, especially larger ones, are best able to train new lawyers.

If you are in law school or can afford to work for free, an internship at an entertainment company can be an effective way to get on-the-job training and set yourself up for a paying position.

Once you obtain experience at a company, you can make the transition to private practice. If you put in enough time at a company, you may be able to do overflow work for them when you set out on your own. After all, you will already be familiar with their policies. You can also use the relationships you develop at the company to obtain referrals. This will give you a headstart in building your own practice.

Many in-house lawyers prefer their work to private practice and never look to move. The in-house lawyer is not required to obtain clients, nor to meet billable hour and receivable quotients. It is also generally believed that in-house lawyers work fewer hours, although many of my friends in legal and business affairs would disagree with this.

Reach Out and Touch Someone

Although you may target a particular area of entertainment law as part of your business plan, it is a good idea to contact as many companies as possible throughout the entertainment industries when searching for your first position. This includes major management firms and talent agencies. Experience is invaluable, even in an area outside your plan. Once you have it, you can virtually write your own ticket and settle wherever you want.

Appendix E gives comprehensive contact information on entertainment lawyers, entertainment companies, management firms, and talent agencies.

Do not blindly send in your résumé to the personnel department; rather, do some investigating and develop personal contacts. This could be a nonlawyer who could put you in contact with a lawyer at the company. Once you develop a contact, stay in touch with that person, even if there are no immediate positions available. As with most things in life, getting what you want is often a function of being in the right place at the right time.

In putting together your résumé, be specific about any entertainment law-related experience you may have, including the types of agreements you may have drafted and negotiated.

It may be a bitter pill to swallow if you have already paid dues in another field, but be prepared to take a hit in compensation at first. Many entry-level in-house entertainment law positions do not pay the same as positions in other non-entertainment companies, especially if you are starting over in terms of seniority. Since entertainment is such a coveted field, lawyers are often asked to take entry-level entertainment law positions at below market salaries.

If you are committed to private practice, focus on firms in Los Angeles, New York, and, in music, Nashville as well. When approaching entertainment law firms, the best selling point you can have is existing clients, or access to clients. Another good approach is a willingness to continue to practice in your current area of specialty in exchange for the opportunity to work on entertainment matters. You should be cautious of this approach, however, as I know many lawyers to whom such promises were not kept.

Target larger firms. Like established entertainment companies, they are more likely to hire an inexperienced lawyer than small firms or solo practitioners are. If you approach a small firm, be flexible. Offer to work at a reduced salary, or even part-time, in exchange for experience. After a year or two, you will magically be transformed into a valuable commodity.

Reach for the Stars

In your search, do not limit yourself to entertainment lawyers. As mentioned earlier, some litigation, tax, and business lawyers may be specializing in the representation of entertainment clients. If any of these practices is more in line with your experience, this may be a good way to get your foot in the door.

Many of the top entertainment law litigators have expertise in entertainment law. This is because not only does effective entertainment litigation require a working knowledge of the underlying transactions that are typically the subject of litigation, but the settlement of those matters usually involves negotiation of new agreements. You may find an entertainment litigation practice rewarding on its own and stick with it.

One good way to come in contact with entertainment lawyers is to attend entertainment law seminars. Another is to join associations and organizations that deal with entertainment law and network within those organizations. A list of leading entertainment law seminars, associations, and organizations can be found in Appendix F.

Up and Coming

To build your own practice, you need to develop clients. The bad news is that there is no easy way to get good entertainment clients. The good news is that it is not difficult to find up-and-coming clients whom you can use to build a practice—there are more entertainment clients who need assistance than there are qualified professionals to service them. Many aspiring entertainment clients do not have the resources to pay for an experienced entertainment lawyer and may be attempting to negotiate deals on their own. In the early stages of your practice, it may be necessary to take chances on clients who cannot afford to pay. You never know when one of them will get lucky and take you along.

The key is to put yourself in places where you will come into contact with prospective clients. This means going to clubs and concerts, the theater, and, if possible, recording studios, television tapings, video shoots, and other venues where entertainment product is produced and performed. It could also include parties and other social functions if you have an entrée into that scene. Clients can also be found at showcases, workshops, industry seminars, and conventions dedicated to aspiring talent. For a list of some of the better-known showcases, industry seminars, organizations, and conventions, refer to Appendix G. Local entertainment trade publications also often contain advertisements by unknown artists and fledgling entertainment businesses seeking representation.

The Slippery Slope

Undertaking representation of unproven talent and start-up entertainment companies requires making subjective decisions about their likelihood of success. To say the least, this is a slippery slope. As a young lawyer, I thought I could recognize talent. It was only after many disappointing experiences that I realized no one can predict artistic success. In deciding which clients to take, look for objective criteria that might earmark them for success. The kind of indicia you should look for include whether they have a résumé of entertainment work, other reputable representatives on board, and/or interest from other industry insiders. However, the bottom line is that you must count on some good fortune along the way. The more experience you get dealing with up-and-coming clients, the more proficient you will become at distinguishing contenders from pretenders.

Down and Out

Although working with developing clients is a good way to start your practice, it is time-consuming and risky. It can be difficult to find meaningful deals even for established clients, let alone untested ones. For tips on shopping deals for entertainment clients, refer to "Shop 'Til You Drop" in Chapter 11, Managing the Workload (Getting the Work Out). Since most companies do not accept unsolicited material, entertainment lawyers are among a handful of people who have access, but you still have to earn the respect of creative executives. If you do not represent quality packages, you will find your access cut off.

Networking

More effective, and certainly more dignified than turning yourself into a talent scout, is to make contact with people who are in a position to introduce you to prospective clients. A personal introduction from a reputable industry insider is infinitely preferable to rushing past security to get backstage at entertainment events. Again, there is no magic formula. The bottom line: *Network as much as possible.* For an interesting discussion of the networking game, read *Dig Your Well Before You're Thirsty,* by Harvey MacKay (Doubleday & Co., 1999).

On the Road Again

A willingness and ability to travel can help broaden your networking potential. Because Los Angeles, New York, and in music, Nashville, are the centers of most entertainment business, promising clients in those areas are likely to be scooped up by established entertainment lawyers. You are less likely to encounter competition for clients off the beaten track.

Two Heads Are Better Than One

If you gain entertainment clients before you have experience, the question remains, how do you provide competent representation without training? As in most business-oriented practices, much of what an entertainment lawyer does relies on common sense and a basic understanding of contracts. There are also many good publications that describe the nomenclature of entertainment contracts and discuss topics in entertainment law. A list of publications can be found in Appendix H. If unsophisticated clients understand that you and they are starting out together, you may be able to meet their expectations through trial and error. If you encounter a client who is in a position to negotiate a contract that is over your head, you might look for assistance from an experienced entertainment lawyer.

I was recently approached, through a mutual friend, by a lawyer practicing in another field who had developed a few entertainment clients. One of those clients was being offered his own production company, and the lawyer asked me to work with him on the matter. On meeting both the lawyer and the prospective client, I was sufficiently impressed with both to agree. In this way, the lawyer got some on-the-job training while still providing quality representation to his client. This also gave him a "foot in the door" for prospective employment with me.

5

Getting Set Up and Creating the Right Image

THE ENTERTAINMENT INDUSTRIES are built on images. Hence, an essential rule is that your *image is everything*. Begin by making sure your office environment projects the image of a thriving practice. This means being in a first-class location with attractive furnishings and artwork, even if you have to lease space from an established firm to start.

Location, Location, Location

Most entertainment law is practiced in New York and Los Angeles, and in music, Atlanta and Nashville as well. Although the practice of entertainment law is expanding beyond these markets, there remains a bias against lawyers in other areas, even though there are many fine lawyers in markets such as San Francisco, Seattle, Chicago, Detroit, Philadelphia, Washington, Boston, Miami, and Houston. Interestingly, regional bias exists even between established practitioners in different cities. New York lawyers tend to have New York clients and Los Angeles lawyers tend to have Los

Angeles clients. More than a function of convenience, there is a perception in many sectors of the entertainment industry that business is done differently on each coast. To avoid being left out, many large firms maintain bicoastal offices.

Within the larger cities, certain locations have a concentration of entertainment-related offices that cater to entertainment professionals. In Los Angeles, for example, Century City, Beverly Hills, and Santa Monica are prestige addresses. In New York, midtown Manhattan is the best place to be.

Whether or not you can afford to be in the high-rent district, make sure you are in a location that is close to the center of the action. This not only facilitates networking, but enhances your credibility.

The Trappings of Success

Your office should be as upscale as possible. Entertainment clients are impressed with the trappings of success, and visitors will scrutinize every aspect of your office, from your choice of lighting to the design of your desk. Expensive furnishings, artwork, and antiques create the impression that you are a winner.

Use artwork specific to your area of practice. In the music business, no self-respecting office should be without its share of gold and platinum records. Ask your clients for records of their successful projects. Offer to pay if cost is an issue. In the film and television industries, posters and other memorabilia are appropriate.

Make sure convenient parking is available. A valet parking option is preferable, but not essential. Validate parking if you can afford to.

Have a Seat

Although the configuration of your office will vary depending upon the size of your practice, there are certain unusual features to keep in mind. Appendix I shows a sample office configuration for a solo practitioner. First, have a large and well-appointed reception area where clients can hang out. Make a guest phone available, and display current publications specific to your area of practice. You can also include books of interest in your area. The reception area should be as separate from the rest of your office space as possible. You do not want clients to overhear discussions with other clients, particularly since some entertainment clients can be loud and disruptive.

Your personal office should be as large as possible with a separate seating area, preferably with a couch. Even if good seating in front of the desk is available, clients will inevitably drift to the couch to feel more at ease.

It is usually best to see clients in your office, as opposed to a conference room, unless you are seeing a large group of people or your media center is located in the conference room. If you are leasing office space in a firm or are in an executive suite and the conference room is better appointed than your cubbyhole, by all means schedule meetings when the conference room is available.

Listen to the Music

Have stereo and audiovisual equipment at your disposal, either in your office or in a conference room. This should include a big screen, high-resolution television and video player (in VHS and DVD formats), and a stereo with music capabilities in various formats (cassette, compact disc, and digital audio tape). This equipment should be as state-of-the-art as possible if you intend to use it to audition projects. Have background music playing, as well as MTV, Black Entertainment Television (BET), or Video Hits One (VH1) for a music lawyer and the Sundance Channel, Entertainment (E) Television, or the Independent Film Channel (IFC) for a film and television lawyer.

Files, Files, Everywhere

Make sure you have sufficient space to expand your filing needs. In order to save space, periodically remove inactive files, box them up, and place them in separate storage facilities. Remember to label the boxes and keep track of the files inside.

Employ a system that allows you to locate files quickly. You may want to keep a few file cabinets close at hand for important, current matters. Other active, but less pressing, client files can be kept in a file room. Keep separate file cabinets for contract forms and billing information, and locate as many of your files as possible out of the sight of clients. You may be comforted by having your most active files on your desk. However, it is more efficient to let your assistant keep track of them. Otherwise, you can find yourself frantically searching for a file at the most inopportune moment.

Larger firms number their client files and keep a central database that logs them in and out. This is not necessary in a smaller office, but you should label your file cabinets alphabetically. Individual client files can be organized by matter and/or by date. Paperwork for large deals is often best kept in separate files that can be numbered sequentially and/or by date.

I recommend using legal-size four- or six-section end tab classification folders with dividers for your individual files. I also use classification pocket holders to keep executed documents separate. For larger clients, entire folders can be devoted to executed documents. I suggest placing these pocket holders on the right side of the folder. It is also useful to print vital client information, like phone, address, and tax identification number, on the front of the pocket holder for quick reference.

There are many ways to organize individual file folders. One way is to place all documents in chronological order from left to right (oldest to newest). Another method is to use the dividers to separate documents by type, such as correspondence, notes, and draft agreements. Still another approach is to use the dividers to separate the file into individual matters. In this case, use different-colored dividers and index them on the front of the file.

Whatever approach you use, don't allow loose papers to collect in your files. Make sure you or your assistant properly indexes all documents according to the filing system you select. When you have reviewed a document, tab it with a Post-it note as to the appropriate file location and put it in your out box. Filing should be done at least once a week. All unfiled material can be kept in a separate "to be filed" folder in case you need to refer to it before it is filed.

Home Sweet Home

Some entertainment lawyers, particularly solo practitioners, work out of their homes or apartments. In the early stages of your practice, this is of course a sensible way to keep your operating costs down. If you choose this option, be aware of certain basic rules. First, segregate your work area from your living area to maintain a professional environment. This means having a separate entrance and separate parking, if possible. You should also have a separate bathroom and office phone lines. A guest house, detached from your living area, is ideal. Second, configure and decorate your office as if you were in a commercial building. Also, maintain it with a regular cleaning service.

Share and Share Alike

Another option for a solo practitioner or small firm is to share offices. The key to making this work is to maintain the identity of your practice by having your name on the front door and your calls routed directly to your assistant.

Unfortunately, the peculiar expectations of entertainment clients may not be met by a traditional law office setting. For example, unless you are office sharing in an entertainment firm, other lawyers in the office may not appreciate your playing music loudly or screening films in the conference room. I recall an amusing experience during the brief time that I shared offices with an entertainment litigation firm. The receptionist was an elderly lady who had been with the firm for many years. One day she came into my office and told me that she was concerned about the type of clients I had. Some of my clients have professional names that suggest a connection with drugs, alcohol, and violence. In taking phone messages, she took their professional names literally and assumed that I was cavorting with degenerates

Dress for Success

Be conscious of your image in all situations where you might come in contact with clients (in other words, not just in your office). You will be judged by the type of car you drive, by how you dress, and by where you live if you entertain clients at your home. A successful entertainment lawyer must keep up appearances.

If you are at a lunch meeting with clients or industry executives, there will be unspoken expectations as the valet pulls up with your car. If you drive an economy automobile, you will not be congratulated for your modesty and good sense; rather, it will be assumed that you are not successful.

How you dress is a bit more complex. The first firm I worked at had a strict dress code that required all lawyers to wear suits and ties. The partners in the entertainment department wore Italian suits, and I assumed that was the profile of a mover and shaker.

When I moved to the boutique firm, I learned that the senior partner was famous for wearing blue jeans and tennis shoes. This had become a trademark for him, sending a message to his clients that he was more relaxed and less stuffy than some of his peers.

I opt for the casually elegant look—designer slacks and shirts, but rarely suits and ties, and tailor my dress depending upon my daily schedule. If I have a meeting with a high-level executive, I may break out the Armani. However, if the prospective client is a young new artist, I may wear jeans and a sports shirt.

You Look Marvelous

Take care of yourself physically and stay well-groomed. Most entertainment clients are obsessed with their appearance and work hard to keep themselves looking good. Whether it is stated or not, they will respect your taking pride in how you look.

Having said that, I know entertainment lawyers who take their image too seriously. One looks like he stepped out of an ad for *Gentlemen's Quarterly* magazine. Not only does he wear the latest designer suits, but I am certain that he dyes his hair blond and spends hours each week under the sunlamp. He always greets me with "Hey, babe" and ends our conversations with "Take care" or "I appreciate you." He is a walking stereotype. Nevertheless, he is successful and his presentation obviously impresses his clients.

New Lease on Life

In approaching your office lease, keep your options open. Since entertainment law is ever-changing, look for a lease that allows you the flexibility to expand quickly, or even to move if another opportunity presents itself. Keep the term short (for example, not more than three years), with options to renew. If you are in a desirable building, it will be easier to find a replacement tenant if you want to get out of the lease early.

Since the appearance of your office is important, negotiate for as many tenant improvements as possible. Finally, since entertainment clients can be loud and out of control at times, pay attention to lease provisions that penalize you for disruptive behavior. Also, make sure the building has sufficient soundproofing to avoid complaints from other tenants.

A pure entertainment practice does not require a law library. Resource materials, such as books, treatises, seminar manuals, and articles, can be stored in the filing room or in your credenza.

Getting Equipped

The basic equipment you will require is not materially different from that in any other area of practice. Because of the heavy reliance on telephones, invest in a quality phone system with multiple line capability. I recommend installing at least one or two more lines than you think you will need. You don't want an important client to get a busy signal or be cut off on call waiting. Depending on the size of your office, you may need a paging system. Caller ID and intercomming are useful features. I also recommend a headset that enables hands-free conversation. It is more personal than a speakerphone.

Finally, employ a reliable voice mail system. This can include a paging option. An answering machine is not appropriate. Your phone carrier can offer low-cost automated options. For a more personal touch you might also consider hiring a company that uses live operators.

Your document production equipment (computers, printers, fax machines, and copiers) should be as state-of-the-art as you can afford. Your practice will be document intensive, so obtain equipment that will perform well under heavy use. This means getting a copier that copies quickly, feeds automatically, and collates large documents. If you have two or more busy lawyers, you may need multiple faxes and printers to avoid logjams. Any equipment features that save time will ultimately save you money. Take out maintenance contracts and extended warranties on key equipment. In the alternative, have reliable service people on call. Make sure they provide loaner equipment while yours is being repaired. Even the smallest equipment malfunction can be incredibly disruptive.

One handy piece of equipment is a label writer (cost: $200–$400) that interfaces with your computer. Your assistant can use it to update your Rolodex and to enter addresses on letters. It can also be an efficient way to print out holiday greeting cards for your important clients. Another useful tool is an extended-arm document holder for freeing up desk space and enabling easy reading of documents.

Rikki Don't Lose That Number

Your Rolodex is a vital information source. Whether you prefer a computerized or manual Rolodex system, or both, use it for more than just keeping track of names, addresses, and fax numbers. Add business information, such as social security or federal identification numbers and bank routing codes. Put in nicknames, the name of an assistant, a spouse, a child, or any significant others that you can use to personalize your communications. Include client birthdays or the names of their favorite restaurants. Anything that helps you make a client feel special is worth its weight in gold. Add possible cross-references, such as managers or partners, which can also be useful in case you need to plug them into a conversation quickly.

If you prefer a manual Rolodex, use a large swivel model and buy two or three. Put see-through color sleeves on your most important cards for quick location.

Keep your Rolodex updated constantly. Instruct your assistant to make new cards or input new data on every new person you deal with. This should be done as a matter of course. Don't take down information yourself—you'll misplace it. Have your assistant do it.

Everything in Its Proper Place

In addition to a computer and a phone, every workstation in your office should have the following basic materials: in and out boxes, a calculator, pens (in various colors for coding purposes), paper clips, Post-it notes, white-out (for cleaning up documents), two-hole puncher, stapler, letter opener, staple remover, binder clips, a clock, and a calendar.

Your assistant's workstation should have an in and an out box where you can retrieve and drop off drafts of letters and documents, filing, and other tasks. He or she should also have a separate follow-up file for important pending matters and documents in progress. It is also useful to give your assistant contracts or correspondence to hold with instructions to bring them to you when a particular person arrives for a meeting or is reached by phone. He or she may find it useful to keep equipment manuals, industry directories, key resource materials, insurance, and bar information at his or her desk as well.

A quality dictation system is important. Purchase at least two hand-held microcassette dictaphones per lawyer. Keep one at your desk and the other in your briefcase. They cost between $100 and $350. Your assistant's transcriber should have a foot control for hands-free typing. These run between $250 and $500.

Also useful is a collection of rubber stamps, not only with your office address but for specific tasks, such as indicating whether a contract is an "Executed Original" or a "Draft," whether bills are "Paid" or "Past Due," and if you are "Still Awaiting Reply" on a matter.

Keep plenty of supplies in case you run short, especially extra stationery, labels, copier and printer ink cartridges, batteries, note pads, and file folders. Set up an account with a local office supply store from which your assistant can order directly by phone. Most office suppliers offer free delivery (subject to certain minimum purchases). It is also a good idea to have basic hardware and first-aid kits in a file cabinet.

If you have a kitchen, stock it with a coffee maker, microwave, toaster oven, mini-refrigerator, and water cooler. Keep snacks and drinks on hand for clients.

Getting Insured

Unless you absolutely cannot afford it, get malpractice insurance. There are close to forty active carriers currently writing policies. Since entertainment law is considered a high-risk area, as many as half of these carriers will not offer coverage to entertainment lawyers or will limit their coverage options. This is especially true for a new practitioner without experience in the area. If you are starting out, you would be well advised to enlist the services of a broker who is familiar with which companies might offer you the most reasonable terms and conditions. Your state and local bars typically also offer low-cost options for solo practitioners and small firms.

Malpractice rates are determined on a case-by-case basis depending on a number of factors including claims history, location and size of your practice, and, of course, the terms of the coverage. Unfortunately, you can expect to pay a higher premium for practicing entertainment law, as opposed to, say, debt collection. This is not only because of the inherently risky nature of entertainment transactions, but also because of the poor track record of entertainment lawyers who have ignored conflict-of-interest issues, and the propensity of juries to sympathize with celebrity claimants. The good news is that as of the writing of this book, the insurance market is soft, and rates are more competitive than they have been in years.

Most commercial leases will require you to have liability insurance for your office, and state law mandates that you carry worker's compensation for your employees. Discretionary coverages include theft protection for valuable items in your office, disability insurance in case you are incapacitated, and health and dental insurance for your employees. Most employees expect you to provide or at least subsidize health insurance. Dental coverage is a more discretionary employee benefit. Another discretionary employee benefit is participation in a retirement program. Check with your financial adviser to familiarize yourself with your options.

Getting Paid (Setting and Collecting Fees)

6

The Color of Money

Entertainment lawyers employ a variety of fee arrangements. The most traditional is billing by the hour, and the most common rates are between $200 and $500 an hour, depending on the lawyer's degree of experience, the location and size of the firm, and the demand for the lawyer's services.

Many entertainment lawyers also employ flat-fee arrangements, either for individual transactions or on a monthly basis. A flat fee can be guaranteed, or can be contingent on the client's receiving money from a deal.

Entertainment lawyers also frequently use percentage-based fee arrangements, most typically between 5 and 10 percent. Some lawyers use percentage-based arrangements on a deal-by-deal basis, while others work exclusively on percentages.

Still another billing method is called value billing. Under this method, the lawyer bills based on an estimate of the value of services rendered. Often, the amount of the bill is presented to the client after a transaction is completed, depending on the size of the deal, the benefit to the client, and the amount of time spent.

Billing arrangements can also be combined, such as an hourly rate against a percentage.

Put Your Money Where Your Mouth Is

The primary advantage of hourly billing is that it is straightforward. It is difficult for a client to challenge the amount of a bill if your time is accurately documented. Another advantage is that it discourages clients from wasting your time (and their money) and helps weed out clients who cannot afford to pay. The primary disadvantage is that the amount you can earn is limited by the number of hours you can bill. Senior partners at prominent firms can charge upwards of $500 an hour. Junior partners are usually in the $300- to $400-an-hour range. Senior associates are typically billed out at around $300 an hour and junior associates at $200 to $250 an hour. Solo or small-firm practitioners may choose to charge less than larger firms to maintain a competitive advantage.

Entertainment clients often request flat-fee arrangements because they like the security of knowing their transaction costs in advance. These work best when you are able to closely estimate the amount of time you will need to invest to earn the fee and are easier to do on a deal-by-deal rather than a monthly basis. Unfortunately, matters have a way of getting out of hand, and you can get burned if you underestimate the amount of time required. One advantage of a flat fee for an individual deal is that since you know the amount of the fee in advance, you can often provide for direct payment from the client in the contract you are negotiating. This eliminates the administrative burden of keeping track of your time and collecting your fee.

Monthly flat-fee arrangements are trickier. To avoid getting in the position of having to do more work than the fee is worth, specify in advance the services covered by the fee. Also, reserve the right to reevaluate the fee on a regular basis to make sure it is equitable for you and your client.

If a flat fee is not guaranteed, you may request a premium for the risk of working on a deal that might not close. Establish a clear understanding with your client about what happens if the deal falls through. Does the fee get wiped out, or is the amount of the fee reduced? If so, by how much? How will the client pay if not directly from the failed transaction? Is there another deal contemplated? If so, are you entitled to charge for the failed deal and the new one?

Going for the Gold

The main reason to use a percentage-based arrangement is to increase your upside potential. On the downside, you risk not being paid for the time you spend. I use percentage-based arrangements when I am asked to create new opportunities for clients. Many entertainment clients are comfortable with a percentage-based arrangement because they are accustomed to paying their manager, agent, and often their business manager the same way, and figure it will motivate you to make them the best possible deals.

For a long time, the standard percentage charged by entertainment lawyers was 5 percent. Recently, many of the more prominent practitioners have started charging 10 percent. A percentage-based arrangement raises several issues for you and your client. One is to what income the percentage applies. In some cases, the percentage will be based solely on the up-front monies payable to your client under a deal. In others, contingent compensation, such as royalties or profits, and/or future product, such as optional albums or pictures, will also be included. Whether you can demand an ongoing participation will depend principally on the bargaining power of your client. For example, if you are shopping a deal for an established client who is likely to command a sizable up-front advance, the client may feel that a piece of that payment is sufficient.

Working Without a Net

There is also the question whether your percentage should be applied to gross or net earnings, and how "net" is defined. Many deals are structured so that an "all-in" advance is paid, out of which your client is responsible to pay the costs of production. Take the case of a client for whom you negotiate a contract that provides for $100,000 to be paid to your client for delivering a video. Let's say the original budget was $50,000, but because of mistakes made during production, your client ended up spending $90,000. Your client may insist that only the $10,000 amount actually retained by her should be subject to your percentage. On the other hand, you may argue that since you had no control over the costs, your percentage should be applied to the $50,000 that your client would have made had she not overspent. One solution is to establish minimum fees. Another is to keep track of your time and have the option of being paid on an hourly basis. In most percentage-based cases, you will just have to take your chances along with your client.

Money Doesn't Grow on Trees

The issues are different if you are being paid exclusively on a percentage basis. Under this arrangement, fees are based solely on your client's income. The first question your client may ask is whether you should commission earnings from activities that do not require legal advice. The answer is that this makes up for your work on non-income-producing matters. As a compromise, offer to cap the amount of fees from income derived from activities that do not require legal advice and/or exclude certain minimum earnings—for example, the first $100,000 of personal performance income.

The next question you are likely to be asked is why you should be entitled to commission monies earned and/or received after the period of your representation. You can certainly argue that it would be unfair for you not to get paid on money that is earned during your representation, just because it is paid afterward. It may be harder to persuade a client to pay you in perpetuity on contracts negotiated during your representation, unless you offer to limit your fees to contracts specifically negotiated and obtained by you. If this issue becomes contentious, offer to limit post-term fees to specific time periods—two years, for example. You can also offer to reduce the amount of your percentage for post-term earnings.

Tracking It Down

One problem with exclusive percentage fee arrangements is that it can be difficult to accurately track your client's earnings. To avoid getting shortchanged, have your client authorize her business manager to account for and pay your percentage directly to you on a regular basis. It is also wise, whenever possible, to have your client authorize direct payment from payers. I have included a sample letter of direction in Appendix J for this purpose. Also, request the right to audit your client's books periodically. Even if you have clear instructions on file with accountants and/or payers, follow up periodically to make sure those instructions are being honored. Develop relationships with the royalty accounting departments of companies instructed to pay you directly and find out when statements are due. Remind them of your payment interest a few weeks in advance. Once the checks have been cut, you may have difficulty getting your client to make it right.

If you are creating opportunities for clients, you can obtain even better fee arrangements than those discussed above. Some entertainment lawyers charge both an hourly fee and a percentage for deals they obtain. I have seen retainer agreements that include an increased hourly rate for shopping services.

Ethical Considerations

Although some of the foregoing billing techniques, particularly value billing, may seem aggressive, they are not unethical as long as they are the result of open negotiation and are generally consistent with fees being charged by others for similar services.

For a discussion of your ethical obligations concerning fee arrangements, see my article in Appendix A, "Crossing the Thin Line Between Manager and Attorney in the Entertainment Industry." These are the basic rules:

1. Fully disclose the terms of the fee arrangement to the client.
2. Obtain the informed written consent of the client.
3. Obtain written acknowledgment by the client that he or she has been advised of and has had the opportunity to seek the advice of independent counsel in the negotiation of the fee arrangement.

Spreading Out Your Risk

For a start-up entertainment practice, I recommend using a combination of billing methods to accommodate clients in different situations. It is also an effective way to balance earning power and stability.

First and foremost, make sure you have enough steady-paying clients to cover your overhead. This is especially important in the early stages of your practice. The most stable billing method is hourly billing, or guaranteed flat fees. Once you become profitable, you can take chances on contingent flat fees and percentage-based arrangements.

If you are starting out, and trying to build a client base, be prepared to accommodate a prospective client's billing demands, even if they are not optimal for you.

First Date

If a prospective client seems promising, don't charge for the initial consultation. In other cases, where the prospective client presents a specific problem, or if you are unsure about the long-term potential of the representation, charge for the initial consultation on an hourly basis and request full payment at the time of the consultation. If you have already agreed to the representation and the initial consultation is to go over substantive matters, it is certainly appropriate to charge for this time.

In most cases, inform prospective clients how you prefer to handle billing and discuss other options only if asked. I see no problem in discussing fee arrangements over the phone. It is never too early to get a sense of a prospective client's ability to pay. One artist I spoke to about representation told me that even though he could not afford to retain me, I should work for him pro bono. When I explained to him that pro bono arrangements are usually reserved for worthy causes, he confidently assured me that his cause was indeed worthy.

Retainers

One effective technique for qualifying clients and minimizing the risk of nonpayment is to use retainers. If you are billing by the hour, the amount of the retainer should be based on your estimate of the work required. To avoid underestimating the retainer, establish minimum amounts for new clients.

A replenishing retainer is even better. Under this agreement, the client agrees to maintain the initial retainer amount on a monthly basis. If you are working on a guaranteed flat fee, request as much of the fee as possible in advance. Even if you are working on a contingent flat-fee or percentage basis, it is wise to request a retainer. In this case, base it on the estimated amount of your fee.

Whatever fee arrangement you employ, establish your expectations regarding payment directly with your client and in your retainer letter. I have included sample retainer letters for the most commonly used arrangements (hourly and percentage) in Appendix K.

Time Keeps On Slipping

If you are billing by the hour, you need to develop a method to accurately monitor your time. There are automated computer programs that keep track of time. I keep track of mine the old-fashioned way, on manual time sheets. Some of the best advice I received early in my career was never to let a day pass without completing my time sheet. I keep mine in the center of my desk and enter time and matters on an ongoing basis during the day. Before you leave the office, review matters worked on and tally up the total time spent.

Instruct your assistant to input your time regularly and not to fall behind in this task. If you are working on a flat-fee or percentage basis, indicate this on the time sheet so that payment can be tracked. Even if you are not working on an hourly basis, you may want to keep track of your time to help you determine if you underestimated the amount of the fee.

Nickels and Dimes

I charge for copies (15 cents a page) and faxes ($1 a page), as well as for long-distance phone calls. To keep track of long-distance charges, employ a client coding system with your telephone carrier. Have your assistant keep a log for faxes and copies. For phone calls made outside the office (such as on your cellular phone or from home), keep a log with you that your assistant can double-check against phone bills.

Make your bills as detailed as possible to give the client a clear sense of the amount of work done. Bill on a monthly basis and send bills out on the first of every month, with a return self-addressed stamped envelope for your client's convenience.

Pay Me Now or Pay Me Later

Do not personally handle bill collecting, unless you cannot afford to hire someone to handle it for you, and do not ask your assistant to do it either. Not only will you be too busy with other matters, but it can be difficult to maintain a nurturing relationship with a client on the one hand and be an effective bill collector on the other. However, if your billing department is stymied on an account, a personal call from you may be necessary. Advise your client that you may be unable to work on new matters unless payment can be arranged. Let your client know she cannot expect you to give her matters priority if she does not give priority to paying your bills.

In any event, stay informed about bill collections. An overaggressive collection effort can damage a relationship and may be inappropriate under certain circumstances. You should also be aware that any action you take could have ramifications with other clients and their representatives. Remember that clients talk to one another and will have no qualms about sharing an unpleasant billing experience.

No one faults you for insisting on payment for your work, but you do not want a reputation for being greedy. If you know a client is going through a hard time, instruct your billing department to offer a payment plan. If you know the client will be receiving royalties or advances from a given matter, have your billing department request payment out of those funds. Under this scenario, have your client sign a letter directing payment to you directly from the payer (see Appendix J).

If all else fails, your only hope of getting paid may be to use your contacts to generate a money-making opportunity for your client.

Getting Stiffed

No matter how effective your billing and collection techniques are, problem accounts are inevitable. As incredible as this may seem, even prominent entertainment lawyers can experience up to 75 percent uncollected billings from time to time. Since the fortunes of entertainment clients are irregular, it can be difficult to identify problem accounts early.

One long-standing producer client of mine was a consistent payer. I hardly noticed when he fell a few months behind. When my billing department made contact with him, he said he had been traveling and had lost track of his bills. That seemed logical and I continued to work for him until several more months passed without payment. At the same time, many of the deals I was working on for him were not closing. I became suspicious and started asking questions of his representatives. I finally found out he was going through a messy divorce that was draining him of funds. When I confronted him, he pleaded with me to help him with a big deal he was putting together that would enable him to pay me. Because of my faith in him, I went along with this for several more months until the deal fell through. Although he has promised to pay when he is able, I am probably stuck with a large uncollectable account.

In another case, I worked for almost two years putting together the sale of a large publishing catalog for a client. Since this was a good client and the deal seemed promising, I agreed to do the work on a percentage basis. During the course of the transaction, I encountered problems, many of which came from the unrealistic expectations of my client. Just when I thought I had vaulted the last hurdle, my client decided not to go forward with the deal. I was left with a tremendous amount of wasted time.

Let's Make a Deal

For truly difficult accounts, encourage your billing department to compromise on the amount of the outstanding bill. The amount of negotiating will depend upon your client's ability to pay and the payment terms. A more drastic option is the use of a collection agency. Agencies charge a percentage (usually 30 to 40 percent) of what they collect. Do not expect great results unless you are giving the agency large accounts. In any event, supervise the process personally and demand regular and detailed reports.

Separation Anxiety

If you are working off retainers, or are responsible for processing settlement or other client monies, you must maintain one or more separate client trust accounts. This includes flat fees unless the fee is earned on receipt. Most commercial banks can assist you in setting up trust accounts in accordance with the rules of your state bar. The general rule is that all client trust funds must be kept segregated from your personal and business accounts and used only for the specific purposes agreed to in writing in advance by your client. The interest earned on these accounts will be automatically forwarded to your state bar. You may only withdraw funds from the trust account as they are earned and you must maintain complete records of all transactions relating to each trust account for at least two years. Your responsibility concerning client trust funds is nondelegable and you must personally sign off on all transactions.

7 Marketing Your Entertainment Law Practice

Do the Right Thing

Your reputation and the relationships you build are the most important assets you possess. To develop these assets, plan the growth of your practice for long-term success. Building a good reputation doesn't happen overnight. The longer you practice, the wider your network will become and the more influence you will possess. Starting a practice is like planting a tree. On the surface it may seem as though your practice is growing slowly, but if you tend to it, its root system will expand. When that root system is strong enough, the tree will shoot up.

Sticking to this philosophy is not always easy. Consider the following scenario. Imagine you are closing a deal that will earn you a healthy fee. Just to make it interesting, let's say you really need the money. Before the closing, you learn that your client has been withholding material information. What do you do? Do you stick your head in the sand and cash the check?

No. You do the right thing and persuade your client to allow you to disclose the information. Unless the problem is insurmountable, you can usually find a solution (even if it means adjusting the deal), and the goodwill you will create with the other party will come back to you in spades, not to mention that you will save your client lots of trouble.

Look Who's Talking

Word of mouth is the best kind of marketing. The music, television, and film industries are relatively small and the same people tend to come in contact with one another on a regular basis. Talent will often ask other talent, or people they work with, to recommend a lawyer. Other lawyers may refer clients in situations where they have a conflict or are too busy. Company lawyers (and their assistants) as well as executives may recommend you to clients with whom they are about to enter into agreements. This means that you must constantly be aware not only of the quality of work you perform, but of how you are regarded by your peers and others with whom you interact.

A reputation for being difficult to deal with will not serve you well. This does not mean you should compromise your representation. However, it points out the wisdom of maintaining good relations with adversaries who may someday be in a position to help you.

Don't Be an Ambulance Chaser

Because entertainment clients are a select group, general advertising techniques will produce limited results. Advertising in industry-specific trade publications or phone books and on television or radio is likely to only bring in unproven clients.

Established entertainment clients will not react positively to these efforts, because "good" clients expect a "good" lawyer to make room for them in an already thriving practice and are likely to assume that any entertainment lawyer who needs to advertise is not worth retaining.

As a result, "advertising" must be done in more subtle and personal ways. The trick in marketing yourself to prospective entertainment clients is to make it seem that they need you more than you need them. In an industry where image is everything, never appear desperate for business. The goal is to increase your name recognition and profile and let the clients come to you. When the first words out of a prospective client's mouth are "I've heard of you," you will have arrived.

In my view, it is not necessary to prepare a brochure or other form of advertising material. A current résumé and client list are sufficient and can be submitted on request.

Making the Scene

Networking is the best way to raise your profile. Because networking is so vital to the development of an entertainment practice, use every conceivable resource at your disposal to make contact with industry insiders. That includes business associates, former classmates, family, friends, and friends of friends. Once you identify people in a position to assist you, arrange meetings with them, preferably over lunch or dinner. The stereotype of the entertainment lawyer zipping from breakfast to lunch to drinks to dinner meetings is not a bad blueprint for success. If you have the time, the energy, and the resources, this is a proven process. If you don't have contacts, start at the bottom and work your way up. Even assistants or low-level entertainment company employees can help you gain access to good networking opportunities.

At lunch and dinner meetings, observe certain etiquette. First, the client/prospective client/invited guest never pays. The exception is an executive with an expense account who insists on picking up the tab. Even in this case, offer to pitch in. Be punctual, but don't expect clients to be. Bring work with you in case your client is late, and always acknowledge a positive meeting with a follow-up note.

The best way to network is through your existing clients. Clients will appreciate your interest in their performances, recording sessions, tapings, shoots, promotional appearances, and rehearsals.

You can also network at industry functions, showcases, seminars, and conventions (see Appendix G). Entertainment law seminars and events can also provide good networking opportunities (see Appendix F). The bottom line is that you cannot be too visible as you build your practice. Every industry insider or other entertainment lawyer you meet may provide an entrée to new business.

The purpose of networking is not just to meet prospective clients. In fact, you should avoid openly soliciting prospective clients at functions. Simply being recognized will improve your reputation.

Golf and tennis are popular sports in the entertainment industry and can be a great way to network if you are athletically inclined. The best-known golf event is the annual "City of Hope" tournament.

In addition to lunch and dinner meetings designed to broaden your network for prospective clients, entertaining existing clients is a classy way to show your appreciation for their business and cement your relationship with them.

The Good, the Bad, and the Ugly

Ultimately, you want prospective clients to seek you out. This will enable you to network on a different level. However, networking for established clients is more complicated than fishing for up-and-coming ones. First of all, a proven client is likely to be represented by another lawyer. Since there are relatively few entertainment lawyers, it is important to be aware of how discussing representation with a prospective client may be perceived by a colleague. If an established client requests your services, make sure that the client has informed the other lawyer and has settled all accounts before agreeing to undertake the representation. It is also politically correct for you to contact the other lawyer personally and make sure there are no hard feelings.

Once the clients start rolling in, you will be in a position to choose between good clients and bad clients. The truth is there may be no such thing as an ideal entertainment client. Except for established company clients, the success of most entertainment clients fluctuates, sometimes rising and falling in a short period of time. In essence, a good client can become a bad client overnight, and vice versa.

Certainly, one looks for clients who have the ability to pay—a viable practice must include clients who pay on a regular basis. However, a client with an exciting opportunity may present himself even though he may not presently have funds. In this instance, you must weigh the potential benefits of pursuing the opportunity against the risk that you might not get paid. The pros and cons of taking chances with developing clients are discussed throughout this book. Refer to "Up and Coming" and "The Slippery Slope" in Chapter 4, Getting Your Foot in the Door, and "Going for the Gold," "Working Without a Net," and "Tracking It Down" in Chapter 6, Getting Paid.

Entertainment transactions are fragile and can unravel for any number of reasons. To avoid being left holding the bag on a deal that doesn't pan out, verify the credibility of the principals involved in advance. Also consider who referred the client to you. In some cases, taking a client will gain you favor with the person who referred him. This may lead to representation of the referring person, or his other desirable clients.

I Want to Thank You

When you receive referrals, show your appreciation. Take the referring person to lunch, buy him a gift, or reciprocate with other business. I have a running joke with one executive that every time he refers a client to me, I send him a gift basket. A tradition I have established with a business manager who sometimes refers me business is that when I close a deal for one of his clients, we go out on the town. He picks the place, I pick up the tab.

One effective marketing technique is to send out greeting cards at the end of each year thanking clients, colleagues, and contacts for a great year and wishing them a happy holiday season. This not only lets key people know you are thinking of them, but gives you a nonaggressive way to advertise your services.

The Rainmaker

Maintaining the image of a successful deal maker is a good way to attract clients. Clients are impressed by a well-connected lawyer who is plugged into who is making deals. Even established lawyers take great pains to preserve this reputation. One successful Beverly Hills entertainment law firm sponsors showcases for new talent. In this way, they get their name in lights and project an image of being at the center of the action. Shopping new projects also puts you in contact with executives who can refer you other business.

Again, this brings you back to working with unproven clients, even if you are past the start-up phase. Making the scene can be a dirty job, but someone has to do it. Appendixes C and G contain lists of informative industry publications and well-known talent/industry organizations, showcases, seminars, and conventions. Once you find an entertainment client you feel has potential, put on your selling hat and let the shopping begin. For tips on how to shop projects and negotiate deals, refer to "Shop 'Til You Drop," "Bidding Wars," "Strike While the Iron Is Hot," and "Control" in Chapter 11, Managing the Workload (Getting the Work Out).

The same firm that sponsors showcases also has a publicist on a monthly retainer to advise them of public relations opportunities. If you negotiate an important new agreement for a client, do your best to get coverage in the industry press. Suggest that the signing be photographed, and get yourself in the picture. If possible, get quoted saying something terribly insightful about the business. If a client receives an award or honor, take out a congratulatory advertisement in trade journals if you can afford it. Speak at symposiums. Write articles.

Whatever you can do to make yourself more visible will enhance your image. This is the essence of marketing an entertainment law practice.

Finding Your Niche

Although it can be prudent to develop a diverse client base as a hedge against shifting tastes, specialization can be an effective marketing tool. If you represent a number of top clients in a particular area, like film composers, or directors, it makes you attractive to other clients in that area. It also gives you clout in negotiating deals and places you at the cutting edge of that market.

8

Keeping the Entertainment Client Happy

What Have You Done for Me Lately?

Do not make the mistake of assuming that providing quality legal work is enough to keep your clients happy. What's more, don't count on you and your clients always agreeing on what constitutes "quality" work. It is not uncommon for entertainment clients to be unrealistic about their market value. If a client who has experienced success is coming off a disappointing project, you will be reminded of this during negotiations. Unfortunately, arguing that your client may have made money in the past is not likely to carry the day. Just because the entertainment industries rely upon artistic endeavors does not mean they are more forgiving of failure than others.

If you ascribe your inability to meet a client's expectations to the client's own shortcomings, he may take this as a vote of no confidence. To keep this from happening, give the client time to accept disappointments on his own. No matter how bad the message is, reassure your client that you remain focused on the positive aspects of his endeavors.

Shooting for the Moon

In approaching negotiations, keep in mind that every client wants you to believe in him wholeheartedly. As a result, even if a client instructs you to request contractual terms that you feel are unrealistic, it may not be wise to advise him to lower his expectations right away.

Interestingly, when you shoot high in a negotiation, your client may be disappointed if you fall short but is not likely to blame you. The client is more likely to commiserate about how unreasonable the other party is and privately blame himself. It is also unlikely to fatally damage a negotiation. Most industry insiders realize that excessive contractual demands are often made to satisfy clients. There will, however, be situations where you are certain that a company will be turned off to a deal by an unrealistic position. In such cases you have to take a harder line with your client.

The Gentle Art of Communication

Although you have an obligation to keep your client informed, exercise judgment in how information is communicated. This requires an understanding of your client's personality. If you recognize that a client you know to be unpredictable is in a particularly bad mood, postpone a difficult discussion. It is not always necessary or wise to transmit messages verbatim. In the heat of negotiations, harsh comments may be made that may later be regretted.

You can keep your client informed without inflaming her by rephrasing unpleasant comments or presenting them in more palatable terms. The degree of editing will depend upon your client and should never go so far as to misinform.

The same is true of client communications intended for another party. For example, in one negotiation, my client became enraged about a company's slow responses. She demanded that I call the head of business affairs and tell him he was unprofessional and had insulted her. I have known this lawyer for some time and understand that he is overworked. If I had done as I was instructed, there is a good chance the negotiations would have ended and the client would have lost the deal. That is the opposite of what she wanted. In the end, I spoke to the lawyer and asked him to give the matter prompter attention because my client was getting frustrated. I told him I knew he was busy, but that I was getting pressured to move things along. He thanked me for the call and promised more prompt responses. My client was satisfied that the company had acknowledged the delays and that my prodding, at her request, had gotten the deal back on track.

Don't Worry, Be Happy

I have always found it best to maintain a calm and confident demeanor. Although some clients want a lawyer who is pugnacious, most entertainment clients prefer to feel at ease with their lawyer on a personal level. No matter how worried I may be about a matter, I never let my clients see me sweat. Interjecting humor into a tense discussion or sharing a laugh with a nervous client is a great way to ease their anxiety.

I often come away from a client interview feeling that beyond my client's expectations about my level of expertise, she wants to feel that I will "take care" of her. This goes beyond caring in a professional sense and comes closer to what I would call nurturing.

Speaking the Language

To keep your clients happy, work on becoming an effective communicator. This means learning how to speak your client's language. Entertainers have distinctive mannerisms and ways of communicating that may seem strange to the uninitiated. In certain cases, clients present themselves not with a foreign language, but what amounts to a language of their own. I find this most often among my rap clients, who use words and phrases with multiple meanings not only as part of their poetry but as part of their daily communication. I was discussing a negotiation on the phone with one client in which I communicated to him an offer I had received of $250,000 for his services. He responded that the offer was too low—that he was "worth at least half a chicken." I was able to discern from this that he wanted to counteroffer at $500,000. Obviously, there is no shame in asking a client to clarify his intentions. Laboring to be too hip can come across as patronizing.

Another amusing story is the day I had a temporary assistant who was accustomed to working with corporate lawyers. On my return from lunch, she told me she had taken several messages that, frankly, she could not understand. One of them was "Yo money, hit me on the hip with the swiftest." I explained to her that this meant for me to page my client as soon as I got in.

The Silent Treatment

A more serious challenge arises when clients become uncommunicative. Entertainment clients are notorious for checking out from time to time and not being reachable. In one deal I was working on, the negotiations had reached a critical juncture and I could not locate my client. Miraculously, he called me at the last minute of the deadline day. When I asked him if he had gotten my messages, he said no, but he had sensed during his daily meditation that I needed to speak with him.

People in entertainment are expected to maintain a "cool" image at all times. This may cause your client to appear aloof. Do not mistake this for a lack of concern; rather, probe for issues that may secretly be worrying the client. Don't be afraid to ask a question like, "If this happens, wouldn't you be upset?"

Terms of Art

The entertainment industries have terms of art that describe concepts unique to them, many of which have become integrated into the legal lexicon. For example, the term "pay or play" means that once a contract for services is entered into, the client is assured of payment whether or not she is allowed to complete her services. Familiarity with these terms will ensure not only good client communication, but effective negotiating. A lawyer unfamiliar with these terms will be identified as a novice.

Study the customs and practices of your industry, and don't request concessions that are beyond customary parameters unless your client has a lot of leverage.

Breaking It Down

Explain contracts to clients in terms they can understand. This can be accomplished by using examples common to their experience. In explaining the concept of exclusivity of services to one puzzled young artist, I asked whether he had a girlfriend. When he said he did, I asked him if his girlfriend would be happy if he went out with someone else. He quickly replied, "Hell no." He may not have liked it, but he understood his obligations better as a result of our conversation.

The same approach can be used in preparing agreements. A standard distribution contract is fifty pages long and loaded with "notwithstanding the foregoings." The definition of net profits in a film distribution agreement can be longer than fifty pages all on its own. Although complicated concepts sometimes require elaborate drafting, many legal concepts can be streamlined and expressed in simpler terms.

Clients will often request that a contract be short and to the point. To appreciate this type of request, take the case of a producer working with a new writer. Part of the producer's job is to collaborate with the writer in the creative process. The producer must inspire the writer, but when it comes to contracts and money, they become adversaries. The producer may fear that a lengthy and complicated contract will damage the trust he is trying to establish, which could inhibit his ability to get the most out of the writer, or worse yet, scare the writer off.

The challenge is knowing which contractual provisions can safely be streamlined. One common device is the use of deal memos, or so-called short forms. The most basic of these are nothing more than outlines of the material terms of a deal. Although this can be an efficient way to start a relationship, deal memos inevitably omit important details. As such, it is good practice to replace them with more formal agreements. Even if this is never accomplished, a basic written agreement is preferable to an oral one.

You Have My Word

Entertainment clients are notorious for relying on conversations. They cannot believe that their friend, their collaborator, would lie to them. However, fame has a way of changing people and making them forget those who helped them achieve it.

One producer client of mine invested significant time and resources developing a young artist. On my advice, he discussed the basic deal he wanted with the artist and presented him with a short-form agreement, but the artist refused to sign it. Since my client was afraid to pressure his artist, I suggested that we meet with the artist and his manager to go over their concerns. At the meeting, I sensed that the artist was skittish and warned my client not to proceed further until a contract was signed. Nevertheless, he arranged a meeting with the artist at a company. The meeting went well and my client excitedly instructed me to work out a deal. However, when I called, the business affairs lawyer questioned me about the relationship between my client and the artist. This raised a red flag and I warned my client again to take care of the contract, but he insisted that the artist didn't like talking about it and that he couldn't force the issue. The next I heard my client had lost contact with the artist. As it turned out, the artist signed with another producer who arranged the deal for him. My client thought about suing until he was advised that he would have a hard time proving his case without a written contract and that the litigation could cost him six figures.

Party Animals

Clients with drug and alcohol problems present other challenges. Many entertainment service contracts prohibit habitual drug or alcohol abuse. If the abuse prevents a client from fulfilling his obligations, breach-of-contract issues will arise even without express contractual prohibitions. The abuse may also inhibit your client's ability to appreciate your advice. I remember one meeting with a client to go over a contract in which he stared blankly ahead and said nothing. The meeting ended with his asking the only question he cared about: "Where do I sign?"

Another time, I had set up a meeting with an executive who was interested in hiring a client of mine for an important project. My client never showed up. When I spoke to him later, he told me he had partied too hard the night before and couldn't get out of bed. Needless to say, he didn't get the job.

The issue is more complex when drugs and alcohol are part of your client's image. It is no secret that many rock stars and actors enjoy partying. They sing about it in their songs, and sometimes make it part of their bad-boy image. Because of this, they rarely exercise caution. An understanding of this will help you to not overreact in uncomfortable situations. You are not a drug or alcohol abuse counselor. Be careful before you try to help a client overcome these problems.

Their Own Worst Enemies

This raises a broader issue. How do you deal with entertainment clients who refuse to act responsibly and seem to constantly self-destruct? It is disappointing to work hard on a deal only to have your client blow it for no good reason. I had one producer client who had tremendous success, but was always getting himself in trouble. He had originally come to me to settle a lawsuit that was unwinnable because it had not been properly attended to. After lengthy and stressful negotiations, I settled the case, one feature of which required him to do future production. When he failed to follow through, the other party went back to court and my client was hit with a large judgment. Amazingly, he was unconcerned and refused to offer money toward a new settlement, or make any commitment about the unproduced product. Eventually, the judgment, along with other bad debts, forced his company into bankruptcy and effectively ended his career.

In another matter, I negotiated a lucrative contract for a client to produce and perform a radio commercial for a nationally known food service company. The contract included fantastic promotional opportunities. All my client had to do was finish a preliminary version of a recording he had turned in that the company loved, but when several deadlines passed without the completed recording, the company finally moved on to another performer. During the last two-week extension, my client decided to take his new girlfriend on a trip to the Bahamas instead of finishing the project.

Your Brother's Keeper

Just as you are not a drug counselor, neither are you your client's keeper. It is not your place to berate a client for his lack of responsibility. Entertainment clients with inflated egos may become offended and take this as a lack of respect. After all, they are the ones who ultimately suffer the consequences. This is particularly difficult when it comes to money. Few entertainment clients are conscientious about managing their finances and often run into tax problems. Although it is a good practice to recommend an accountant, it is not your job to manage your client's money.

May I Help You?

To keep your clients happy, you must be aware not only of your own behavior, but of that of your support staff. Your receptionist/assistant is the first person a client encounters when reaching out for you. Entertainers are sensitive to other people's emotions and can detect a person who is unhappy or stressed out. Your assistant sets the tone for your client's experience and can either heighten your client's anxiety or calm him down.

Encourage your staff to be friendly and to make clients feel at ease. Your assistant is particularly important when you are too busy to speak to a client. No client likes being refused access to you, but your assistant can make your client feel better by assuring him that his issues will be handled as soon as possible.

Instruct your assistant to take detailed messages. This allows your client to get a problem off his chest and also informs you about what may be bothering him. Your assistant may also reassure a client by being able to report that you have already placed a call on a matter of concern to him or have sent out a contract or letter.

Obviously, your assistant should not express an opinion on matters to clients, but the mere act of communicating information can ease a client's anxiety. This won't work with every client. One well-known client of mine chewed me out because I asked my assistant to deliver a message to him. He told me the only person in my office he wanted to hear from was me.

One caveat is that some clients will misinterpret a friendly demeanor as an invitation to a personal relationship. Assistants have told me about clients who have become too familiar. This can be as innocent as a client who wants to have a long personal conversation with your assistant in the middle of a busy day, or as serious as harassment. Entertainers and executives are used to being fawned over by groupies, and it can be difficult to maintain the line between a professional office environment and a comfortable one.

How You Like Me Now?

In most cases, it will not be difficult to assess whether your clients are happy with your services. Entertainment clients are not shy about expressing displeasure. Similarly, they can be effusive in their appreciation. Nevertheless, it is wise to ask clients periodically whether they are satisfied with the way certain matters are being handled.

I do not conduct regular client surveys. If I sense that a client is uneasy, I may ask what is bothering him. The difficulty is how to respond to a client who may be unhappy for no good reason. Unless you are prepared to lose the client, it is best to swallow your pride and share the blame. For example, one client complained to me that I did not warn him about the ramifications of a trademark issue, even though I had advised him to consult a trademark lawyer (and had even given him a referral). Nevertheless, I apologized for not helping him follow up on the referral. This calmed him down and he told me he was not really upset at me, but was drunk, and had just had a fight with his wife.

I Need You

The most common complaint I hear is that the client does not feel that she is being paid enough attention. Take time to make every client feel important. Ask her how her new project is coming or what her upcoming plans are. If a client requires more attention than you can give, recommend new representation. Although you may tempted to placate a client with promises that cannot be kept, this will only make matters worse.

Who's on First?

Since most entertainment clients have a variety of ongoing matters, review your files on a periodic basis and prepare status reports. Offer to present those reports to your bigger clients.

Not only do entertainment clients have a variety of matters to deal with, they also have an assortment of representatives and parties interested in their affairs. It is incumbent upon you to make sure that key people are kept in the loop. Forgetting to copy a key person will irritate a client more than you might think. This situation is complicated by the ever-changing nature of a typical client's representation. A client may want a person in the loop one day and out of the loop the next. Worse than forgetting to copy an important person is sending a copy of a sensitive document to someone the client does not want to know her business. As a result, it is best to err on the side of caution and only copy people you are certain about. This may seem like a trivial matter, but can raise the ire of a client faster than almost any other mistake.

Can You Keep a Secret?

Beyond your ethical obligation not to disclose confidential client communications, don't engage in gossip. For example, you may learn something about a client or his associates from an outside source. Even though this may not be a confidential communication, it is not wise to disseminate it. Entertainment clients are paranoid about their business getting out and will lose trust in you if you are indiscreet. On the other hand, keeping abreast of executive comings and goings is one way to maintain the image of an industry insider.

Have I Got a Deal for You!

One surefire way to make an entertainment client happy is to be proactive on her behalf. This means not simply taking care of business matters presented to you, but creatively seeking out new opportunities. Nothing will make a client happier than a lawyer who is making her money. This can be as simple as informing a client or her manager or agent about a new project that might be right for her, or as involved as pitching a client for projects.

Matchmaker, Matchmaker

A more ambitious undertaking is matchmaking your clients. Let's say you have a producer client who is looking for new screenplays. If you encounter a writer looking for a producer, it may benefit both clients to introduce them. The irony is that you may be conflicted out of representing either of them in the matter.

You Can Take It to the Bank

Another way to assist clients is to help with financing relationships. A young client who comes into money for the first time in his life may not even have a bank account. There are banks and investment brokerage firms, especially in Los Angeles, New York, and Nashville, that have departments devoted to the entertainment industries. One example is City National Bank in Beverly Hills. Their entertainment department caters to clients in the industry and offers assistance with everything from asset management to short-term loans against future income.

One particularly interesting new development in entertainment finance is the emergence of investment groups that specialize in lending money (through securitization) against royalty income streams. Conventional lending institutions are hesitant to lend money against intellectual property because of the perceived instability of its earnings. As a result, clients wanting to capitalize on the value of their copyrights have traditionally been forced to sell them outright.

Investment issues can also arise in a private context. It is not uncommon to represent a client looking to make a deal with a private investor who may be enticed by the idea of owning a piece of a star or an entertainment project. For larger investments, a savvy investor will require a business plan. Unless you are trained in this area, have financial projections prepared by a certified public accountant or other financial expert.

Negotiating investment arrangements raises tax and securities issues. As long as the transaction involves a few private investors, no formal securities rules apply. However, a large offering to numerous investors may require registration with the Securities and Exchange Commission and compliance with their regulations.

In the area of film financing (or "packaging"), investment relationships are essential. There are a handful of banks that dominate the area. Two of the currently most active institutions are Imperial Bank for independent projects and Chase for more mainstream films. Financing relies heavily on due diligence and issues such as rights clearances and insurance, like errors and omissions (which is designed to protect against infringement claims) and completion guarantees (which are designed to ensure completion of a project). Often, independent and conventional financing sources are not sufficient and rights (such as foreign exhibition or home video) must be sold off or licensed to bridge the gap.

9

Keeping the Entertainment Lawyer Happy (General Tips for Managing Stress)

CLIENTS ARE NOT THE ONLY ONES who deserve to be happy. Lawyers need love, too. Like any other area of law, entertainment law is stressful. However, effectively managing the unique set of pressures presented by an entertainment practice is especially important when dealing with clients who are often on edge themselves.

On the Run

The first step is to prepare yourself to feel overwhelmed. Unlike many other areas of legal practice, entertainment law involves work on a number of tasks in any given day. This requires constantly shifting gears and jumping from matter to matter quickly. It is not uncommon to be in the middle of one negotiation and have two or three people on hold waiting to speak to you about other matters. Rarely is there time to reorient yourself before you pick up the next line. Out of necessity, you learn to pull up information during discussions and bring yourself up to speed as you go. Unfortunately, if you employ a more methodical approach, you may find yourself unable to keep pace.

Since the volume of phone calls can be enormous, use a phone log. Periodically go over the log and have your assistant place calls for you. This saves you from wasting time leaving messages and allows you to keep track of important calls. A phone log is a simple 8½-by-11 notebook-style register with the date at the top of each page. Each log entry should include the time of the call, the name of the caller, a brief message (usually what the call is regarding), and the phone number. Indicate completed calls with an "X" and messages with an "LW" for "left word." Make sure your assistant keeps track of LW calls and repeats them after a few days unless a particular call is urgent and you want it placed sooner. Your assistant should rewrite the outgoing list for each day and go over it with you first thing so that you can prioritize important calls.

Take copies of the log with you when you are out of the office and indicate on those copies completed calls or messages left. Return them to your assistant for updating on the master log. This system is infinitely preferable to the traditional use of individual message slips, which are easy to misplace and create clutter.

Sign Language

Since it is common to be in the middle of a call when other calls come in, a system must be employed to inform you of incoming calls. There are automated phone systems that print messages on a viewing screen without interrupting the call that is in progress.

You can also use e-mail. With a Windows interoffice e-mail program called WinPopup, your assistant can alert you to an incoming call and you can type in a response while you are on another call. In a smaller office, handwritten notes or even nonverbal cues will suffice. An assistant who is familiar with your clients will be able to use judgment about when to interrupt you to avoid a constant barrage of distractions. Although it is tempting to ask either the current or incoming caller to hold, it is usually best to tell one of the callers that you will call back. If someone is put on hold, instruct your assistant to get on the line every 30 seconds or so to reassure the caller on hold that you will be with them shortly. Never leave someone hanging for an extended period of time.

Out of Touch

Most people in the entertainment industries understand the nature of busy workloads and are forgiving of a lawyer who does not return calls promptly. Clients are less forgiving, and it can create real problems if you get a reputation for being chronically unresponsive. If several days pass without your being able to return a call, have your assistant phone or e-mail to apologize. Ironically, getting a reputation for being "hard to reach" is not necessarily bad. Clients will take pride in the fact that their lawyer is so in demand. Obviously, this is a fine line.

One helpful tool in managing a busy workload is to make time for drafting or reviewing lengthy agreements when you do not expect heavy phone activity. This can be either before or after normal business hours.

Come On and Take a Free Ride

Another way to maximize your efficiency and minimize stress is to avoid people who waste your time. In the entertainment business there is no shortage of hustlers looking for a free ride. They are often charming and will dazzle you with grandiose schemes. Less sinister, but no less time consuming, are wanna-be's who have no realistic chance of making it. Don't let them distract you from concentrating on people with whom you can have a productive working relationship.

Only in situations where your assistant recognizes that a prospective client may be valuable should you speak with him during the initial phone call. It is safer for your assistant to get as much information as possible and take a message. This affords you the opportunity to check things out. If you decide the client is not worth representing, have your assistant tell them you are too busy or refer the prospective client to a lawyer who may be more willing to take a chance on them.

My assistant uses the following checklist to weed out undesirable prospective clients:

1. They must be prepared to pay a minimum retainer or have a viable source of payment (such as a deal in progress).
2. They must be referred by an existing client or reputable industry insider.
3. They must have pending business matters of substance.
4. They should make their living primarily from the entertainment industry.

Of course, how strictly you are able to adhere to the foregoing checklist will depend on how developed your practice is. For example, if you are in a start-up mode, you may not have the luxury of insisting on a retainer or rejecting clients who have no pending business. However, even a brand-new entertainment practice will benefit from some criteria to avoid clients who are certain to be a waste of time. The following modified checklist could be employed by a start-up entertainment lawyer to screen out deadbeat clients:

1. Do they have a job?
2. Do they have any contacts in entertainment?
3. Do they have any interest from entertainment companies?
4. Have they worked in entertainment since their high school play?

Who Let You In?

Although screening prospective clients works in most situations, an occasional crackpot will slip through. Excessively temperamental or unstable clients can be difficult to spot until the initial interview. One "pre-qualified" prospective client came to our initial meeting with her dog. She explained that she couldn't leave it at home because it had been sexually abused. During our interview, she repeatedly complimented me on my physique and at one point walked behind my chair and offered to rub my shoulders. When I told her I was too busy to represent her, she left in tears.

One telltale sign of trouble is a client who is leaving another capable lawyer. Although the question is sometimes indelicate, it is not inappropriate to ask a prospective client why he is making a change.

Toeing the Line

Another warning sign is a client who insists on taking unethical or unsupportable positions. On more than one occasion, I have had to toe a line that a client wanted to cross. In one case, a client asked me to prepare a contract for services he wanted to perform. When I reminded him that he was prohibited from rendering those services by a prior agreement, he said he needed the money and asked me to do it anyway. I refused and eventually talked him out of doing the deal (to the best of my knowledge). In another instance, a client asked me if he could avoid his obligations under a recently signed contract by changing his name.

If a client insists on taking unsupportable positions, your best option may be to resign your representation. It is not enough to excuse your client's behavior by disclaiming responsibility for actions taken against your advice. Your reputation is still on the line and there is little to be gained in providing counsel that is consistently ignored.

Why You Treat Me So Bad?

Equally problematic is an overly demanding client. Although most executives and lawyers are forgiving of a lawyer who is representing a difficult client, you will be judged by how you conduct negotiations. An unreasonable and unreliable client can damage your reputation.

One successful client would call me five times a day even if she was told I was out at meetings. If she did not hear back from me immediately, she would leave irate messages threatening to fire me. When I would finally make contact with her, she would apologize for being a pest, and tell me how much she needed me. She would also make unrealistic demands in the course of negotiations and become furious when those demands were not met. Although duty-bound to carry out her instructions, I found myself taking positions I could not support and embarrassing myself with colleagues. In spite of this, I persisted in my representation of her for many months until one negotiation became so acrimonious I told her that if she insisted on maintaining certain positions, I could not continue to represent her. She laughed this off and told me she was too good a client for me to terminate. She was wrong.

The most troubling type of client is a volatile one. The illegal activities of some well-known stars are front-page news, and the recent murders of prominent rap stars and assaults by them have focused attention on the seriousness of the problem. Investigate prospective clients who seem suspicious and avoid those with a history of disruptive behavior.

Out of Sight, Out of Mind

Avoiding problematic or unproductive clients does not guarantee you a manageable workload. Sometimes the only solution is to prune existing clients and limit new ones. No one likes turning away business, and every successful entertainment lawyer has stories of the "big ones" that got away. If you become too busy, however, you may lose good existing clients, which can damage your reputation.

In an entertainment practice, the issue is complex. Because of the volatile nature of the entertainment business, it is prudent to take on more work than you can handle as a hedge against shifting tides. Entertainment clients are fickle and can switch representation for no good reason. In addition, the fortunes of entertainment clients are unstable. If you are not overcommitted and you lose a few key clients, you can find yourself with free time on your hands. That is every private practitioner's worst nightmare.

The downside is dealing with the stress of a crushing workload. Murphy's law in entertainment is that just when you take on a new matter to fill up some perceived spare time, a client who has not required your services in months will ask you to quickly get in the middle of a new deal. The end result is that no matter how proficient a juggler you may be, expect to drop some balls now and then. This is especially true if you are expanding your client base as part of a plan to hire a new associate. At those times when your workload seems about to overwhelm you, employ the tips in this book to maximize your efficiency and minimize your stress.

Where Are They Now?

Keep track of prospective clients you turn down and refer out. Have your assistant keep a list with contact and other relevant information. You might find it useful at a later date when the prospective client resurfaces, either on your doorstep or on the other side of a deal.

I Can See Clearly Now

Although it may seem like a hopeless battle at times, keep your desk organized. It is easy to allow stacks of paper to accumulate. Unfortunately, important documents can get lost and forgotten this way. I have tried several solutions. One is to set up several stacks on your desk in order of importance. In other words, one stack, the one located closest to you, would consist of the most important or urgent matters and should be tackled first. The second, third, and, hopefully, not fourth, would contain less important matters. The problem is that you will never get beyond stack number two and the other stacks will become black holes where matters disappear forever. To avoid this, periodically review everything on your desk and carefully sort incoming material. As unruly as this technique can be, I suspect it is the closest to what most people instinctively do to organize themselves.

Another method is to label and sort the material on your desk by client so that you can find things when you need them. You can do this by setting up working files, each labeled with a client's name.

I use a combination of these two techniques. I keep my most pressing matters in a "to do" stack and less pressing matters in separate working files organized by client.

Organize It

To keep your desk organized, separate and delegate incoming and outgoing matters. The following is a list of some effective organizational tools you can employ:

1. Have your assistant place the mail in a file every day and go over it with him or her at an appointed time.

2. Deal with perfunctory mail, such as circulating copies of executed contracts or filing correspondence, promptly following receipt.
3. Send out copies of important incoming material that requires client input right away.
4. Unless you are expecting an urgent fax or e-mail, follow the same procedure as with the mail. Have your assistant assemble faxes and e-mails regularly, say twice a day, and go over them together.
5. Have your assistant separate bills into a "Bills to Be Paid" folder, periodicals in a "Periodical" folder, and other nonlegal material into a "Miscellaneous" folder. Deal with those matters when necessary or when time permits, but keep them separate from legal matters.
6. When you receive instructions on a new matter from a client, immediately memorialize them, either by dictating a memo or by taking notes, and place those written instructions in your "to do" stack. Do not scribble notes on a Post-it note or loose piece of paper and leave it dangling. Accurate note taking is critical to effective drafting and deal making. If a dispute over terms arises, it is invaluable to be able to refresh opposing counsel's memory by identifying the exact date and nature of prior conversations. This means that all your notes should be dated at the top of the page and identified by client and matter. You should also specify whether the notes were taken during a meeting or telephone conversation, as a result of research, or just to memorialize your thoughts. Also identify everyone who was involved in the discussion. If your notes are supplemented by subsequent information, color-code the new material by date. Use abbreviations such as "T" for telephone conversation and "Mtg" for meeting.

   When out of the office, keep notes in your day planner or pocket computer and create a written memo immediately on your return to the office. Alternatively, instruct your assistant by phone to create the memo for you. While on the subject of day planners, it is good practice to periodically review previous appointments and notes to yourself. This may trigger a contact or client you may have forgotten to stay in touch with or a matter you may have forgotten to follow up on. Cross out pending matters from your appointment book as you handle them.

7. Have separate incoming and outgoing trays on your desk. Instruct your assistant to check the outgoing tray regularly.
8. Keep work in progress separate from completed matters. My assistant places drafts in a manila folder labeled "Rough Drafts for Approval" and completed matters in "For Your Signature" folders. When working on a document or letter, have your assistant attach the last draft you worked on to the new version of the document for easy reference. Don't toss out prior drafts—in some cases you may need them to review the history of a negotiation. Don't print on letterhead until you are certain that a document or letter is in final form.
9. Have your assistant log in materials from prospective clients (such as tapes, screenplays, and résumés) and go over them at designated times. If you don't have time to deal with rejected material personally, send out a courteous form letter. The best reason for rejection is that you are too busy to take on the matter at that time.

Although no amount of organization will make the work disappear, the more you can separate matters into distinct categories, the easier it will be to complete them efficiently. Don't expect to keep yourself organized without help. E-mailing your assistant when you place a note in, say, stack "A" can save you from frantically searching your stacks for the missing link several days later.

Rising to the Challenge

Part of dealing with the stress of entertainment law is maintaining the correct mind-set. I suspect most lawyers share the feeling that ennui leads to sloppy work. Although you might think that juggling a busy workload and making quick decisions would make you prone to mistakes, I find the opposite to be true. It raises your level of concentration and teaches you to trust your instincts.

Unfortunately, burnout among entertainment lawyers is common. In the first firm I worked at, one of the associates in the entertainment department was a closet alcoholic who kept a fifth of scotch in her desk drawer, and one of the partners was a chain-smoker whose hands shook constantly. On an even more serious note, a respected colleague of mine recently suffered a heart attack at his desk at the age of fifty-three.

There are also stories of entertainment lawyers who have become addicted to amphetamines or other supposedly energy-enhancing drugs. As a young associate, I heard about lawyers at one prominent entertainment firm who routinely snorted cocaine together in the bathroom during the workday. In the high-pressure world of entertainment law, it's important to be aware of these dangers and take care of yourself. Regular exercise and good eating habits will give you more energy and enable you to cope.

After Hours

Unless you are the type of person who thrives on long workdays, allow yourself time off. From my first day of practice, I was deluged with work. When I was young and eager to learn, my answer was twelve-hour workdays, seven days a week. As I became more established, I realized that the work would always be there and that it is important to let it go when you leave the office. Entertainment law is taxing. You need time to recoup your faculties.

Most active entertainment lawyers, especially those in larger firms and companies, put in long workweeks that typically include weekends. If you factor in networking outside the office, almost every waking hour can be devoted to an entertainment practice.

Because entertainment clients are so demanding, they may request that you be on call after hours. Many entertainers have unusual schedules and may be able to discuss business only at unusual times. While this may be unavoidable in some circumstances, entertainment clients will have no qualms about crossing the line if you allow them to. I once received a call at one in the morning from a client at a concert who decided to render an impromptu performance and wanted my advice on a release agreement from the concert promoter.

On Call

Keeping work and personal matters separate is difficult in an entertainment practice. You are likely to encounter clients and colleagues at social events, where, inevitably, the conversation drifts to business matters. With the proliferation of cellular phones, beepers, and two-way pagers, private time is even more difficult to find. In Hollywood, everyone at a restaurant instinctively looks to their belts at the sound of a cell phone ringing.

When cellular phones first came out, mine became my best friend. I took it everywhere with me and marveled at the additional amount of work I was able to accomplish. Over time, I realized that for every hour of billable time I gained, I lost valuable downtime. The turning point for me came at a lunch meeting with a client during which he and I never spent more than two minutes talking to each other in between phone calls.

Even commuting time, which may seem like an ideal opportunity to take care of business, may be better spent listening to music and winding down from (or gearing up for) your workday.

Perks of the Trade

Some of you may not want to separate your personal and professional lives. One of the perks of being an entertainment lawyer is access to entertainment events, such as screenings and concerts, on a V.I.P. basis. It is unthinkable for an entertainment lawyer to attend a concert without backstage passes, or a premiere without an invitation to the after party. These are premium networking opportunities.

Wanna Dance?

It probably will not surprise you to learn that many entertainment lawyers date their clients. Even more common are entertainment lawyers who become partners with, or invest in, their clients. Because the lawyer is often among the first people to hear about a project, it is easy to get in on the ground floor. If you comply with your ethical obligations, there is no legal prohibition against it. However, before entering into these relationships, consider conflict-of-interest and disclosure issues carefully. Also consider how such a relationship with a client might affect your objectivity. Can you be honest with a client with whom you are personally or professionally involved? Will you be inclined to cut them too many breaks on billings, or unwisely give their matters priority over those of other clients? And what happens if the relationship turns sour? You will lose not only a friend, but a client as well.

Pitfalls of an Entertainment Law Practice

10

Lord, Won't You Buy Me a Mercedes-Benz?

One of the keys to maintaining a profitable practice is to keep control of your overhead. This means expanding carefully and not overextending yourself. Just because you are doing well with a client or two doesn't mean you should rush out, buy a Benz, and lease a penthouse suite on Madison Avenue. Remember, a client can be big today and gone tomorrow. Before you expand, revise your business plan and weigh the risks.

Keeping control of overhead does not mean scrimping on your image. Even during tough times, let everyone think you are thriving, and never complain about billings.

Beggars Can't Be Choosers

When first hanging up your shingle, you may not be able to turn away paying clients just because they are not exactly the type of clients you are after. There is no shame in taking on non-entertainment matters to pay the rent. Over time, you can become more selective until you are able to practice entertainment law full-time.

Out of Bounds

The area of conflict of interest is particularly difficult in entertainment law. Because the entertainment industries are so intertwined, conflicts are common. One entertainment lawyer remarked to me that if he refused to take every new client who presented a potential conflict, he would be out of business. In fact, conflicts often are coveted by entertainment clients looking to use their lawyer's relationships to further their careers. A client interested in a company you represent is less likely to be concerned about your duty of loyalty to him than about your ability to use that relationship to get him a deal.

Some commentators have argued that entertainment lawyers should have a different set of standards applied to them because of the unique aspects of the specialty. For two interesting viewpoints on this question, read Edwin McPherson's article "Conflicts in the Entertainment Industry? . . . . Not!" and Owen Sloane's article "Serving Two Masters May Jeopardize Client Interests," both reprinted in Appendix L.

Edwin McPherson argues that the defining issue should be whether the conflicted parties are truly adversarial. For example, let's say two of your entertainment clients decide to collaborate on a project and split everything down the middle. To make it even clearer, suppose the deal terms have already been negotiated by your clients' respective managers/agents and presented to you for the sole purpose of documenting the agreement. In this instance, it seems remote that either client will be harmed by your concurrent representation. McPherson goes on to point out that even two entertainment clients who ask you to negotiate deal terms between them may not be as adversarial as they would be in a typical litigation context. Since the material terms of most entertainment transactions are determined largely by industry custom, it is not hard to fashion a deal that is fair to both clients.

Owen Sloane, on the other hand, argues that arriving at a fair result is not sufficient and that most clients expect you to be more than impartial. He suggests that the real issue is the sophistication of the clients involved, and the degree of confidence each client reposes in you. In his view, even though not expressly required by the ABA Model Rules of Professional Responsibility, you should withdraw your representation whenever you are not able to provide uncompromising counsel.

Both perspectives have merit. However, debating this proposition is a purely intellectual exercise since the Rules of Professional Responsibility are not likely to be changed for entertainment lawyers anytime soon. It doesn't help that entertainment lawyers have a history of not only ignoring conflicts but of using them to their advantage. If two partners in the same firm cut a deal between two of the firm's clients during a coffee break, can they be trusted not to put the interests of the more important firm client over those of the less important one? Even more disturbing, would a lawyer be inclined to betray client confidences to curry favor with a powerful industry executive who is in a position to refer him business?

Since entertainment clients often insist on proceeding in spite of conflicts, be mindful of your disclosure and written waiver requirements. If a deal goes bad, you may become the scapegoat, and a conflict of interest is a red flag. Before taking on a new client, identify all adverse and interested parties. In larger firms, circulate a memo for all lawyers to sign off on. For direct conflicts, you must obtain the informed written consent of all parties. I have included a sample conflict waiver in Appendix M. The client should be advised to have the waiver reviewed by outside counsel and perhaps the underlying transaction as well. In an indirect conflict situation, a written disclosure is sufficient.

It's a Jungle Out There

The competition for clients among entertainment lawyers is fierce, and some lawyers will go to great lengths to steal clients. I was in the middle of shopping a deal for one client when he told me that his previous lawyer had called him demanding to be involved. My client said that although he refused at first, this lawyer threatened to sabotage the negotiations with one of the interested companies if he was not included. Since this lawyer represented the president of that company, my client took the threat seriously and asked me to collaborate with his former lawyer with respect to negotiations with that company. As it turned out, my client did the deal with another company. After the fact, however, I learned that my client's previous lawyer had actually phoned the president of the new company and trashed his own client in an effort to steer the deal back to his other company client.

There is an old saying that there is no such thing as a secret in Hollywood. This means that you should assume that comments made about others, even if in confidence, may end up being thrown back in your face. Clients come and go, but you are likely to deal with the same lawyers and executives over and over again.

Keep It to Yourself

It is also helpful to keep in mind that entertainment clients sometimes talk merely to entertain themselves. It is not uncommon for a client to call me one day insisting that I fire his manager, only to change his mind the next day or forget he ever gave me the instruction in the first place. As a result, it may be prudent to delay carrying out requests that you feel are being made in haste. I often ask clients to reflect upon emotional decisions for a day or so.

Don't Take It Personally

If you are going to weather the storms of an entertainment practice, learn how to let criticism run off your back. One long-standing client of mine has a reputation for flying off the handle in stressful situations. However, this client is successful and hardworking. Colleagues have praised me for putting up with her over the years, but the truth is I have learned how to deal with her tirades and not to take them personally.

Don't Put All Your Eggs in One Basket

One common mistake is to rely too heavily on one or two successful clients. This may be unavoidable in the early stages of your practice, but you should expand your client base as quickly as you can. If you lose a client who represents a substantial percentage of your billings, you will have nothing to fall back on.

I will never forget one painful experience early in the development of my practice. I was referred an artist by a record company that was interested in signing her. Upon meeting the artist and listening to her material, I felt this company was not right for the musical direction she wanted to pursue. She agreed and after months of listening to new material, I shopped her tape. I was turned down at every major record company. Undaunted, I shopped her tape to music publishing companies and finally found someone who shared my belief in her. Throughout this process, she and I became close, and I spent many nonbillable hours reassuring her about her personal and professional insecurities.

Once at the publishing company, she hired a personal manager who stepped in and took control of her life. As a result, her reliance on me diminished. After she signed her first record deal and started to achieve success, the manager perceived me as a threat and fired me. The artist admitted that she was embarrassed about this but had to defer to her manager's decision. The artist has since gone on to become one of today's leading new artists and yours truly receives no credit or billings. Luckily, I had other clients that I focused on and the loss was not fatal to my practice.

To avoid overreliance on any one client, delegate work for that client to your partners/associates and use the extra time to cultivate new clients. Even if you are thriving, you must constantly plant new seeds and build new relationships. Invariably, some of these seeds will sprout into important clients, just as others fade away.

11 *Managing the Workload (Getting the Work Out)*

Sink or Swim

Managing the workload and getting the work out in entertainment law presents many unique challenges. I realized this from my first day of work when I walked into a stack of files, memos, and phone messages. There was no orientation, no friendly chat from a supervising lawyer—only deadlines. To make matters worse, all the entertainment lawyers at the firm were too busy to give me guidance.

I will never forget my first negotiation. The firm's client was a prominent film composer. Attached to the file I was given was a composer's agreement with numerous comments written on it. A short memo from the partner explained that he had discussed these comments with the studio's lawyer, who was waiting for our responses. He instructed me to review his notes and close the deal as soon as possible.

This would have been a daunting task for an experienced lawyer, let alone a brand-new associate. Nevertheless, I studied the agreement, pulled up previous agreements involving the same client, and even read a few law review articles on the subject. When I asked the partner for some time, he cut me off after five minutes to deal with an "emergency." Needless to say, much to my chagrin, I fumbled ineptly through the negotiation.

Most entertainment lawyers I know had the same experience of being thrown off the deep end of the pool at the outset of their careers. If you have trouble with that kind of pressure, pick another field.

Hook, Line, and Sinker

Although your level of expertise will improve over time, you will never feel in control of your workload. The key to sinking or swimming is *effective time management.* All entertainment lawyers find themselves in the same boat at one time or another, and avoiding calls or making up excuses will only make matters worse. Be honest with clients and their representatives, but do not expect the same level of understanding. Often, the only way to calm a client down is to give him a date by which you expect to complete a task; however, in doing so, do not set unrealistic deadlines for yourself. The best approach is usually to simply tell your client that you will get to the matter as soon as you can.

First Things First

Prioritizing matters is essential. Matters involving your most important clients should be given priority, but should also be weighed against the time pressures of each deal. For example, if you are working on a deal for a less important client that must be completed by a certain date, you might prioritize it over a matter for a more important client that is not time-crucial. There is no shame in explaining to your more important client that you have an emergency for someone else that requires your immediate attention.

Wait and See

Everyone agrees that time-wasting endeavors should be avoided. Having said that, deciding what is a waste of time is not always easy. For example, spending time with a client who cannot afford to pay may seem pointless. However, if the client is on the verge of a big deal, it might be worth seeing if the deal comes to fruition.

Spending time going over a matter with a prospective client or even a nonclient may also seem like a waste of time. However, this can be a good investment if the nonclient is in a position to refer you business or assist you in other matters. This is what networking is all about.

The more influential people with whom you have working relationships, the more powerful you become. As I have said before, *the golden rule in entertainment law is that what you know is less important than who you know.* Doing a favor for another lawyer, or a key executive, by giving free legal advice will often be repaid at a later date.

Getting to the Heart of the Matter

The bottom line is that you will not be able to crank the work out until you become familiar with the issues that should be addressed in negotiations. An experienced entertainment lawyer will spot issues instinctively. A less experienced lawyer will benefit from a checklist.

Making a List and Checking It Twice

When dealing with entertainment contracts, that checklist should include the following basic issues:

1. Term of the agreement. All agreements should specify the period of time for which services are being provided and/or rights are being granted.
2. Territory covered by the agreement (for example, North America only, the world excluding North America, Europe, etc.)

3. Scope—what the agreement entails (for example, services and/or rights)
4. The commitments/duties of each party (including delivery and scheduling requirements, budgetary, creative, and administrative responsibilities)
5. Payment terms—fixed (meaning guaranteed) and contingent (meaning profit-based)
6. Accounting and audit provisions
7. Credit provisions (for example, the size and placement of billing, which may include name and/or logo identification)
8. Warranties/representations/indemnifications
9. Assignability
10. Dispute resolution, choice of law, and notice provisions

Getting to Know You

One habit to avoid is the tendency to assume that every client and every agreement is basically the same. Once you are trained to recognize issues, it is easy to spew them out. It is much more difficult to cull critical issues from nonessential terms. Take the time to find out which issues are important to each client and concentrate on those.

If a negotiation drags on because you raise every conceivable issue, you will not make your client happy. You may think you are being thorough, but you may actually be alienating not only opposing counsel but your own client as well. This problem can be exacerbated when your client is presented with a huge bill for the time you spent negotiating points that your client did not care anything about.

Just as your reputation can be damaged by unreasonable demands from your client, so your client will be judged by how you conduct negotiations on his behalf. Bad blood created as a result of overaggressive lawyering may poison the reputation of a client at a company and brand your client as difficult or hard to work with.

Getting to Yes

If you are having trouble resolving important issues in a negotiation, get a sense of the other side's reasons for refusing to concede them. Discuss these points with your client and brainstorm creative solutions that address everyone's concerns. For example, let's say opposing counsel is not offering your client sufficient compensation for a project. His client may have the money, but may be skittish about risking too much up front. If your client is confident about his chances of success, he might accept additional payments that are based on performance. Opposing counsel in this scenario is likely to embrace the idea of your client earning the extra money he wants.

Shop 'Til You Drop

Pitching clients for projects is an art form unto itself. Start by evaluating the entertainment package. In a music context, a typical package will consist of a demo (preferably in compact disc or digital audiotape format), a picture, and a biography. The demo should consist of three to five songs. In that regard, quality is more important than quantity. If your client has only two good songs, go with that rather than add mediocre material to fill up space.

In film and television, the typical package consists not only of a screenplay or teleplay, but also of key elements "attached" to the project, such as a star actor or a well-known director.

Make a list of prospective buyers and go over it with your client. Discuss the pros and cons of different companies and list them in order of preference. In music, there are a handful of record companies, producers, and music publishers who have the ability to finance, promote, and distribute music. In film, the primary sources of funding include private investment groups, distributors (major and independent), foreign sales agents, and banks.

Make personal contact and pitch the project personally before sending the package. Don't apologize for the material even if there are flaws. If you cannot deliver the package personally, send it by messenger or FedEx and follow up to make sure it is received. Get reactions as soon as possible. If there is interest, set up a meeting or invite key executives to a performance or screening. Invite multiple companies to fill in for no-shows and to create hype.

Find out who else will be involved in the shopping process and what their role will be. In music, personal managers often shop deals. In film and television, agents typically assume an active role.

In some cases, it is better to pitch a manager or agent first before directly approaching companies.

Be energetic and passionate, and keep your lawyerly pride in your briefcase.

Bidding Wars

When negotiating a new deal for a client, use offers from other companies to improve your bargaining position. Competing companies will often outbid each other for a coveted deal. However, during the feeding frenzy, don't lose sight of which company will do the best job of marketing your client's project. Some companies will outbid a competitor merely for the satisfaction of winning, even if they are not properly set up to market the project. Up-front money is certainly important, but not at the expense of long-term success. Work with your client's manager/agent to ascertain each company's plans and ask the following questions: What other projects are on the company's roster that might compete with your client's? What is the first available release date? What marketing commitments is the company prepared to make?

Although most companies accept bidding wars as part of the shopping process, some will insist that their offers not be used to obtain better offers. If you are pursuing multiple offers, do not mischaracterize them. Competitors talk, and if you are found to have been deceptive, this will not only hurt your deal but will damage your reputation.

Strike While the Iron Is Hot

In any event, keep the shopping process moving along and settle on the best offer as quickly as possible. If your client takes too much time considering offers or trying to improve them, they may disappear by the time your client is ready to accept them. This is especially true if you are negotiating a deal for an unproven client. Often, deals can be improved after the fact. See "Renegotiation" later in this chapter. In addition, the longer the process takes, the more likely you are to lose control of your client. Remember that other entertainment lawyers may be whispering in your client's ear that they could do better.

Control

Once your client accepts an offer, consummate the deal immediately and instruct your client not to discuss it with the other party. If you are negotiating an agreement, client contact can only hurt, especially if your client is unpredictable. I was in the final stages of one negotiation when my client demanded to speak with the company's vice president for creative affairs. Over my objections, I asked this executive to phone my client. The executive told me later that she spoke to someone at the number I had given her who rudely rebuffed her. It turns out it was my client's bodyguard, who confused the executive with a groupie. Fortunately, the executive was able to laugh off the incident, but it could easily have soured the deal.

Although deals are made year-round, companies tend to be more active in the first half of the year when their budgets are fresh. By the middle of the summer, those budgets may be depleted as companies focus on their summer and Christmas releases. Many entertainment executives also take vacations during the summer and at the end of the year.

The Power of the Pen

Case management has many applications in entertainment law. The most common tasks involve contracts. Your role in negotiating agreements will depend on whether you or opposing counsel will be preparing the paperwork. Although there are no hard-and-fast rules, if you are representing creative people who are dealing with a company, the company's lawyer will typically insist on using his or her form of agreement. Being more familiar with its terms than you are gives the opposing lawyer an advantage.

One way to even the playing field is to study a contract you may have previously negotiated with that company. This will refresh your memory about that company's policies and inform you about which concessions you are likely to achieve. Most companies have forms of agreement that have concessions built in. These are commonly referred to as the "A form" or the "B form." Ask opposing counsel to send you as prenegotiated a form as possible.

In-house lawyers are under pressure to close deals. As a result, most will cooperate to expedite the negotiation process. If you have done a deal with that company recently or, even better, with that lawyer, it will be easier to persuade him/her to start with concessions from the last deal you and he/she worked on. However, company lawyers are also expected to hold the line and not to concede points easily. Therefore, some may not be willing to automatically include prior concessions in a first draft.

Opposing counsel's willingness to prenegotiate will also depend upon your client's bargaining position. If the prior deal involved a highly coveted client, but the new negotiation involves an unproven one, opposing counsel may appropriately argue that not all of the prior concessions should apply.

Chasing Your Tail

Even if you are assured by opposing counsel that you are receiving a form of agreement that you previously negotiated, it is incumbent upon you to read the agreement thoroughly. It is not uncommon to review an agreement in this circumstance and find changes.

Some lawyers prefer to raise issues in letter form, but the more efficient method is to notate comments directly on the draft and send it to opposing counsel. This is commonly called a "markup." Either way, copy your client and reserve his right to request additional modifications. In negotiating comments, note opposing counsel's responses (and your counteroffers) in different-colored ink and identify them by date and source. When you receive a revised draft, use your last markup as a road map to identify which concessions were made and which issues remain open.

Form over Substance

If your client is dealing with a smaller company, or a collaborator, or if you represent a company, offer to prepare the agreement yourself. Drafting agreements is time-consuming, but it puts you in the driver's seat. The key to effective document preparation is selecting the right form. Ask yourself, have I done a similar agreement recently? If so, use that form as a starting point. To help you develop your form file, I have included in Appendix N a few of the forms commonly used in an entertainment practice (a personal management agreement, a recording artist agreement, a songwriter agreement, a screenwriter agreement, a film producer agreement, a music producer agreement, and an actor agreement). For more forms, refer to Mark Litwak's book *Contracts for the Film and Television Industry,* 2d ed. (Silman-James Press, 1998); *Entertainment Law,* 2d ed., by J. Selz, M. Simensky, P. Acton, and R. Lind (West Group, 1998); and Matthew Bender's entertainment law form book series (Matthew Bender & Co., Inc., bender.com).

Before putting pen to paper, go over the deal points with your client and obtain all relevant information. One good way to avoid mistakes is to ask your client to send you an outline of the deal terms to work from. If you are unclear about how to address an issue, call your client and discuss it. Offer suggestions on deal structure and additional provisions your client may not have considered. Send a rough draft to your client for approval before furnishing it to opposing counsel if you have time, and always reserve your client's right to modify the provisions of any document you send out.

Mix and Match

If you are drafting an agreement that does not fit with anything you have done before, decide what form you have that can best be adapted. Don't be afraid to call other lawyers to see if they have a form that is more on point. In some cases, you may have to mix and match provisions from different agreements.

I recently prepared an agreement for a client who wanted a finder's fee in the event he was able to obtain a deal for an artist, as well as the option to manage the act and co-own the act's material. He requested that all of this fit in no more than two pages. This presented me with the challenge of condensing three separate agreements, each of which could have been ten to twenty pages, into a two-page document.

A Form for All Seasons

As you build your form file, develop various types of agreements for different situations. For example, I have several personal management agreements: a long form that is favorable to the manager and one that is favorable to the artist, as well as medium-sized forms and deal memos.

One of the most challenging aspects of entertainment law is that just when you think you have seen every form, a client will ask you to prepare an off-the-wall agreement that has nothing to do with anything you have ever done before. Rather than trying to adapt a form, you may be better off pulling out your dictaphone and creating the document from scratch. Here are a few hints to help you prepare a complicated agreement:

1. Outline the material issues in your head before putting pen to paper.
2. Begin the draft with recitals and definitions to set up your working premises.
3. Create defined terms for concepts you intend to use more than once.
4. Avoid wordy, redundant sentences and unnecessary legalese.

Caveat Emptor

If you are the drafting party, you may be called upon to draft negotiated changes. Most in-house lawyers have form variations they use when drafting concessions. The problem is that many of these variations are so loaded with caveats and exceptions that they simply create new issues to resolve.

One prominent company had a senior lawyer on staff for years whose sole job was to refine that company's forms so that they were as favorable to the company as possible. These forms and form variations became notorious for their hidden meanings. The ill-fated strategy behind this was to wear down opposing counsel, but it often backfired when deals took too long to close and other companies interceded to steal coveted signings. As a drafter, strive to phrase concessions concisely to avoid prolonged negotiation over the same issues.

Indicate changes from prior drafts by "red-lining" (sometimes also referred to as "black-lining") drafts of an agreement. This can be done either by hand or by computer. Do this each time you send out a new set of revisions. If you are red-lining by hand, indicate added material by underlining. If an entire paragraph is new, you can draw a vertical line in the lefthand margin of the paragraph without having to underline each line. Identify deletions by inserting an upside-down caret (^) where the deletion occurred. Most computer redlining programs, such as Microsoft Word, put a line through deleted provisions and either underline or highlight additions.

Hung Up over You

In more cases than not, I find that a willingness to concede nonmaterial points is a good way to move a negotiation along. Too many lawyers get bogged down negotiating meaningless provisions. Sometimes the situation is unavoidable if opposing counsel makes endless comments. It may be that opposing counsel is inexperienced and afraid to depart from his or her checklist. In this instance, lines need to be drawn. In all likelihood, opposing counsel will get pressure from his client to conclude the transaction, especially if your client is holding the check.

One particularly annoying type of negotiator is one who constantly raises new issues. The only way to deal with this is to set limits lest you be dragged into a quagmire of endless negotiation.

Handle with Care

Whether you are drafting or reviewing, handle and disseminate documents carefully. Since time is usually a factor, your first consideration should be the quickest method of delivery. Faxing or e-mailing is instantaneous. However, it is best to follow up faxes and e-mails with original copies by mail or express delivery. Always keep copies of original documents you send out.

In addition to time, cost is a consideration. Although you can bill back most costs, you still need to cover the initial outlay. In addition, you cannot always count on reimbursement. Finally, clients appreciate your saving them money. Regular mail is the cheapest way to send documents. It is usually reliable, but things have been known to get lost in the mail, and it is difficult to pinpoint an exact delivery date. Express mail service costs more but offers the advantage of speedy delivery and the ability to trace misplaced items. Most express couriers offer options that are more or less costly depending on how quickly you require the delivery to be made.

The most costly but fastest method of delivering documents is by personal messenger. Check with other businesses in your area for reliable referrals. Make sure the messengers are bonded and ask them about discounts for nonurgent deliveries. Messengers are most often used to send checks or original contracts. They also make an impression on the receiver of an important package. You can use messengers to retrieve documents for you or even to accomplish a round-trip task such as sending a contract to a client to sign and then having it returned to you.

Certain notices require registered mail or personal delivery to be effective. Always check the notice provision of an agreement before sending out an official letter. You can also use "return receipt requested" for proof that a parcel or letter was received on a given date. Many office buildings have a central mail room that can handle this for you.

To save time, order postage by mail, and have a current postage scale to calculate postage for larger packages. If you are sending out contracts to be signed, tab (with colored "sign here" flags) the exact places that require signature and give detailed signing instructions in your cover letter. Also indicate (with colored "initial here" flags) the exact places that require initialing. If you are sending contracts to a client to be signed, include a self-addressed stamped return envelope or return FedEx pouch for convenience. Follow up to make sure documents are received. Be careful of notarization or witness requirements.

If multiple parties are signing a contract, you can provide for the agreement to be signed in counterparts. This enables you to send out individual copies to each party and assemble them later, rather than having to wait for each party to sign before forwarding the agreement on.

Make enough copies of contracts so that you, your client, each opposing party, and their counsel can have a fully executed original copy. Don't ask the other side to make copies for you unless time is short and you are sending a contract by fax or e-mail.

Perfect in Every Way

In all things, strive for perfection. Sloppy contracts or letters with typographical errors stick out like a sore thumb. Proofread outgoing correspondence before you sign it, even if you have already edited it. Do the same for documents you prepare. One good practice is to stamp every page of a final contract with your initials to indicate that you proofread it before it went out. Don't let anyone pressure you into sending out a document before you are satisfied with it. People will soon forget that it was late, but will never forget if it was wrong.

Breaking Up Is Hard to Do

The next most common task in entertainment law is dispute resolution. This does not mean dispute resolution in a formal sense, such as through litigation or arbitration; rather, it involves the informal settlement of disputed matters through negotiation.

Often, a dispute will center on the interpretation of a preexisting contract, and whether the parties have fulfilled their obligations. If there is no written contract, you may be called upon to advise your client about what the customary terms would have been had there been a formal agreement.

Unless you have experience in litigation, advise your client that any dispute resolution effort will not include the filing of formal action by you. However, be aware that any communication or negotiation undertaken may impact subsequent litigation. If your client has sufficient resources, involve litigation counsel on a consulting basis early in the process. It can also be useful to get an opinion in advance from an experienced litigator about the merits and weaknesses of your client's position. This will give you a better idea about how to approach settlement discussions.

If you are not a litigator, avoid arguing points of law. Confine yourself to the business issues and the expectations of the parties involved. No matter what the merits, the resolution of most disputes ultimately boils down to money.

Sometimes the key to resolving a dispute lies beyond the merits, relying more on the financial and political strength of the interested parties. For example, if your client is going up against a major entertainment company, you need to take into account that companies are not generally intimidated by litigation. In addition, it may not serve your client to get a reputation for being contentious, even if he has a good claim. Many talented people in entertainment have found doors closed to them simply because of disputes early in their careers.

Quid Pro Quo

One effective way to resolve disputes is to look for quid pro quo solutions.

In one matter I handled, a production company discovered an artist and was getting him signed to a company. Unfortunately, the company had failed to conclude a written agreement with the artist. By the time I was hired, the artist's first product had already been released and was showing signs of success. The production company knew I had a good working relationship with the distributor and hired me to negotiate their distribution agreement. However, in reviewing the matter, I advised my new client that the first order of business was to get the artist signed and that they were at risk of losing the whole deal until they did so. I immediately prepared an agreement with the artist.

When several weeks passed without a response, I suspected something was up. My suspicions were confirmed when I received a letter from the artist's lawyer stating that the artist did not feel that he was under contract to my client. Neither the artist nor my client had the resources for a legal battle over the enforceability of their oral agreement. Accordingly, I focused my attention on the distributor. Even though the underlying dispute was between the artist and my production company client, the distributor was the only one with the resources to settle the dispute. In the end, the distributor gave my client a share of the profits from the artist and a deal for another artist of theirs as a reward for allowing the artist to sign directly.

Let My People Go

The most common disputes involve disgruntled clients looking to extricate themselves from bad deals. Often there are no clear legal grounds for termination of an agreement. Rather than inventing phantom breaches, sometimes the best approach is to simply ask the other side for permission to find another deal. If your client is unhappy, chances are the other side may be just as dissatisfied and will accept a profit participation in a new deal rather than force your client to perform for them. Even if the other side is not anxious to let your client go, they can often be persuaded if your client is resolved not to perform for them and the exit price is right. Although some companies will not interfere with contracts under any circumstances, many in entertainment are only too willing to jump into the fray for a coveted deal. Contract jumping in many segments of the entertainment industry is practically an accepted business practice.

Renegotiation

Another common request from unhappy clients is to renegotiate the terms of a bad deal. Since unproven clients have little bargaining power, they often enter into long-term contracts at the beginning of their careers that do not keep pace with their market value once they achieve success. As a result, most entertainment companies accept renegotiation as a customary practice. Nevertheless, don't expect market value concessions. After all, you can't use a bidding war to drive up the price when your client is already under contract.

Pride of Ownership

Another common task in entertainment law is the securing of rights. This generally encompasses copyrights, trademarks, and patents.

Of the three, patent law is the most arcane. You should not approach this area without experience. Patents are less prevalent in entertainment than copyrights or trademarks since they involve the protection of processes and designs, as opposed to artistic product.

Ownership of rights in intellectual property is crucial to entertainment transactions. Once product is exploited embodying uncleared copywritten material, or under an infringing trade name, the infringing parties are at the mercy of a plaintiff and the resulting settlement can be costly.

Clearing the Air

When dealing with copyrights, identify which portions of a work are owned by your client. For example, if a producer is hired to write music, find out if he interpolated other material into his work. If so, negotiate clearances in advance for the right to use that interpolated material. If there is a question about whether preexisting material is protected, seek the advice of a copyright specialist.

In film and television, establishing a clear chain of title is fundamental to production. Make sure the underlying literary property is free and clear and that all underlying rights have been properly secured.

Get It in Writing

If the issue of underlying rights does not center on preexisting material, but on collaborators, another set of issues arises.

Artistic collaboration is a personal undertaking, and collaborators commonly ignore the business aspects of their relationship during the creative process. If your client is skittish about agreements, advise him to set out the arrangement in his own words. A more formal agreement can be prepared later, but at least this will document the basic understanding of the parties before it is too late.

Prepare basic confirmation forms that your client can feel comfortable going over with a collaborator. These forms may simply identify the name of the work being created, the parties involved, and the nature of their respective contributions. See Appendix O-2 for a basic form. Encourage clients to handle this business immediately after the creation of a work. The longer your client waits, the more likely problems are to arise.

Out of the Woodwork

If your client is contracting with others for services, as opposed to collaborating, prepare "work-for- hire" releases for them to have signed. "Work-for-hire" is a term found in the United States Copyright Act that allows the transfer of ownership of the results and proceeds of a person's work to that person's employer at the moment of creation. For example, a producer may hire a musician to perform guitar parts for a song. Have the guitarist sign a release acknowledging that the services are owned exclusively by your producer client and were paid for in full. Otherwise, the guitarist may pop up when the song is successful and claim to have done more than simply played parts. In retrospect, it may be difficult to prove who created what. I have included a release agreement in Appendix O-1.

A Rose by Any Other Name

Trademark issues arise whenever you are representing a new client or establishing a new business. Performers, producers, and writers often adopt professional names. On the local level, your client must obtain a fictitious business license. This is a simple process that can be handled through any local or regional legal publication for a nominal fee.

National protection is more involved. Engage a service that specializes in trademark searches that include not only an examination of the trademark registry, but common-law uses. Thomson & Thomson is an established search service: 500 Victory Road, North Quincy, Massachusetts 02171-3145. The telephone number is (800)692-8833. The fax number is (617)786-8273. Their Web site address is thomson-thomson.com. Another service is Trademark Express: 2025 Pennsylvania Avenue, Suite 1004, Washington, D.C. 20006. The telephone number is (800)340-2010. The fax number is (203)496-1601. A new online service is Trademark.com. A search report will identify all potentially competing uses and provide whatever information is available on them. It is up to you to analyze this information and advise your client. If you are not a trademark specialist, you might consider referring this work out. If you do advise on this area, familiarize yourself with the issues and case law.

Clients may ask whether an extensive search is necessary. As in many businesses, name recognition is an important asset. If a client starts to build a reputation under a performing or company name, only to find that the name has already been used, valuable marketing efforts will have been wasted. The registration of domain names for Web site use, or URLs, has also become an essential task. One company that handles the searching and registration of domain names is Network Solutions, Inc. Their Web site is networksolutions .com.

Name rights should also be flagged when negotiating agreements. For example, if members of a group are forming a partnership, pay attention to who has rights to use the group name if they break up. If this issue is not addressed, it can cripple the future endeavors of the individuals involved.

Business as Usual

A final task often performed by entertainment lawyers is the establishment of business relationships, such as setting up a partnership or a corporation. Deciding on the actual form of association may involve issues beyond your expertise, such as tax considerations. If you are not expert in this area, consult a specialist.

If you represent one of the partners, advise the other partner(s) to get separate representation. If the other partners ask you to represent them as well, obtain conflict-of-interest waivers.

Get a sense of what work the business will require and whether you will be able to offer those services. If a particular project is crucial to the venture (such as acquiring rights to someone's life story), secure those rights simultaneously with the cementing of the business relationship.

I'm Late, I'm Late, for a Very Important Date

Keeping track of important dates is difficult in an entertainment practice. Automated computer programs, such as Microsoft's Outlook, can calendar important dates and tickle follow-up matters. You can also set up a manual tickler system by writing reminders on a calendar or by placing an extra copy of correspondence in a calendaring file. A week to ten days later, the item can be retrieved and given to you for further instructions. At that time, you can either put it back in the calendaring file for an additional period of time or ask your assistant to place a follow-up call concerning the matter. You can also follow up on matters by stamping "Still Awaiting Reply" on prior correspondence and sending it out again with the new date. You can do this once every two weeks or so to keep a record of your follow-up efforts. Copy clients to let them know you are staying on top of things.

For specific contractual option dates, it may not be possible to be accurate in all circumstances. For example, many entertainment agreements provide for options that are triggered by the occurrence of a future event, such as the commencement of principal photography of a film. Since the client is in a better position to monitor these events than you are, it is wise to advise him to assume primary responsibility for keeping track of option dates, and your retainer letter should specifically address this point.

Every company has its horror stories of the prized property that got away because someone missed an option date. As a result, more and more companies are insisting upon language that provides for a notice and cure before an option lapses. Others include options that are automatically exercised, unless there is a notice to the contrary. The danger in this is that an option may inadvertently be exercised, creating obligations the exercisor may not wish to assume.

Computer Love

Advances in automation have revolutionized the practice of entertainment law. It is difficult to imagine practicing in this area without computers and e-mail. Since the area relies heavily on document preparation and correspondence, purchase effective word processing software, such as Microsoft Word or WordPerfect. Appendix Q describes a good hardware and software setup.

Unless you are preparing spreadsheets, you do not need special software in this area. However, you do need software for billings. Timeslips is an effective program.

I Remember

Have sufficient memory to store your documents, and network the computers in your office. This assures you that you are working on the most current draft of a document. Install a tape backup system that periodically saves what is on your hard drive. It might also be worth investing in a document scanner that allows you to input agreements. If you receive a well-crafted document, ask for it to be e-mailed to you and store it in your form directory. You can also input your Rolodex and access calls from your computer. This can be tied in directly to your cell phone and pocket computer as well. Install modems and CD-ROMs so that you can receive and send documents directly from your computer and audition interactive client material.

Hide and Seek

Your ability to locate documents easily is crucial. The key is to carefully organize your database by clients and matters. Keep separate directories for "forms," "retainer letters," "conflict letters," and other commonly used documents, and create subdirectories within each client directory for larger files. Label each document you prepare clearly. List the parties, the type of agreement, and the version of the document (either by indicating the latest date and/or document version number). For example, "Smith/Disney/ Stars License 6/12/97." You can also employ a numbering or coding system in the footer of your documents. Periodically delete older documents and save them to disk for storage. Label those disks by date and by matter, and keep them handy in case you need to retrieve a stored document later.

Surfing the Web

E-mail is streamlining the process of communicating with clients and other lawyers. It not only allows you to communicate instantaneously with anyone anywhere in the world, but eliminates the need for internal memorandums in your office. Many clients and lawyers prefer e-mail to phoning or faxing.

The Internet contains unlimited information. Resource materials, such as industry news, names and numbers of client representatives, and dates of conventions and seminars are available. You can subscribe to industry news services and catch up on the latest happenings first thing every morning. (See Appendixes C, E, F, G, and H for informative Web sites.) Set up your own Web site to advertise your services, or to discuss controversial issues.

12 Managing the Workload (Information Gathering and Fact Investigation)

Gather Your Thoughts

When a client presents you with a new matter, the first step is to gather as much information as possible. In a prospective client interview, the initial conversation/meeting should include questions about the background of the client, how the client came to you, the specific matters that require your attention, and fee arrangements. Explore the client's expectations and level of sophistication right off the bat. Ask the client to bring any relevant documents to the initial meeting or, if possible, send them in advance. Also request a sample of the client's work, if applicable.

Artist and Repertoire

If the prospective representation includes shopping, start with an evaluation of the product. In a music context, this would consist of auditioning demonstration recordings. In film and television, this would involve reading an underlying literary property, such as a treatment, screenplay, teleplay, series concept, novel, or life story. Find out as much as you can about what you will be shopping. Where/how was the product created and who was involved? Is the client happy with the quality of the product or does he feel that additional work is necessary? How old is his material? Is there more-current material he is working on? Does the client have a track record in entertainment, and if so, is any of his previous work available for review? Does the client have a budget and/or business plan prepared for the project? In the case of a performer, what is his image? Does he have pictures and a biography? Are those materials current? Can the client supply his own packages, or does he expect you to make copies? Has the product been shopped before, and if so, by whom and what were the results? Are there current copies of the product in the hands of other shoppers?

Can We Talk?

To assist you in conducting a typical client interview concerning a new matter, consider the following questions:

1. **Who Are the Players?**

   In other words, who are the relevant parties to be involved in the matter? This involves not only the person or company with whom your client is doing or is about to do business, but the representatives of that person/company, if known. This area of inquiry should be broad enough to encompass anyone with whom your client has had contact in connection with the matter. Perhaps you will recognize someone involved and gain a personal entrée.

   Playing the "Who do you know/work with?" game can also flag potential conflicts. This should include current business associates, as well as prior relationships. Hearing a client's perspective on former deals can also instruct you in how to keep your client satisfied with your work.

Finally, find out who will handle the matter for the other party, if known. If that person is not a lawyer, the additional question to ask is whether a lawyer will be involved.

2. **Who's in the Loop?**

Once you have a feel for the nature of the matter, the next step is to find out who your client wants Involved. First and foremost, ascertain what your role will be in the negotiation and how your client wants you to interact with her other representatives and/or partners. In some cases, a client will ask you to spearhead a negotiation from scratch. In other situations, a client or her manager or agent will ask you to work with them in arriving at the basic deal terms. It is also possible that the client or her manager or agent will negotiate the basic deal terms and turn the matter over to you for negotiation of the actual contract. There may also be other interested parties, such as a publisher, producer, business manager, family member, investor, or partner. Get clear instructions from your client about how involved these other individuals should be in the negotiation and whether their approval or input is required. If another person will be involved, find out how your client wants you to communicate with them. For example, does your client want to be told of developments first, or is she satisfied to have the last word?

Sometimes, who your client wants involved flags other issues. For example, if your client asks you to apprise an investor, ask what the investor's role in the matter is. It may be that your client's arrangement with the investor needs to be examined before proceeding further with the matter at hand.

If your client is comprised of a group of individuals, ascertain the dynamics of the group members. For example, are there key members? In other words, who are the decision makers and key contributors without whom the project could not continue? What would happen if a key member left the group? If everyone is to be involved in the group's business affairs, appoint a spokesperson so you don't have to repeat the same advice over and over. Do any individuals have separate concerns, and how will addressing those individual issues affect the rest of the group?

3. **Where Have You Been?**
   After you have a clear picture of who is involved, investigate the history of any negotiations. This means questioning your client and her representatives in detail about conversations they have had or information they have received. This may involve discussions with other interested parties that may not have resulted in an agreement but may have bearing on your handling of the matter. Obtain any correspondence or notes relevant to the matter and question the genesis of such materials. An examination of those materials may raise other questions or spark a client's memory about other discussions or matters.

4. **Where Are You Going?**
   Perhaps the most important area of inquiry is finding out what your client's objectives are. Is your client happy with the person/company with whom she is about to do business? Is your client pleased with the discussions to date, or does she have concerns? If a deal has been negotiated in principal, does your client want you to improve upon those terms, or merely negotiate the boilerplate provisions (that is, non-deal terms, such as warranties and indemnification)? Are there special instructions about how to handle the negotiation? If your client wants the deal improved, what does she expect? Are those expectations realistic? If not, is there a way you can bring your client's expectations down to earth? Are there other issues that might be of concern to your client, such as where and how she wants her money sent (for example, directly to her or to an accountant; by check or by wire transfer)? Is she properly set up to perform her obligations in connection with the matter? If not, what advance planning can you recommend, such as setting up a corporation or affiliating with a union, to assist your client?

5. **Tell Me Everything**
   At this point, you should have a good idea of what the matter will entail. However, to avoid problems down the road, it is always a good practice to exercise some due diligence. This includes finding out whether there are other matters that could impact your client's ability to perform the services required or grant the rights contemplated. Often you will be familiar with other matters that might have bearing on the matter at hand. If this is the case, bring them to your client's attention. Remember, it is not uncommon for a client to keep secrets. He may be too embarrassed to tell you about an ill-advised agreement he previously entered into, or may hope that no one finds out. It is also possible that your client has forgotten about another matter or does not realize its relevance to the matter at hand.

   Skeletons in the closet are all too common for entertainment clients, who are often taken advantage of in the early stages of their careers. Almost every successful entertainment client has at least one horror story about a bad deal he made on the way up. As you go through a client's past, be on the lookout for warning signs. Making a client recall an unpleasant past business experience is not easy for either of you. However, you can do a client no greater service. If you are in the middle of a new deal and someone from your client's past pops up with an unfinished piece of business, it can cripple the new deal and/or lead to an expensive settlement.

6. **Time Is of the Essence**
   The last area of inquiry involves the timing of the matter. Since most clients want their matters handled as quickly as possible, probe deeply to get a sense of the real timing issues. For example, has your client started working on the project, or is he not permitted to do so until the agreement is finished? Is there a release schedule that hinges on the completion of the agreement? Does the other party have specific timing requirements—for example, before the end

of a certain fiscal period? Has any money changed hands? What additional sums are due on completion of the deal?

Go Fish

You would certainly hope that your client or his representatives would have copies of important paperwork. Unfortunately, this is not always the case. If you are familiar with opposing counsel, you may not need written authorization to obtain copies of agreements, but if necessary, have your client sign a letter authorizing you to receive information pertaining to him. Some companies will not provide copies of accountings or backup for expenditures, even with client authorization, insisting that your client must avail himself of his contractual audit rights.

Pulling Teeth

If you are handling a dispute resolution, an extra level of awareness needs to be applied to information gathering. The parties to a dispute are almost always upset. This is particularly true with entertainment clients, whose egos may be easily bruised. At best, assume that your client will relate facts in the light most favorable to him. At worst, a client may omit important details. If your client is unable to answer simple questions like "Did you sign anything?" you may need to look elsewhere for answers.

Let Me See Your Registration

If you are asked to negotiate for rights, find out whether the rights involve acquiring intellectual property or rendering personal services. If services are involved, ask what the relationship of the parties is and the exact nature of your client's expectations. Are those expectations realistic, and on what are they based? If property rights are being acquired, what is the most effective method of protection?

Registering copyrights is relatively simple, requiring no special expertise. Determining what works require copyright protection is more complex. Ascertain whether the work in question is original or is based on other material, and whether the preexisting material is copyrighted. This may require a copyright search. Copyright searches can be done either directly with the copyright office or by clearance companies for a fee. Search registrations with industry organizations, such as the American Society of Composers, Authors, and Publishers (ASCAP) for songs and the Writers Guild of America for treatments and screenplays.

If preexisting material your client wants to use is protected, negotiate for rights to use the underlying material. This raises a number of questions:

1. Does your client want to purchase all or part of the rights?
2. Is your client satisfied to license rights for a period of time, or does he want ownership in perpetuity?
3. Does he need worldwide rights?
4. Is he better off optioning, as opposed to purchasing, rights while he develops and shops the property?

Free Samples

Advising clients who use preexisting material in a new work can be difficult, since many clients won't admit to having done so. They may feel that they can sufficiently disguise or change the preexisting material so that no one will detect it. Discourage your clients from playing this game of Russian roulette.

In reviewing new work by your clients, be on the lookout for familiar themes that may indicate copying. It is also advisable before shopping to hire a clearance specialist to give an opinion as to the existence of preexisting material.

Let's Get Together

If rights involve not the use of preexisting material but the work of collaborators, obtain information about the nature of those relationships. Find out whether discussions or agreements have been reached among the collaborators and whether your client is happy with those arrangements.

If you are asked to set up a new business venture, walk the parties through the basic issues. Gather as much information as possible about their relationship and understandings, as well as their objectives and resources. Ask the following basic questions:

1. Who are the participants in the venture and what are their roles?
2. What are the financial requirements of the venture and each parties' respective responsibilities?
3. Who will be making day-to-day and/or major decisions?
4. How are profits and losses to be split?
5. What are the restrictions, if any, on withdrawal or transfer of a partner's share?

13 Managing the Workload (Working with Other Professionals)

THE MOST TRIED-AND-TRUE WAY to manage your workload is to delegate work. This includes not only your internal staff (legal and nonlegal) but outside professionals as well (legal and nonlegal).

Ringy, Ding, Dingy

The first position you must fill is that of receptionist. Since entertainment lawyers deal with a tremendous volume of phone calls, this job should not be entrusted to just anyone. Your receptionist must be able to juggle callers and not get flustered. Hire someone with initiative who is able not only to receive messages but to transmit them accurately.

Help! I Need Somebody

Other than associates, the most important employment position in your office is your personal assistant. Hire at least one full-time assistant for each lawyer.

Some firms require lawyers to share assistants. This is not a good idea in an entertainment practice. In fact, a busy entertainment lawyer can make use of multiple assistants.

A good assistant becomes your eyes and ears. He or she keeps you organized, reminds you of important matters, keeps your appointments, and commiserates about difficult clients.

Obviously, your assistant must have word processing and secretarial skills, but should be able to do much more. In between telephone calls and correspondence, your assistant may handle document preparation, filing, and billings. Since your assistant must exercise judgment about the importance of certain inquiries, educate him or her about which clients and types of matters should be given priority. Discuss personality traits of certain clients and how best to deal with them.

Star Gazing

In the early stages of my practice, I thought it would be helpful to have an assistant who had a passion for the entertainment business. I also thought it would be beneficial if my assistant went to events that I was too busy to attend. Over time, I realized that this can create problems. One assistant I had became so obsessed with "making the scene" that she would often come in to work exhausted from a night out partying with my clients.

When You're Smilin'

You want an assistant who helps you keep an upbeat atmosphere in the office. I had one assistant who was very capable, but not at all friendly in manner. She would constantly complain about the workload and dealt with my clients in a perfunctory way. I tried to overlook her behavior because she was efficient, but she not only alienated my clients, she adversely affected my ability to manage my workload.

One note of caution is that you cannot always trust complaints about your staff from clients. If a client tells you that your assistant "blew me off," this may be the client's way of telling you that he does not like being refused access to you. The bottom line is that it takes a mature and grounded person to deal with the eccentricities of entertainment clients.

Take a Load Off

If you hire a capable assistant, you can delegate quasilegal tasks to him or her. For example, an assistant can handle information gathering and client research. He or she may be able to handle basic registrations and affiliations, such as with performing rights societies and unions/guilds. Encourage a resourceful assistant to develop his or her own contacts at these organizations.

A capable assistant can process executed agreements, send out copies of correspondence, and draft basic forms and retainer letters. This only works if your assistant is willing to undertake this responsibility and only if you are willing to invest the time to teach him or her the issues.

Paralegal Operations

Paralegals are used extensively in entertainment law. The advantage in hiring a paralegal is that his or her salary expectations are lower than a lawyer's. The downside is that you will not be able to charge as much for the paralegal's time, no matter how well qualified he/she is, because clients will expect a significant difference in hourly rates between legal and nonlegal personnel. Nevertheless, hourly rates for paralegals can be significant, even if only a fraction of those charged by lawyers. In firms that bill exclusively on a percentage basis, the cost–return ratio of using paralegals to negotiate and draft agreements can be even more advantageous.

Practicing Law Without a License

There are some paralegals who have been practicing with entertainment lawyers for so long that they handle the same type of work as lawyers. These paralegals have their own assistants and are expected to meet billable quotients. However, paralegals with this level of experience are rare and command salaries commensurate with those of associates.

The use of paralegals in entertainment companies is even more prevalent. One of my first assistants has made a career for herself in the area of licensing and has run the copyright clearance department at a prominent publishing company. Companies need not worry about how clients will interact with nonlegal personnel or how to charge for their time.

Many tasks in the entertainment business that are typically considered "legal," such as contract negotiation, are handled by nonlawyers. Such "legal duties" as starting negotiations with entertainment lawyers are often performed by creative executives.

On-the-Job Training

Law clerks and interns can also provide useful support. Because entertainment law is such an attractive field, it is not difficult to find law students willing to work for little or no pay. Many prominent law schools offer internship programs for their students in entertainment law, and I know several lawyers who got their foot in the door by interning.

However, the use of law students presents the same problems as with any other inexperienced personnel. Even a law student who has studied contract law, copyrights, and entertainment law is not capable of handling anything but the most basic matters without supervision.

If the law student is doing a formal internship, it is incumbent upon you to spend time teaching. Although this can be rewarding in a personal sense, it is not likely to improve your bottom line. The use of interns makes more sense in large firms and companies where the responsibility can be spread out among several lawyers. If the company or firm is serious about hiring the intern, these training efforts can pay dividends when the law student passes the bar. At that point, the young lawyer will be able to hit the ground running and will already be familiar with basic entertainment law concepts and firm/company policies.

Who Needs Lawyers Anyway?

Less direct, but sometimes just as effective, is the use of nonlegal professionals in connection with specific matters. As mentioned earlier, managers in music and agents in film and television can be instrumental in developing opportunities for your clients. In some cases, it can be useful to enlist their services on a consulting basis.

Number Crunchers

Another beneficial association for an entertainment lawyer is with a business manager. Many accountants specializing in entertainment are excellent deal makers and have a good working knowledge of entertainment contracts. It is not uncommon for me to receive instructions on behalf of a client from the client's business manager, who may have already negotiated the basic compensation structure of a deal.

In all situations where you are working with nonlegal professionals, observe the following basic rules:

1. Fully disclose the arrangement to your client.
2. Obtain your client's informed written consent to the association.
3. Negotiate your own fee arrangements.
4. Maintain a clear distinction between your responsibilities and the responsibilities of all nonlegal coworkers.

Guilt by Association

The traditional way to ease your workload is to work with other lawyers. One of the primary advantages of law firms and large legal departments is the capacity to allocate work according to expertise. For a solo practitioner, a small firm, or a new company, the more common solution is to contract out work to other lawyers until you can afford to hire a full-time associate. Contract work can be handled at your office or in some cases at the contract lawyer's office. If you use contract lawyers, all work should be subject to your supervision. Correspondence should be on your letterhead, if possible, and you need to arrange payment terms with the contract lawyer. Typically, the contract lawyer will bill you for his or her time at a discounted hourly rate. Since most contract lawyers expect immediate payment, only delegate work that you are certain of being paid for by your client.

Contracting work out is not just helpful in easing your workload, but may be indicated to assure you of quality representation in an area in which you are not expert. In this instance, choose contract lawyers that you trust not only to provide quality service but to respect your relationship with your client.

On the flip side, rendering services for an established entertainment lawyer as a contract lawyer can be an effective way to gain experience and get your foot in the door. For a detailed discussion of how to get the most out of being a contract lawyer, I recommend *Practicing Law Without Clients,* by David A. Robinson (American Bar Association, 1996).

One colleague of mine has set up what he calls his "virtual law firm." It consists of a group of young entertainment lawyers sharing office space and practicing under his banner. They all contribute to the group's overhead and are free to work on their own matters. When working for each other, they are paid like contract lawyers.

Hiring and Firing

The concept of hiring associates to lessen your workload and generate additional fees is a tried-and-true formula for both firms and solo practitioners. As a private practitioner, there is only so much time you can bill, but as a partner in a firm, the amount of billable time your firm can generate is limitless. This also allows you to delegate simpler tasks and devote more time to deal making and networking.

There are plenty of talented lawyers eager to gain experience in entertainment law. Some may even be willing to work at a below-market salary, or work part-time. However, it takes time to train an inexperienced lawyer. You will not necessarily notice any lightening of your workload or improvement in your bottom line right away. The other problem is that the market value of an associate you have trained increases dramatically. Without a substantial raise in salary you will lose him or her to another law firm. Having your years of training benefit the next employer more than you can be difficult to stomach.

The problem with hiring a more senior lawyer who does not require training is that experienced entertainment associates are in short supply and command above-market salaries. If you cannot afford an experienced associate, offer the lawyer a partnership or a piece of his or her own client billings as a salary supplement. Typically, one-third of the lawyer's billings would go toward overhead, and the remaining two-thirds would be available to divide up.

Before adding an associate, revise your business plan to determine how much you can afford to pay and how many billable hours you need your associate to generate to cover the additional expenses. Depending on the associate's level of experience, be prepared to write off significant amounts of time for training. When calculating the additional costs, include not just salary, but additional taxes, benefits, support staff, and office space.

Pedal to the Metal

If you have gotten to the point where you are considering adding an associate, you have more work than you can handle. The question is, do you have so much extra work that you can keep an associate busy? Be prepared to work extra hours for a while to increase your client base. If you get overwhelmed, contract out work until your associate can take over, while you devote extra time to developing new clients. Encourage your associate to develop new clients as well. Depending on your arrangement, remember to factor in the additional costs of allowing your new associate to network.

One alternative to hiring an associate is to partner with an attorney in a similar situation and share the costs of an associate. There is always the possibility of becoming a partner at a firm that either specializes in entertainment or is looking to build an entertainment division. This may be an attractive option once you have established yourself and are looking for a way to get to the next level without taking on the financial risk of expansion. Many firms who represent Internet companies are on the lookout for entertainment lawyers to advise their clients on content-related issues.

A more creative option is to enter into an "of counsel" arrangement with a firm to take advantage of their associates and lawyers in related specialties. Under this arrangement, you can delegate work and share in the billings, as well as perform work for partners in the firm. For example, suppose you have experience in film law and want to offer music-related services, such as soundtrack album deals, to your clients. You may find a music law firm that is not necessarily ready to make you a partner, but may like the idea of your using their associates for these projects. Not only will you benefit financially from the arrangement, but you will gain experience and develop contacts in related fields of entertainment law.

If you are looking to gain the credibility of an established firm but prefer to remain on your own, there are firms that may allow you to use their letterhead under an even looser "of counsel" agreement.

The Other Side of the Table

Another route is to leave private practice for a position in an entertainment company. Interestingly, this does not necessarily mean that you must give up your practice. In some cases, you can negotiate for the right to continue to represent key clients from your in-house position. Of course, if you are at a firm, you can arrange for your clients to continue to be represented by the firm. You may also be in a position to refer additional business to your firm from your new company, although this can create conflict-of-interest issues. I know more than one entertainment lawyer who left private practice to work for a company only to return to private practice later. Although the process of rebuilding a client base requires effort, it does not take that long if you have a good reputation and contacts.

A final option is to leave the field of law for nonlegal pursuits. As mentioned earlier, many prominent entertainment executives and successful entertainment entrepreneurs are former lawyers. I guess my mother was right when she told me, "A legal degree can't hurt you, no matter what you do."

Conclusion 14

IF YOU ARE AN ENTREPRENEURIAL LAWYER with a passion for entertainment, this is an excellent time to consider starting your own entertainment law firm. Emerging technologies are not only creating new areas of specialty but are streamlining the day-to-day practice. Even more exciting, the trend toward the consolidation of entertainment lawyers into larger firms is leaving many small but promising clients looking for representation. Put yourself out there and you might just find yourself with a new career.

One of the beauties of entertainment law is that there is no one road to success. Every prominent entertainment lawyer is unique, with his or her own style of doing business. Ultimately, you must find the path that works for you. Along the way, have fun and keep in mind the seven basic rules repeated throughout this book:

1. *There Is No Substitute for Experience*
2. *Expect the Unexpected*
3. *Build Relationships*
4. *Network As Much As Possible*
5. *Protect Your Reputation*
6. *Manage Your Time Effectively*
7. *Image Is Everything*

Appendix A

ENTERTAINMENT LAW ARTICLES BY GARY GREENBERG

Reprinted from *The Entertainment and Sports Lawyer*

A-1 "Crossing the Thin Line Between Manager and Attorney in the Entertainment Industry," Fall 1996

A-2 "Seven Years to Life: The Fight for Free Agency in the Record Business," Fall 1994

Appendix A-1

"Crossing the Thin Line Between Manager and Attorney in the Entertainment Industry"

By Gary Greenberg

Reprinted with permission from *Entertainment and Sports Lawyer,* a publication of the ABA Forum on the Entertainment and Sports Industries, Volume 14, Number 3, Fall 1996.

Introduction

Entertainment law is a commonly misunderstood specialty. I often find myself in conversations that go something like this: "So what do you do?" "I'm an attorney." "What's your specialty?" "Music law." "You mean you handle trials for rock stars?" "No, I'm not a litigator." "Oh, so you draw up their contracts?" "Yes, but I also negotiate their deals and help them decide which deals they should do." "Isn't that what agents and managers do?" "Yeah, but in a different way. Anyway, could you excuse me, I'm being paged by a client."

An artist's "team" of representatives typically includes a personal manager, a talent agent, a business manager/accountant, a publicist and an attorney.[1] The roles played by these representatives, however, are not always clearly delineated and often overlap. This article will focus on issues which confront entertainment attorneys who find themselves in one of the more common instances of such overlapping representation—the thin line between attorneys and personal managers.[2]

The Thin Line

Attorneys wield considerable influence throughout the entertainment industry. They function not just as dispute resolvers, but as deal makers and trend setters. Many prominent industry executives are or were attorneys, and those executives who are not attorneys rely heavily on their legal and business affairs departments, as well as on their personal attorneys.[3] There are attorneys, although some are not actively practicing law, who openly act as artist managers.[4]

The more interesting discussion, however, centers on the management-like functions routinely undertaken by entertainment lawyers who are not functioning in a formal management capacity. Many of the services typically required of a manager are often performed by the artist's attorney. This point is illustrated by examining the provisions of a standard management agreement which calls for the manager to advise and counsel the artist "with regard to general practices in the entertainment industries and with respect to such matters of which the manager may have knowledge concerning compensation and privileges for similar work, and in connection with the negotiation of all agreements affecting the artist's career."[5] Although this provision is taken from a management agreement, it is one of the most succinct descriptions of the services performed by entertainment attorneys I have found. This also indicates that managers are arguably giving legal advice when they perform the above services. In fact, most management agreements confer a power of attorney on the manager to execute agreements and other legal documents on behalf of the artist. Another function which is typically considered "managerial," but which is often performed by entertainment attorneys, is the use of contacts to generate opportunities for clients. Since most companies will not accept unsolicited material directly from people with whom they do not have a relationship, attorneys are among the handful of individuals who can give an artist that access. This often requires the attorney to make creative evaluations of an artist's ability.

Crossing the Line

I would argue that, as opposed to being a burden, the opportunity to provide career guidance and development to artists presents attorneys with an opportunity for growth, both professionally and personally, and may serve to make them better attorneys. Attorneys called upon to fulfill managerial duties can improve their client relation and deal making skills, and broaden their understanding of the industry. In addition, the opportunity to provide management services may be of particular interest to a young attorney who is trying to build an entertainment practice. It may be easier for such an attorney to do so if she can supplement her income during the difficult early years with management commissions from up-and-coming artists.

I would further argue that attorneys who are willing to perform management services can fill an important need for artists who, for one reason or another, do not have management. This can occur in a number of instances. For example, an artist may come to an attorney for help extricating himself from an existing manager. During and even after that process, the artist may be hesitant to hire a replacement manager and may look to the attorney to assist the artist on an interim basis. Another instance is the new artist who may not be in a position to attract an experienced manager. Yet another case is the artist who decides that she would rather take an active role in the direction of her own career, but with the help of advisors who are not formal managers.

I believe that attorneys are uniquely qualified to provide this assistance for a number of reasons. First, attorneys are governed by a code of ethics which discourages abuses of the fiduciary relationship that is formed between a manager and an artist. Second, attorneys receive special training in contracts and negotiation. Last, since legal considerations form such an integral part of the complicated transactions which involve intellectual property rights, attorneys are best able to safeguard the artist's interests.

The foregoing discussion is not meant to imply that artists don't need managers. In fact, personal managers perform vital roles in the entertainment industry. Nor am I suggesting that attorneys can or even should permanently replace managers. I should also point out that being a manager is not all fun and games. Management can be a thankless job filled with late-night calls and detail-oriented days (such as booking hotel reservations and making sure the dressing room is properly outfitted). As such, an attorney should carefully weigh the risks and the rewards before agreeing to manage a client.

"Everybody's Doing It": Percentage and Flat Fee Arrangements

One issue immediately raised by such representation involves an attorney's disclosure obligations concerning potential conflicts of interest and fee issues. Most managers are compensated in the form of a commission. In the music industry, the vast majority of personal managers receive between 10% and 20% of the artist's gross earnings as compensation.[6] In the motion picture and television industries, the personal manager generally receives 15%.[7] In contrast, attorneys traditionally charge an hourly rate for their services. However, many entertainment attorneys also employ percentage-based fee arrangements (usually 5% of the artists' gross earnings) and flat fee alternatives (for certain types of services such as the negotiation of a record contract).[8] Actually, it is common for entertainment attorneys to employ all of the foregoing fee methods (i.e. hourly, percentage and flat fee) depending on the type of services they render.

An attorney's latitude in charging fees is limited only by the California Civil Code's prohibition against unconscionable contracts,[9] a prohibition which is expressly applied to attorney retainer agreements by current California State Bar Rule of Professional Conduct 4-200 and its similar predecessor, former Rule 2-107.[10] What constitutes an unconscionable fee is determined primarily by the percentages charged by other attorneys or managers in the same community for the same services. In the leading case on this subject, *Shaffer v. Superior Court,* the court held that the presence of "not disproportionally dissimilar" fee agreements in the same marketplace is a strong indicator of conscionability.[11] Therefore, so long as attorneys charge the percentages customarily charged by entertainment attorneys and personal managers, they are not likely to run afoul of current judicial standards. This is because compensation of 5% to 20% is well below both the traditional 33% contingent fee for personal injury cases and the informal 50% unconscionability threshold.[12] The same general rule would apply to flat fee arrangements so long as the amount of the fee is consistent with fees being charged by other attorneys for similar services, and the client has given an informed consent to the fee. Case law seems to indicate that even a fee that is higher than the prevailing price for comparable services would not be unconscionable so long as the parties bargained fairly over the fee. In *Cazares v. Saenz,* the court held that "where the bargaining process is a fair one, courts traditionally defer to the parties' agreement as the best measure of the value of the contract performance."[13] One variation on a flat fee arrangement which deserves scrutiny is so-called "value billing," where a fee is not established in advance but is determined after a transaction has been consummated. Although this arrangement could lead to overcharging, there is no reason to conclude that value billing is any more inherently unconscionable than any other fee arrangement.

"Be Up Front with Your Client": Disclosure Requirements and Conflicts of Interest

All attorneys are aware of the need to obtain informed written consent from each client before representing two or more clients whose interests actually or potentially conflict.[14] Because entertainment is such a closely knit industry, it is common for entertainment attorneys to find themselves in conflict situations. However, so long as the conflict is fully disclosed, and the attorney does not place the interests of one client over another, the conflict does not necessarily mean that the attorney cannot provide fair representation.

An interesting question is whether an attorney who is also acting as a manager automatically puts himself in a conflict of interest situation, either with that client, or with other clients. In theory, one of the attorney's roles is to police the activities of the artists' other representatives. However, if an artist is dissatisfied with her manager, the artist may lose a valuable balancing mechanism if her manager is also her attorney. Whether an attorney's other clients would be prejudiced by an attorney's decision to manage seems more remote. Although such other clients may feel that an attorney might prioritize matters in favor of a management client, this is really no different than similar choices attorneys make on a daily basis in managing their case loads.

Because of the varied tasks that entertainment attorneys perform and the non-traditional fee arrangements which are often utilized, entertainment attorneys must pay particular attention to disclosure requirements regarding fee arrangements. A percentage-based fee agreement must comply with the disclosure requirements of California Business and Professions Code section 6147 and the California State Bar Rule of Professional Conduct 3-300.[15] The relevant disclosures are the rate, how costs or other fees will be deducted, an opportunity to receive consultation from independent counsel, and a statement that the rate is negotiable. In addition a copy of the fee contract containing the client's written consent must be provided to the client. Failure to comply with these requirements renders the fee agreement voidable at the option of the client.

Another set of disclosures must be made pursuant to California State Bar Rule of Professional Conduct 3-310 when the attorney "has or had a legal, business, financial, or professional interest in the subject matter of the representation."[16] Taken literally, this rule applies to virtually every attorney, even those charging by the hour, since everyone has an interest in getting paid for the services they render. However, rule 3-310 raises unique issues for entertainment attorneys working on a percentage, flat fee or value billing basis who may be tempted to compromise their representation of the client in order to advance the attorney's own financial or personal interests.[17] The rule has obvious implications for attorneys who become partners with their clients in certain ventures, engage their clients on behalf of other clients with whom the attorney is in business, or acquire copyrights or other rights from clients.

However, rule 3-310 also raises more subtle questions: If the attorney stands to make a significant commission or fee on a given transaction, might that attorney be more apt to emphasize the benefits of the deal to the client and downplay the potential problems? Similarly, would an attorney who has tasted a 10–20% management commission advise a client to seek outside management when the client's career might benefit from such advice? These are the types of issues that attorneys should discuss with their clients in advance so that the client can decide how much authority to give the attorney, what is fair compensation, and when to hire a manager. Only by making such disclosures can an attorney fulfill the ethical obligation to act in the best interest of the client.

Managers, Beware of Your State Bar

The foregoing issues need to be considered not only by practicing attorneys but by anyone who is an active member of a state bar, even members who are acting in a purely managerial capacity. This is because some courts have held that such a person is still bound by the rules of conduct governing attorneys.[18] This is especially true where a fiduciary relationship exists between the non-practicing member and the client.[19] Because of the control managers assume over virtually every aspect of the artist's affairs, this is exactly the type of relationship that would likely trip the wire of state bar disciplinary action. In other words, although a member of a bar may be acting in a manner that is customary for personal managers, but which does not conform to the requirements placed upon an attorney, that attorney may find himself subject to disciplinary action and liability for the failure to comply with those requirements.

In a 1951 decision, the Illinois Supreme Court held that "it is not necessary that [a disciplined attorney's] acts be strictly in the discharge of professional duties. Any act which evidences want of professional or personal honesty, such as renders him unworthy of public confidence, affords sufficient grounds for disbarment."[20]

Conclusion

Entertainment law is a popular specialty among law school graduates primarily because it promises the opportunity to reach beyond the boundaries of legal dogma. In this era of growing disenchantment with the practice of law, entertainment law should be viewed as an encouraging example of how attorneys can play an important role in non-legal areas. Our rigorous training and code of ethics have become highly prized in the entertainment industry, where the seductive and unstable nature of the underlying product has fostered abuse and neglect. In my view, as long as attorneys have a passion for the industry and a commitment to honestly serving the needs of clients, the thin line between attorney and manager need not be one they should fear crossing.

Notes

1. An artist may actually have a number of attorneys, including a transactional attorney, a litigator, a corporate attorney, and an intellectual property specialist.

2. For a more detailed discussion of the overlapping relationship between a personal manager and talent agent, see my article *The Plight of the Personal Manager in California: A Legislative Solution,* 6 Hastings Comm. & Ent. L.J. 837 (1984).

3. The examples of former attorneys who are now prominent executives are too numerous to enumerate. A few examples are: Jeff Fenster, who was a music lawyer before becoming Senior Vice President of A & R for Jive Records; Robert Flax, who was a partner at Grubman, Indusky & Schindler before becoming Executive Vice President of EMI Music Publishing; Gary Gilbert, who was a partner at Bloom, Dekom and Hergott before becoming Senior Vice President of Business Management at Capitol Records; and David Simone, who is President of Polygram Music Publishing and was also an entertainment attorney.

4. A few examples are: Michael Lippman, who left entertainment law to become a successful producer's manager; Randy Phillips who, after earning his J.D., managed such acts as Rod Stewart and Toni Braxton and is currently president of Red Ant/Alliance Entertainment; and Mickey Shapiro, who, during his many years of practicing law, has managed several acts, including The Wilson Sisters and Jefferson Starship.

5. Standard personal management agreement. The other services enumerated in a typical management agreement are as follows: To "advise and counsel in the selection of literary, artistic and musical material; advise and counsel in any and all matters pertaining to publicity, public relations and advertising; advise and counsel with relation to the adoption of a proper format for presentation of Artist's talents and in the determination of proper style, mood, setting talents and characterizations in keeping with Artist's talents; advise, counsel and direct in the selection of artistic talent to assist, accompany or embellish Artist's artistic presentation; advise and counsel concerning the selection of talent agencies and any other persons who may be engaged to counsel and advise Artist and to seek and procure contracts of employment and engagements for Artist; and only to the extent permitted by law, seek to obtain employment for Artist as a recording artist in the recording industry."

6. David Naggar and Jeffrey D. Brandstetter, The Music Business (Explained in Plain English) 14 (1995).

7. Mark Litwak, Reel Power 46 (1986).

8. A fee of 5% is the norm for an attorney (who is not also a personal manager) to negotiate an entertainment employment contract for contingent compensation. *Starring in the Biggest Deals in Hollywood,* L.A. Times, Jan. 12, 1996, at A14.

9. Cal. Civ. Code section 1670.5.

10. Current Rule 4-200 became operative May 27, 1989. Former rule 2-107 was operative from January 1, 1975, to May 26, 1989.

11. *Shaffer v. Superior Court,* 33 Cal. App. 4th 993, 1002, 39 Cal. Rptr. 2d 506, 512 (1995).

12. The "conventional wisdom" is that a contingent fee in excess of 50% bears an informal presumption of unconscionability. Lester Brickman, *Contingent Fees without Contingencies: Hamlet without the Prince of Denmark?* UCLA L. Rev. 29, 30 (1989).

13. *Cazares v. Saenz,* 208 Cal. App. 3d 279, 287, 256 Cal. Rptr. 209, 213 (1989).

14. Rule 310(C). Case law has interpreted this rule, and its predecessors, broadly to maintain the attorney's duty of undivided loyalty, without which public confidence in the legal profession would be undermined. *See Santa Clara County Counsel Attorneys Ass'n v. Woodside,* 7 Cal. 4th 525, 547 fn. 6, 28 Cal. Rptr. 2d 617, 629 fn. 6, 869 P. 2d 1142, 1154 fn. 6 (1994).

15. California Business and Professions Code section 6147 applies with equal force to both litigation and non-litigation representation. The Court of Appeal held that an earlier version of section 6147 applied only to contingent agreements for *litigation* services because the earlier statute referred primarily to a "plaintiff," not to a "client." *Franklin v. Appel,* 8 Cal. App. 4th 875, 879, 10 Cal. Rptr. 2d 759, 760 (1992). In 1994, the Legislature amended the section, replacing "plaintiff" with "client." "Thus, AB 3219 overturns *Franklin.*" California Committee Analysis, Aug. 9, 1994 (LEXIS, CAL library, CACOMM file). The current version of Business and Professions Code section 6147 becomes inoperative January 1, 1997.

State Bar of California Rule of Professional Conduct 3-300 states that an attorney shall not "enter into a "business transaction" with a client nor "knowingly acquire an ownership, possessory, security, or other pecuniary interest adverse to a client" without having made specific, written disclosures to the client and receiving the client's written consent.

16. California State Bar Rule of Professional Conduct 3-310(B)(4).

17. *See Buehler v. Sbardellati,* 34 Cal. App. 4th 1527, 1544, 41 Cal. Rptr. 2d 104, 114 (1995).

18. *See, e.g., State ex. rel. Nebraska State Bar Ass'n v. Bremers,* 200 Neb. 481, 484, 264 N.W.2d 194, 197 (1978) ("An attorney may be subjected to displinary action for conduct outside the practice of law or the representation of clients . . .").

19. *See, e.g., Cutler v. State Bar,* 71 Cal. 2d 241, 251, 78 Cal. Rptr. 172, 178, 455 P.2d 108, 114 (1969) ("A member of the bar, however, is held to a high standard of conduct when dealing with his clients and their funds, even though not in an attorney-client relationship, particularly when the relationship has fiduciary aspects.") For a detailed discussion of an attorney's fiduciary obligations outside the traditional attorney-client relationship, see Edward D. Spurgeon & Mary Jane Ciccarello, *The Lawyer in Other Fiduciary Roles: Policy and Ethical Considerations,* 62 Fordham L. Rev. 1357 (1994).

20. *In re Melin,* 410 Ill. 332, 337, 102 N.E.2d 119, 121 (1951).

Appendix A-2

"Seven Years to Life: The Fight for Free Agency in the Record Business"

By Gary Greenberg

Reprinted with permission from *Entertainment and Sports Lawyer*, a publication of the ABA Forum on the Entertainment and Sports Industries, Volume 12, Number 2, Fall 1994.

Introduction

Section 2855 of the California Labor Code[1] or the so-called "seven year rule" states that an employee may not be bound to an exclusive employment contract beyond seven years.[2] As such, it provides a statutory form of free agency for exclusive employees who are bound to long term personal service contracts such as those contracts which exist between an artist and a record company. The Statute, which is largely untested in the courts, contains many important, but unresolved, issues for exclusive recording artists. For example, in 1987, a provision was added to the Statute allowing a record company to bring an action for damages against a recording artist who terminates his recording agreement by invoking the Statute.[3] However, since the courts have not addressed this new provision, it is not known how strictly they will apply it, nor how they will measure damages. Another issue which is not specifically addressed in the Statute, but which the courts have addressed, with varying results, is whether the modification of an agreement during the seven years in question extends the statutory time period.

Case History

The early cases addressing the seven year rule concerned motion picture icons who were signed to multi-picture exclusive contracts under the old film studio system. For the last fifteen years, most

---

of the litigation concerning the Statute has involved sound recording stars seeking to free themselves of lengthy recording commitments.

The Existing Cases

DeHaviland v. Warner Bros.[4]

In this seminal case, Olivia DeHaviland brought an action for declaratory relief seeking to invalidate her personal services contract with Warner Bros. Pictures. The contract provided for a one-year initial term with six successive one-year options, all exercisable by Warner. All of the options were exercised, and the actress rendered her services over a period of approximately seven and a half years. However, this period of service was interrupted by several periods of suspension which were solely the result of her actions. In each instance of suspension, Warner exercised its right to extend the term of the contract for a time period equivalent to the period of suspension. Nevertheless, DeHaviland sought to invalidate the contract by invoking the Statute. Warner challenged this by arguing that Section 2855 should be interpreted to mean seven years of actual service. The court, however, adopted a literal interpretation of Section 2855 and held that enforcement applied to seven calendar years only. In response to Warner's argument that the actress had waived her rights under Section 2855 by agreeing to extend the term of the contract beyond the seven year period, the court stated that to uphold such an argument would render Section 2855 meaningless. Therefore, the court concluded that an employee cannot waive these statutory rights either by conduct or agreement.

Autry v. Republic Productions, Inc.[5]

In September, 1938 the parties in this matter entered into an employment contract for an initial term of one year, with four successive one-year options. In May, 1942 a second contract was signed providing separately for an additional one-year term of employment to run after the 1938 contract expired. Autry served as a member of the armed forces from 1942 to 1945, and was unable to render the services required under the 1942 contract. Republic nevertheless sought to enforce that contract. Autry argued that this was contrary to Section 2855 because it would have required him to be bound to Republic for more than seven calendar years from the date he commenced rendering services. The court held that since Republic had lost Autry's services through no fault of its own, the 1942 contract was enforceable against Autry. The court further held that employer and employee should be free to bargain for extensions during the term of an exclusive agreement without the Statute's depriving them of the benefits of that bargain. This decision was never taken on appeal and it has been argued that it might have been overturned in the face of the pro-employee public policy pronouncements of *DeHaviland*.[6]

Manchester v. Arista Records, Inc.[7]

In 1973, Melissa Manchester signed an exclusive recording contract with Arista Records for an initial term of eighteen months, with four consecutive one-year options, exercisable by Arista. Manchester was required to deliver two albums in the first eighteen months and two albums in each additional contract year. The contract contained a standard extension/suspension clause; namely, if the albums were not timely delivered, Arista had the right to extend the term of the contract (and suspend its obligations during any such extension periods) until all required albums were delivered. Manchester failed to deliver all albums on time and Arista extended her contract, so that by the eighth calendar year of the contract, only the obligations applicable to the fifth contract year had been fulfilled. In addition, in 1976, Manchester and Arista signed an amendment pursuant to which Arista agreed to pay Manchester's former producer $145,000 in exchange for Manchester's granting Arista an additional one year option to commence at the end of the 1973 contract. In 1980, Arista informed Manchester that it would exercise the additional one-year option. In 1981, Manchester filed an action to declare that option unenforceable by reason of Section 2855. Although the court dismissed the action on jurisdictional grounds, in an obiter dictum, the court held that midterm extensions could be upheld on a case by case basis. In viewing the facts in this case, the court decided that the modifications made in 1976 were material. As a result, the court concluded that the 1976 contract was not dependent on the 1973 contract.[8]

Future Decisions. There have been no reported decisions in over ten years involving the Statute. One reason for this is that few artists have a career that lasts for seven years. Another is that given the present uncertainty about how crucial issues concerning the Statute will be decided by the courts, an artist who is in a position to invoke it is likely to settle with his record company rather than risk an adverse judgment. This is true in spite of the potentially high cost of such a settlement.[9]

An example of the foregoing is the matter of *Geffen Records, Inc. v. Henley*,[10] a Los Angeles County Superior court case that recently settled out of court.[11] In that matter, it was alleged that Henley, a recording artist for almost twenty years, sought to free himself from his recording agreement with Geffen Records in 1992 by invoking Section 2855. In response, Geffen filed a complaint against Henley for breach of that recording agreement. It was alleged that Henley and Geffen entered into the agreement in 1984. Geffen alleged that because the 1984 agreement was modified in 1988, the seven years had not run and that Henley's alleged repudiation was premature. In a cross complaint, Henley alleged that the 1988 agreement was merely a midterm modification of an already existing agreement that was signed in 1984. On that basis, he alleged that his cancellation of the agreement was valid under the Statute. In the alternative, Geffen alleged that because Henley only partially fulfilled his recording commitment before he repudiated the agreement, Geffen had a claim pursuant to subsection (b)(3) of the Statute for damages for Henley's non-delivery of the agreed upon number of albums during the seven years in question. Since the *Henley* case involved all of the crucial issues concerning the Statute, it would have been an ideal opportunity for a clear statement of the current state of the law.

An even more recent case is *We're Only in It for the Music v. Elektra Entertainment, Inc.*, filed in San Francisco Superior Court on

September 27, 1994.[12] In that complaint, the members of the rock band Metallica allege that they entered into an exclusive recording agreement with Elektra on or about September 11, 1984. The complaint requests that the court declare that agreement invalid because of the application of the seven-year rule. Despite a provision in the recording agreement that New York would govern the interpretation and enforcement of the contract, the band alleges that Elektra used its superior bargaining power at the time the agreement was signed to force the members to agree to this provision with the intent of depriving them of the protection of Section 2855. At the time of the writing of this article, Elektra had not yet responded to the complaint. Therefore, it is not known whether Elektra will allege that there were midterm extensions to the 1984 agreement, and/or whether Elektra will cross complain for damages. However, it seems clear that Metallica expects Elektra to challenge the case on jurisdictional grounds. If such a challenge is successful, the case will be dismissed. If it is not, the case will probably settle for the reasons discussed in this article. Either way, a decision on the merits is unlikely.

Record Companies—Recording Agreements

In order to appreciate why recording artists need protection like that afforded in Section 2855, it is necessary to understand the extreme bargaining power that record companies possess in the negotiation of most recording agreements and the one-sided provisions which are the result.

Dominating the Market; The Imbalance of Power in the Record Company/Artist Relationship. In the recording industry, the six major production/distribution companies[13] control an overwhelming share of the market. These record companies not only form a powerful lobbying group, but establish industry custom and contractual guidelines. While some provisions in recording agreements are negotiable, many are not. The reason for this is that most artists are so anxious to embark on or continue their recording career that they are willing to accept almost any terms. The result is an agreement which unilaterally favors the company. Since Section 2855 deals with the amount of time which a record company may exclusively employ an artist, understanding that the portion of a standard recording agreement which relates to term and the artist's recording commitment is essential to appreciate the importance of the Statute.

The Inequitable Structure of Term and Recording Commitment Provisions in a Typical Recording Agreement. The typical recording agreement provides for a minimum recording commitment of one album with options (exercisable exclusively by the record company) for six or seven additional albums. The options are exercisable one at a time, except in unusual circumstances where the record company must commit to up to two or three albums as part of a single option. Companies also reserve the right to terminate a contract while an artist is in the middle of recording an album if the company anticipates that the album being produced will not be satisfactory or will exceed the budget approved by the company. In addition, the company has the right to suspend and/or terminate the term of the contract for various reasons, including delays caused by an event of "force majeure," the illness or incapacity of the artist, the artist's failure to timely deliver product, and other alleged breaches by the artist of his representations, warranties, covenants and agreements under the contract. In other words, since the company, in its sole discretion, can terminate the contract virtually at any time, while the artist cannot, the company controls the length of the relationship. Since the financial terms applicable to all albums which may be recorded under a long-term contract are established at the outset of the relationship, the typical recording agreement can become exceedingly inequitable when an artist's talents suddenly rise in value and that value is undermined by the terms established during the original negotiations.

Key Issues Involving the Interpretation of the Statute

New Subsections (b)(2) and (b)(3)—The Right to Sue for Damages. As part of the 1987 amendments to Section 2855, the Statute now provides that even if a recording artist removes himself from the obligation to render personal services to a record company by reason of the Statute, under subsection (b)(2) of the Statute, the company retains the right to sue the artist for any breaches which occurred during the seven years in question.[14] In addition, under subsection (b)(3) of the Statute, a record company can sue a recording artist for damages for the artist's failure to render all services required (or optionally required) to have been rendered in connection with the production of the number of recordings required pursuant to the recording agreement during the seven years. Neither subsection has been interpreted by the courts.

Subsection (b)(2) seems reasonable on its face. Since nothing in the Statute prior to the 1987 amendments specifically limited a company's right to bring actions against employees for breaches which occurred during the term of a contract, it could be said that this new subsection merely codified a self-evident proposition. However, it would be unfortunate if, in applying this subsection, the courts broadened this proposition. I contend that it should only apply to provisions which are necessary to protect the ongoing business between an artist and his former company after the expiration of their agreement. Virtually all recording agreements specify that certain obligations will survive the expiration or earlier termination of the agreement. This would include re-recording restrictions, representations and warranties, and the obligation to account for and pay royalties on previously delivered product. Both parties have a legitimate interest in ensuring that any breaches of these provisions remain actionable. However, any broader interpretation would give a company the ability to thwart the policy underlying the Statute. Faced with the possibility of losing an important artist, a company which would otherwise overlook certain non-material breaches could use the threat of a lawsuit to discourage an artist from leaving by reason of the Statute.

New subsection (b)(3) is more problematic. The threshold issue in analyzing subsection (b)(3) is whether the courts will interpret this subsection literally (i.e., uphold a claim for damages for all albums included in an artist's recording commitment during the seven years in question which were not delivered during that period), or whether the courts will weigh the reasonableness of the provisions of each contract against the history of the parties involved and the realities of the recording process. In other words, what approach will the courts take in deciding whether and to what extent an artist may have "failed" to satisfy his recording commitment according to the Statute? In my opinion, this new language should be repealed. As a result of this amendment, the Statute presents recording artists with a difficult decision; whether to sign with another company and risk forfeiting the financial reward of a new deal (in addition to undertaking the expense of litigation), or to forego the benefits of the Statute and continue to perform for the artist's current company. The only realistic option for an artist who is resolved to change companies after seven years, but who has a portion of his recording commitment remaining at that time, may be to approach his current company and negotiate a settlement.[15] In sum, under current circumstances, a recording artist must be prepared to pay a price to avail himself of the Statute. In addition, I would argue that in singling out recording artists, this new language unfairly discriminates against them and may be invalid on constitutional grounds.

Notwithstanding the foregoing, until this subsection can be repealed, any court faced with the task of applying it must do so only with an understanding of the unrealistic nature of the provisions of a recording agreement which govern recording commitments and term.[16] I believe that the only reasonable interpretation of this subsection in its current form is that so long as an artist was pursuing his career during the seven years in question (other than for reasons beyond the artist's control, such as illness or disability), no such failure should be actionable. In other words, the only instance in which a court should consider a claim for damages for undelivered product is where the record company can demonstrate that the artist, without cause, willfully failed to record albums, on a consistent basis according to generally accepted industry practice.

Another issue raised by subsection (b)(3) is how the courts will determine what damages are appropriate for undelivered albums. Presumably, damages will be based upon a record company's lost profits on such undelivered albums. Under basic principles of contract law, this could be measured either by: (i) the profits made by the new record company on such albums; or, (ii) the profits which the prior record company could have reasonably expected to make on such albums. However, neither method may be accurate. It could be argued that since not all record companies are equally successful, or capable of exploiting artists of a particular genre, it is not possible to measure damages accurately according to the results achieved by the prior record company. On the other hand, since it is difficult, if not impossible, to predict the success of a given album, no matter how successful or consistent the prior success of that artist may have been, the courts may not be able to rely upon the profits made from previously released albums either. This problem is further complicated by the difficulty a court may have in ascertaining exactly what constitutes "profit" for a record company in connection with its sale of records. In sum, since damages for undelivered recordings are speculative, they may not be recoverable at all.

Finally, if lost profits are awarded, a recording artist could be liable for damages far in excess of the "profits" that the artist could expect to realize under a new recording agreement. To be specific, an artist could be faced with a judgment for each undelivered album pursuant to the Statute in favor of his prior record company which would require the artist to disgorge all of the profits he could expect to receive for each three or four albums to be recorded under his new deal.[17] As a result, this portion of the Statute may be difficult to enforce on an equitable basis.

Midterm Modifications. Another crucial issue concerning the interpretation of the Statute is what type of modifications to an employment agreement during the seven year period concerned should constitute the commencement of a new seven year period for purposes of the Statute. This issue arises often because, during the term of most employment agreements, it is common for there to be changes in the parties' working relationship. In fact, all of the decisions discussed in this article addressed the issue, while coming to different conclusions. In *DeHaviland,* the court took a strict view of the issue and held that no midterm extensions, regardless of whether they were intended as amendments, or as new contracts, could initiate a new seven-year period for purposes of the Statute.

This decision was made in spite of evidence showing that DeHaviland herself had approved and initiated the midterm extensions and was aware that they would extend her contract beyond seven years. The court in *Autry,* however, refused to follow the strict pro-employee lead of *DeHaviland* and upheld the midterm extension in that case, saying that Republic, through no fault of its own, lost the services of Autry, and should not be penalized as a result. The *Autry* court went even further to state that mid-term extensions offer permanence and stability to the employee/employer relationship and should be viewed in a favorable light. The court in *Manchester* also upheld the midterm contract extension in that case, and declared that the issue should be determined by future courts on a case-by-case basis. Since neither *Autry* nor *Manchester* is a reported decision, the holding of *DeHaviland,* even though it is almost fifty years old and has not been followed by subsequent courts, remains the only cited authority on point.

In their article on the subject, Bushkin and Meyer conclude that no such modifications should vitiate the policy of the Statute.[18] I agree with their analysis and would argue further that unless the Statute is applied as written, litigation over this issue will undermine the benefits of the Statute. One example of this is the unfortunate reasoning of the court in *Manchester.* In deciding that the 1986 amendment in that case was material, the decision did not seem to fully understand the economic realities of the relationship between Manchester and Arista. All monies paid by record companies to or on behalf of artists must ultimately be paid back out of the artist's royalties. Typically, when an artist asks his record company for money above what is guaranteed in the contract, the company will review the artist's account to ascertain what royalties are in the "pipeline" (royalties earned but not yet paid) and agree to accommodate the artist based on those projected royalties. In this way, what appears to the artist to be a generous concession is actually a prepayment of money which the artist has already earned. Even though *Manchester* is an unreported decision, it illustrates the complexity of this issue. If a successful artist hopes to improve his recording agreement within the first seven years, the artist must accept the risk that these improvements may serve to disqualify the artist from later taking advantage of Section 2855. If, on the other hand, the artist refuses to take advantage of his success at the time, that success may wane before the seven years are up, and that opportunity may be lost forever. Even if the artist remains successful, a decision to forego deserved improvements in his contract makes a deal that was unfair from the outset, increasingly unjust.

Notwithstanding the foregoing, I accept that certain courts have had and likely will continue to have difficulty strictly applying Section 2855 in situations where individuals are purported to have freely bargained to the contrary. If in future cases, courts are uncomfortable upholding the sharp lines drawn in *DeHaviland,* I would urge them to view the issue within carefully constrained boundaries. As mentioned above, during the term of most recording agreements, it is not uncommon for there to be amendments. Courts should exercise restraint before deciding that such changes form the basis of a new contract for the purpose of calculating the statutory seven year period. I propose that unless a company can demonstrate that changes given to the artist were the equivalent of what the artist could have obtained had the artist been given the opportunity to negotiate freely with other companies at the time, not even seemingly material changes should be so construed. Proving this would require a company to point to other agreements negotiated by unsigned artists with similar sales bases at the time. Essentially, a record company would have to prove that the modification in question accomplished the same goal as the Statute was meant to achieve.

The Need for Change—Lessening the Time Period and Enacting a National Law

In addition to construing the Statute in favor of the artist and repealing subsection (b)(3) as argued above, I believe the current time period of seven years is too long and that a national law is needed to ensure uniform enforcement.

Lessening the Time Period. Section 2855 should be amended to provide for not more than five years before an artist can invoke its protection. The current seven year period is anachronistic in the modern day record business in which careers, and sometimes entire genres spring up, flourish and disappear in that amount of time.

In deciding what period of time is reasonable to keep a recording artist under an exclusive contract, it is illuminating to compare the terms of a recording agreement with the terms of other significant exclusive contractual agreements that involve recording artists. Perhaps the most important employment relationship a recording artist enters into, other than with a record company, is with a music publishing company. In a typical exclusive songwriting agreement, the initial term will be for approximately one year, subject to delivery of the minimum number of songs required, with an average of three one year options. In other words, a total time commitment of four years. A four-year exclusive commitment affords the publishing company a sufficient period of time within which to acquire valuable copyrights, without unduly binding the writer. Record companies might argue that this comparison is inappropriate because publishing companies do not normally make as significant an investment in developing writers as record companies make in developing recording artists.[19] While this may be true in most cases, neither does a publisher typically stand to make as much profit.[20]

Circumventing the Statute—Enacting a National Law. One of the shortcomings of the Statute is that since it only applies in California, it is relatively easy for record companies to circumvent. This is accomplished, as is alleged in the *Metallica* case, by forcing artists to consent to jurisdiction in a State outside of California.[21] Most major record companies require a new act to agree that New York law will apply to the interpretation and enforcement of their recording agreement, even if the artist resides in California, intends to record in California and does most of his business in California. The main reason for this is to attempt to avoid California's artist oriented statutes, Labor Code Section 2855 and its sister provision Civil Code Section 3423 (the so-called "Six Thousand Dollar Statute").[22] In addition, it is generally assumed that California courts are more sympathetic to artists' rights than are New York courts. Even though California is the only State with these types of artist protection laws (other than Louisiana, which has a statute which limits the duration of employment contracts to five years),[23] California remains the leader in the recording industry and many contracts are or could be subject to California law. Therefore, record companies must be aware of the possibility that Section 2855 could be used against them in spite of contractual statements to the contrary. In this way, the Statute helps maintain the boundaries of how far record companies will go in their quest for album commitments. In order to avoid forum shopping, a national exclusive recording artist protection act should be adopted which would mirror the terms of California Labor Code Section 2855 (with the changes recommended herein) and California Civil Code Section 3423.[24]

The Record Company Rebuttal

The Return vs. Investment Argument. Record companies may argue that the seven-year (or longer) length of a recording commitment is justified because of the significant investment the company makes in developing a new act which only begins to pay off for a record company after several albums have been marketed. This argument is flawed for several reasons:

Many new acts actually achieve their greatest success with their debut albums which become profitable for the record company from the outset. In fact, many artists whose debut efforts are remarkable find it difficult to match that success on future albums and may actually find a record company investing less in them over time.

Record companies regulate their investment in an act depending upon the performance of that artist's records. In other words, a record company will only spend money promoting successful acts. Rarely will a company continue to spend money promoting an act that is not selling merely because it hopes that the act will sell in the future. This is especially true in these cost-cutting times. The more common scenario is that when an act ceases to be profitable, a record company will simply cut the act from its roster.

The system of recoupment which is built into virtually every record agreement favors the record company. The artist is responsible to recoup one hundred percent of the recording costs and typically fifty percent to one hundred percent of promotional costs out of his share of the profits (the artist royalties). In addition, some of the company's overhead costs are deducted directly from the artist's royalty, such as packaging deductions and the cost of promotional records. The result is that the record company uses the artist's royalties to recoup most of the company's investment. At the same time, the company is realizing its profit margins on all records being sold.

The Law of Averages Argument. Record companies might also argue that even if it is true that they make substantial profits on a successful act, those profits are necessary to offset the losses they incur on the numerous unsuccessful acts that they have invested in. First, it is difficult to understand why a successful artist should bear any responsibility for a company's failures. Second, although the fortunes of record companies are unpredictable, the profitability of most major companies has been well documented.

The Myth of Renegotiation. Record companies may argue further that Section 2855 is unnecessary because most companies will reward success by renegotiating contracts. However, since whatever renegotiation occurs is done while an artist is under contract, unless an artist becomes enormously successful, the record company will maintain the upper hand in any renegotiation. The only exception to this rule is the rare circumstance where the company fears losing an act it covets to a competing label. This only happens when a new act is being pursued by a number of labels or when an established act is about to get out of an existing contract. It is precisely to protect this small window of opportunity that the seven year rule is so crucial.

Conclusion

Even though there have been few reported decisions concerning Section 2855, the Statute remains an important piece of legislation for recording artists and record companies who are parties to long term exclusive employment agreements. Unfortunately, until certain key issues involving the interpretation of the Statute can be finally determined in a current reported decision, the law will remain unclear. In addition, until recording artists and their representatives join together to lobby both state and federal lawmakers to expand the current protection afforded them in the Statute, the RIAA (Record Industry Association of America) is likely to continue to try to undermine its effects. Preservation of the policy underlying Section 2855 is essential for recording artists who are almost always in an unequal bargaining position with record companies. For some time, our nation has lamented its slipping role in the world as an exporter of American products. One area in which America has maintained a prominent position is in the creation of music which is sold throughout the world. In order to ensure that America continues to lead in this area, it is important for our lawmakers and our courts to nurture the source of that music by preserving and expanding the protection provided by the seven-year rule.

Notes

1. California Labor Code Section 2855 (West 1974).

2. The history of Section 2855 of the California Labor Code as contained in the Industrial Relations Act begins with former Civil Code §1980. Civil Code §1980 was enacted in 1872 and underwent a number of amendments, relating to its enforceability in respect of time periods. The first amendment to §1980 occurred in 1901, which amended §1980 to provide that an employee could not be bound to a contract to render personal services for a period exceeding two years. In 1919, the time period was increased to five years, and in 1931 the period was further increased to seven years. In 1937, §1980 became Labor Code §2855.

3. In 1987, the RIAA (Record Industry Association of America) lobbied for several amendments to the Statute, including an increase in the time period from seven to ten years. While this request was denied, the RIAA was successful in obtaining some significant concessions for record companies. First, the Statute now requires a recording artist to give written notice to the record company of the artist's intention to cease rendering services to the company by reason of the Statute. Second, record companies may sue for damages for breaches of the contract which occurred during its term. Third, record companies may bring an action for an artist's failure to render all of the services required during the seven years in question pursuant to the recording commitment specified in the contract.

4. 67 Cal. App.2d 225 (1944).

5. (No. 503481) (Los Angeles County Superior Court Case Jan. 14, 1946).

6. See, "The enforceability of Mid-Term Extensions of Employment Agreements Under California Labor Code §2855" by Henry I. Bushkin and Rauer L. Meyer, Article 15, Beverly Hills Law Journal #1 385, Page 392, and another version of the same article entitled, "Employee Emancipation in California: The 7 Year Itch Under Labor Code §2855" California State Bar Journal (1981) 56 State Bar Journal 20.

7. No. CV81-2134 (CD Cal., Sept. 17, 1981) (Judge Robert J. Kelleher chose not to publish the case).

8. For a full critical discussion of *Manchester,* as well as *Autry, DeHaviland* and other relevant cases, see, "Legislature Developments Affecting the Midterm Renegotiation of Recording Contracts under California Labor Code §2855" by Jonathan Blaufarb, 1986 Entertainment Publishing and the Arts Handbook (Viera and Thorne, Editors), p.175.

9. This type of settlement would typically involve payment of a portion of the artist's royalties under his new deal to the artist's prior company, as well as payment of advances directly by the new record company to the prior company, which would typically be recoupable from the artist's royalties under his new deal.

10. No. BC073696 (Los Angeles County Superior Court Case).

11. The terms of the settlement are not available.

12. No. 964007 (San Francisco County Superior Court Case).

13. Sony, WEA, EMI, Polygram, BMG and MCA, and their affiliated or distributed labels.

14. It is important to note that any such action must still be brought within the applicable period prescribed by law.

15. For discussion of the likely terms of such a settlement, see note 9, supra.

16. The record company typically has until the later of twelve months from the commencement of a given contract period, or seven to ten months from delivery of a previous album, to decide whether to exercise an option for future product. Assuming an artist can consistently write hit songs on demand, put all the creative elements together quickly and deliver great performances without any difficulties, an artist can theoretically satisfy a seven album recording commitment in seven years. Except in rare circumstances, however, this is not realistic. Once a record company exercises an option, the artist must write or find the songs to be recorded, select and schedule the producers, studios, engineers, musicians and other creative elements for recording the album, prepare a detailed

budget and get all of the foregoing approved by the record company. Many record companies employ staff producers, or hire "Artist and Repertoire" representatives who are producers, who control virtually every aspect of the production process. This means that in many instances, the company has more "control" over whether an artist "fails" to render the services required under the contract on a timely basis than does the artist himself. This pre-production process often takes several months, and in some cases years, to complete. The actual recording, mixing and mastering process usually takes three to six months, but frequently longer. Accordingly, even in a best case scenario, it will take an artist five to six months from the time a record company exercises an option to deliver the applicable album. Nor does the paradigm of an album a year leave any room for a career decision (often made at the request of a record company) to take time off between albums. It is not uncommon for an artist to require additional time at stages in his career to re-evaluate the style of his artistic presentation or to regenerate his creative energy.

17. The typical recording agreement provides for compensation to artists (excluding mechanical royalties for songwriting) for record sales through a combination of advances and royalties. After deducting royalties to third parties (e.g., producers and mixers), an artist can expect to receive a royalty of between 75¢ and $1.25 per record, depending on how successful the artist is, and the configuration of the record that is sold (e.g., CD or cassette). On the other hand, the record company may realize three or four times that amount, as its share of the profits, from the sale of that same record.

18. See note 6, supra.

19. See discussion under *The Return vs. Investment Argument,* infra.

20. In general, a record company can expect to make three dollars or more per record sold, while a publisher can expect to make around twenty cents in mechanical royalties for its share of the songs on that record (unless the record contains several hit songs that are re-recorded by other successful artists).

21. Record companies would no doubt deny that they attempt to circumvent any laws. Unfortunately, given the power that the major record companies wield, lawmakers should view any such denials suspiciously.

22. California Civil Code Section 3423 (West 1970).

23. L.A. Civ. Code Ann. art. 167 (West 1952).

24. In order to enact a national exclusive recording artist protection act, artists and their representatives would need to organize pressure groups to lobby Congress. One example of how state legislation became

national as a result of strong lobbying is the domestic violence laws of 1984. During the late 19th century, many states enacted statutes which criminalized domestic violence. Through the efforts of pressure groups, it became clear that these laws needed to be extended nationally to be effective. In 1984, the house and senate passed legislation designed to provide funding for battered spouses, which both made these protections uniform throughout the country and provided assistance in states where none had previously existed. Unfortunately, recording artists have not historically proven themselves to be capable of joining together to fight for changes in their industry. By contrast, the RIAA has been an effective lobbying group.

Appendix B

RECOMMENDED LITERATURE ON HOW TO START A NEW BUSINESS AND PREPARE A BUSINESS PLAN

1. *The Entrepreneur's Guide to Business Law* by Constance E. Bagley and Craig E. Dauchy, West Publishing Company, 1997.
2. *Entrepreneur Magazine's Start Your Own Business: The Only Start-Up Book You'll Ever Need,* Inc. Entrepreneur Media, Entrepreneur Media, 1998.
3. *The Entrepreneur Magazine Small Business Advisor,* John Wiley & Sons, 1995.
4. *Managing Small Businesses* by Robert Lee Anderson, John S. Dunkelberg, and Maggie Jarpey, West Publishing Company, 1993.
5. *The Portable MBA in Entrepreneurship* by William Bygrave, John Wiley & Sons, 1997.
6. *Starting Your New Business: A Reference Guide for Entrepreneurs,* Charles L. Martin, Crisp Publications, Inc., 1994.
7. *Successful Small Business Management* by Leon Megginson, Charles Scott, and Williams Megginson, McGraw-Hill Professional Publishing, 1991.
8. *How to Start and Build a Law Practice,* Fourth Edition, by Jay Foonberg, American Bar Association, 1999.
9. *Writing Business Plans That Get Results* by Michael O'Donnell, NTC Publishing Group, 1991.
10. *Your New Business: A Personal Plan for Success* by Charles L. Martin, Crisp Publications, Inc., 1993.

Appendix C

INFORMATIVE ENTERTAINMENT INDUSTRY PUBLICATIONS

1. Magazines/Periodicals/Web sites

A. Music

- *Billboard*, weekly publication containing information on all facets of current news and trends in the business. Album sales, video sales and rentals, and top radio play are all charted. One Astor Plaza, 1515 Broadway, New York, New York 10036. Phone (800)745-8922. Web site: billboard.com
- *Hip-Hop Newsletter*, free newsletter sent out twice a month to subscribers that features exclusive interviews with Hip-Hop/Rap and R & B artists, news from around the world, freestyle showcase, and album reviews.
  Web site: visionol.net
- *Hip Hop Central (formerly The Source)*, Web site offering a collection of links, sounds, and album reviews.
  Web site: hiphopcentral@hotmail.com
- *Hits*, weekly fact sheet with chart information and industry news, including yearly publication with contact information. 14958 Ventura Blvd., Sherman Oaks, CA 91403. Phone (818)501-7900. Fax (818)789-0259.
  Web site: hitslosers@aol.com
- *The Music Paper*, national publication for musicians with reviews, industry news, and ads. P.O. Box 5167, Bay Shore, New York, New York 11706. Phone (516)666-4892. Fax (516) 666-7445. Web site: musicpaper@hotmail.com
- *The Musician's Guide to Touring and Promotion*, publication from *Billboard* magazine dedicated to musicians, featuring up-to-date information on the art, business, and technology of making music. Phone (800)407-6874.
  Web site: musicianmag.com

- *Music Row Magazine,* publication that covers Nashville's music industry with record reviews, music videos, current news items, interviews, or new talent information. Phone (615)321-3617. Fax (615)329-0852. Web site: musicrow.com
- *Music Connection Magazine,* entertainment trade magazine for musicians. 4731 Laurel Canyon Blvd., North Hollywood, CA 91607. Phone (818)755-0101. Fax (818)755-0102. Web site: musicconnection.com
- *MusicNewsWire*, compilation Web site offering daily updates on news stories and information from various music Web sites. Web site: musicnewswire.com
- *Rap Sheet, Rap Pages,* Web site with latest hip-hop news. Web site: rapsheet.com
- *R & R (Radio & Records, Inc.),* industry newspaper providing the radio and recording industries with the latest in news, sales, marketing innovations, and airplay data. Located in Los Angeles at 10100 Santa Monica Blvd., 5th floor, Los Angeles, CA 90067-4004. Phone (310)553-4330. Fax (310) 203-9763. In Nashville at 1106 16th Avenue South, Nashville, TN 37212. Phone (615)244-8822. Fax (615)248-6655. In Washington, D.C., at 888 17th Street, NW, Suite 310, Washington, D.C. 20006. Phone (206)463-0500. Fax (206) 463-0432. Web site: rrdc@rronline.com.

B. Film/Television

- *Creative Planet.com,* Web site featuring daily film/T.V. and music industry news.
- *Entertainment Employment Journal,* national entertainment career magazine for professional, creative, technical, production personnel, and others interested in a career in the motion picture, broadcast, or cable television business. EEJ Publishing Company, Dept. 5000-2000, P.O. Box 7382, Van Nuys, CA 91409. Phone (800)640-4836. Web site: eej.com.html

- *Filmmaker Magazine,* publication geared to independent filmmaking with interviews and articles. 5455 Wilshire Blvd., Suite 1530, Los Angeles, CA 90036. Phone (323)932-6060. Fax (213)932-6111.
- *Hollywood Reporter,* guide to entertainment industry information. 5055 Wilshire Blvd., Los Angeles, CA 90036. Phone (323)525-2150.
  Web site: hollywoodreporter.com/
- *Production Weekly,* guide that provides the entertainment industry with a comprehensive breakdown of projects in preproduction, preparation, and development for major studio as well as independent films, network and cable television movies, pilots, and series, both domestic and international. Phone (818)951-0298. Fax (818)951-0248.
  Web site: productionweekly.com
- *Show Biz Wire,* online source that compiles the latest news on films, television, and celebrities
  Web site: showbizwire.com
- *Variety,* daily and weekly entertainment magazine featuring news and information on film, TV, and music. 5700 Wilshire Blvd., Suite 120, Los Angeles, CA 90036. Phone (323)857-6600. Fax (323)857-0494. In New York at 245 West 17th Street, New York, NY 10011. Phone (212)645-0067. Fax (212) 337-6977. Web site: variety.com

2. Books

A. Music

- *The Billboard Guide to Music Publicity,* Jim Pettigrew, Jr., Watson-Guptill Publications, 1997.
- *The Business of Artist Management,* Xavier M. Frascogna and H. Lee Hetherington, Watson-Guptill Publications, 1997.
- *Career Opportunities in the Music Industry,* Shelly Field, Facts on File Inc., 1995.

- *Everything You'd Better Know About the Record Industry,* Kashif Michael Jones and Gary Greenberg, Brooklyn Boy Books, 1996.
- *How to Be a Working Musician: A Practical Guide to Earning Money in the Music Business,* Mike Levine, Watson-Guptill Publications, 1997.
- *Inside the Music Industry: Creativity, Process, and Business,* Michael Fink, Macmillan Library Reference, 1996.
- *Making It in the Music Business: The Business and Legal Guide for Songwriters and Performers,* Lee Wilson, Allworth Press, 1999.
- *The Music Business: Career Opportunities and Self Defense,* Dick Weissman, Crown Publishing Group, Inc., 1990.
- *The Music Business (Explained in Plain English): What Every Artist and Songwriter Should Know to Avoid Getting Ripped Off!* Jeffrey Brandsetter and David Naggar, DaJe Publishing, 1996.
- *Platinum Rainbow—How to Succeed in the Music Business Without Selling Your Soul,* Bob and Riordan Monaco, NTC Publishing Group, 1990.
- *The Real Deal: How to Get Signed to a Record Label from A to Z,* Daylle Deanna Schwartz, Watson-Guptill Publications, 1997.
- *Tim Sweeney's Guide to Releasing Independent Records,* Tim Sweeney and Mark Geller, TSA Books, 1996.
- *Welcome to the Jungle: A Practical Guide to Today's Music Business,* Joe Owens, Harper Perennial, 1992.

B. Film/Television

- *Contracts for the Film & Television Industry,* Mark Litwak, Silman-James Press, 1998.
- *Dealmaking in the Film & Television Industry: From Negotiations to Final Contracts,* Mark Litwak, Silman-James Press, 1993.

- *The Hollywood Job Hunter's Survival Guide: An Insider's Winning Strategies for Getting That (All-Important) First Job . . . And Keeping It,* Hugh Taylor, Lone Eagle Publishing Co., 1992.
- *How to Make It in Hollywood: All the Right Moves,* Linda Buzzell, HarperCollins Publishers, Inc., 1996.
- *The Movie Business Book,* Jason E. Squire, Simon & Schuster, 1992.
- *Opening the Doors to Hollywood: How to Sell Your Idea, Story, Screenplay, Manuscript,* Carlos de Abreu and Howard Jay Smith, Random House Publishing, 1997.
- *Reel Power: The Struggle for Influence and Success in the New Hollywood,* Mark Litwak, 1994, Silman-James Press.

Appendix D

D-1 Typical Office Expenses

D-2 Typical Start-Up Expenses (One-Time)

Appendix D-1

TYPICAL OFFICE EXPENSES

1. Office rent (omit if home office or barter for services)
2. Parking expenses (parking validation extra)
3. Support staff salaries: assistant/secretary, receptionist
4. Temporary-personnel wages
5. Associates/paralegal salaries
6. Salary for owner
7. Local phone bills
8. Long-distance phone carrier
9. Computer hardware (maintenance, upgrade, and repair)
10. Computer software (maintenance, aid, and program updates)
11. Internet charges (monthly)
12. Cellular phone bills
13. Phone system service (update service, repair work)
14. City business taxes (yearly)
15. County business taxes (yearly)
16. Payroll taxes (state and federal)
17. Health insurance (monthly)
18. Dental insurance (monthly)
19. Malpractice insurance (monthly)
20. Worker's compensation insurance (yearly)
21. Office liability insurance (yearly)
22. Federal Express/UPS charges
23. Messenger charges
24. Office supplies
25. Water charges
26. Office machinery maintenance/repairs (copier, fax, and printer)
27. Postage
28. Coffee/tea service
29. Plant service

30. Subscriptions to magazines, newspapers, and industry/legal publications
31. Meals and entertainment
32. County bar dues (yearly)
33. State bar dues (yearly)
34. State bar continuing legal education—compliance class fees
35. Stationery/printing
36. Banking charges
37. Accounting fees
38. Contingency funds
39. Research and development (for example, CDs, movies, cable, theater)
40. Client gifts

Appendix D-2

TYPICAL START-UP EXPENSES (ONE-TIME)

1. Moving expenses
2. Lease deposit, including first and last month
3. Phone system
4. Phone system installation
5. Phone line installation
6. Computer and software
7. Computer installation
8. Office furniture/filing cabinets
9. Office supplies
10. Fax machine
11. Copier
12. Stationery
13. Advertising and promotion for opening

Appendix E

CONTACT INFORMATION ON ENTERTAINMENT LAWYERS, ENTERTAINMENT COMPANIES, MANAGEMENT FIRMS, AND TALENT AGENCIES

1. Music

- *The Album Network's Yellow Pages of Rock,* "rock Rolodex" for personnel for radio networks, record labels, music retail, distributors, recording studios, CD duplication and mastering facilities, press and public relations consultants. 120 N. Victory Blvd., 3d floor, Burbank, CA 91502. Phone (800) 222-4382. Web site: musicbiz.com
- *Billboard Directories,* P.O. Box 2015, Lakewood, NJ 08701. Phone (800)223-7524 or (212)536-3174.
  - A. International Talent and Touring Directory
  - B. International Buyer's Guide
  - C. Record Retailing Directory
  - D. International Tape/Disc Directory
  - E. Nashville 625/Country Music Sourcebook
  - F. International Recording Equipment & Studio Directory
  - G. Fall Edition—The Power Book Directory of Music Radio & Record Promotion
  - H. International Latin Music Buyer's Guide
- *The CMJ Directory,* published annually, contact guide for the college radio and "alternative" areas of the music industry. 810 7th Avenue, 21st floor, New York, NY 10019. Phone (646)485-6600. Web site: cmj.com
- *In Charge, Music Row Magazine,* yearly publication of the who's who of Nashville (see Appendix C for information).
- *Music Books Plus*, directory of major and independent record labels, publishers, recording studios, entertainment

attorneys, and services geared toward the working musician. P.O. Box 670, 240 Portage Road, Lewiston, NY 14092. Phone (800)265-8481 or (905)641-0552. Fax (905) 641-1648.

- *Musician's Guide to Touring & Promotion,* annual *Billboard* publication containing listings and contact names for clubs, press, record stores, and rental/repair shops throughout the United States and Canada. Also contains information on major and independent record labels, fanzines, music business services, and Web sites pertaining to the musician. 1515 Broadway, 11th floor, New York, New York 10036. Phone (800)344-7119.
  Web site: musicianmag.com
- *The Music Business Registry, Inc.,* 7510 Sunset Blvd., Suite 1041, Los Angeles, CA 90046-3418. Phone (818)769-2722. Fax (818)769-9818.
  Web site: musicregistry.com.

  Separate publications are:

  A. *A & R Directory,* contains regional A & R contacts with all major and independent labels in Los Angeles, Nashville, and London.
  B. *Film and Television Music Guide,* lists all movie studio, TV network, and independent production company music departments, all music supervisors in film/TV, film composer managers and agents, music clearance managers and agents, music libraries, music editors, and ASCAP/BMI film/TV divisions.
  C. *Music Attorney, Legal & Business Affairs Registry,* contains all music business attorneys, legal and business affairs personnel at all of the record labels, music publishers, and film studio/TV network music departments.
  D. *Music Publisher Registry,* registry of major publishers and independents in Los Angeles, New York, Nashville, and London.
  E. *Talent/Personal Management Directory,* registry of leading talent agents and personal management companies.
- *National Directory of Record Labels and Music Publishers,* Barbara Taylor, Rising Star Music Publishers, 1995.

- *Performance Guide Series,* 1101 University Dr., Suite 108, Fort Worth, Texas 76107-3000. Phone (817)338-9444. Fax (817)877-4273.
  - A. Talent/Personal Managers
  - B. Manufacturers/Production Personnel
  - C. Promoters/Clubs
  - D. Booking Agencies
  - E. The Black Book (an industry-wide phone and fax directory)
  - F. International Markets
  - G. Country Talent/Variety
  - H. Concert Production
  - I. Transportation/Accommodations
- *Pollstar Magazine,* 1998 edition. 4697 West Jacquelyn Ave., Fresno, CA 93722. Phone (800)344-7383. Fax (559)271-7979. Web site: pollstar.com. Separate publications are:
  - A. Record Company Rosters
  - B. Agency Directory
  - C. Management Directory
  - D. Connection Directory
- *The Recording Musician's Association Directory*, a listing of RMA-affiliated studio musicians. Includes information on recording studios, music equipment, sample contracts, and other useful services. 817 Vine Street, Suite 209, Hollywood, CA 90038-3715. Phone (323)462-4762. Fax (323)462-4762. Web sites: rmala.org.com (Los Angeles–based) or rmaweb.org.com (nationally based).

2. Film/Television

- *Hollywood Creative Directory,* complete directory listing of agents and managers, published quarterly as a series of books with up-to-date who's hot and what's in, in motion picture development. 1024 N. Orange Dr., Hollywood, CA 90038. Phone (323)308-3490 or (800)815-0503. Fax (323) 308-3493. Web site: www.hcdonline.com.

Also published by *The Hollywood Creative Directory*:

A. *Agents & Managers Directory,* listing of agents and managers for actors, writers, directors, producers, comedians, dancers, voice-over artists, models, composers, lyricists, below-the-line talent, and photographers, published twice a year.

B. *Hollywood Distributors Directory,* film and television distributors.

C. *Quick Phone Directory,* phone numbers for companies in directories.

D. *New Media Directory,* Internet and CD-ROM companies.

- *Hollywood Film Institute (HFI),* a movie resource center and film educational facility teaching everything from how to produce a film, find an agent, and direct a feature to selling your script. 223 Olympic Blvd., Santa Monica, CA 90409. Phone (310)399-6699 or (800)366-3456. Fax (310)851-0919. Web site: filmschool@hollywoodu.com
- *Hollywood Reporter Blue Book,* yearly film and television production company guide (see Appendix C for more information).
- *Careers in Film, Television, and New Media,* site featuring descriptions of film, television, and new media professions, sample films created by students, chat rooms, and suggestions for creative ways to break into the film industry. Web site: www. mediacareers.com
- *Global Film & Media Access,* searchable database of industry professionals and companies with free listings and downloadable production forms. P.O. Box 70, East Chatham, New York, NY 12060. Phone/fax (518)392-5604.
- *Mandy's International Film and TV Production Directory,* detailed information about technicians, facilities, producers, and job listings worldwide. Also features an industry homepage service, where filmmakers can list their credentials and projects. Web site: mandy.com

Appendix F

LEADING ENTERTAINMENT LAW SEMINARS, ORGANIZATIONS, AND ASSOCIATIONS

1. Seminars

- *University of Southern California,* Entertainment Law Institute seminars. USC Law School, Suite 124, University Park, Los Angeles, CA 90089-0071. Phone (213)740-2582. Fax (213)740-9442. Web site: www.usc.edu/dept/law/cle
- *University of California at Los Angeles* extension programs, symposiums. 10995 Le Conte Ave., Los Angeles, CA 90024. Phone (310)825-9971. Web site: uclaextension.org
- *CLE (Continuing Legal Education),* 100 Van Ness Avenue, 28th floor, San Francisco, CA 94102-5238.
- *Loyola Law School,* entertainment law seminars. 919 South Albany Street, Los Angeles, CA 90015. Phone (213)736-1000. Fax (213)380-3769. Web site: loyolalawschool.com
- *PLI (Practicing Law Institute),* 810 Seventh Avenue, New York, New York 10019. Phone (800)260-4754. Fax (800)321-0091.
- *CEB (Continuing Education of the Bar),* 2300 Shattuck Avenue, Berkeley, CA 94704-1576. Phone (510)642-3974 or (800)232-3444. Fax (510)642-3788. Web site: ceb.ucop.edu/
- *Glasser LegalWorks,* seminars on intellectual property. 150 Clove Road, Little Falls, NJ 07424. Phone (973)890-0008. Fax (973)890-0042. Web site: legalwks@aol.com
- *Communications Media Center of New York Law School,* 57 Worth Street, New York, New York 10013. Phone (212)431-2100. Fax (212)966-2053. Web site: info@cmcnyls.edu

2. Organizations/Associations

- *ABA Forum on Entertainment & Sports Law,* American Bar Association, 750 North Lake Shore Drive, Chicago, IL 60611. Phone (312)988-5000. Web site: www.abanet.org

- *BESLA (Black Entertainment & Sports Lawyers Association),* 1502 Fairlakes Place, Mitchellville, MD 20721. Phone (301)333-0003. Fax (301)333-0013. Web site: www.besla.org
- *CLA (California Lawyers for the Arts),* Southern California, 1641 18th Street, Santa Monica, CA 95814. Phone (310)998-5590. Fax (310)998-5594. Northern California, Fort Mason Center, Building C, Room 255, San Francisco, CA 94123. Phone (415)775-7200. Fax (415)775-1143.
Web site: cla@sirius.com
- *The Jewish Federation, Entertainment Division,* 5700 Wilshire Blvd., 2d floor, Los Angeles, CA 90036. Phone (323) 761-8000. Web site: jewishla.org
- *California Bar Association,* an entertainment law section. 180 Howard Street, San Francisco, CA 94105-1639. Phone (415)538-2000. Web site: calbar.org
- *Beverly Hills Bar Association,* a special section on entertainment law. 300 South Beverly Drive, Suite 201, Beverly Hills, CA 90212. Phone (310)553-6644. Web site: bhba.org
- *The Association of the Bar of the City of New York* committee on entertainment law. 42 West 44th Street, New York, New York 10036. Phone (212)382-6600. Web site: abcny.org
- *Stanford Entertainment and Sports Law Association,* Stanford University, Stanford, CA 94305. Phone (650)723-2300. Web site: www.stanford.edu
- *Chapman University Law School—Entertainment and Sports Law Society,* 370 N. Glassell Street, Orange, CA 92866. Phone (714)997-2400.
Web site: www.chapman.edu/law/index.html

3. Entertainment Law–Related Web Sites

- www.stanford.edu for SESLA (Stanford Entertainment and Sports Law Association).
- www.abanet.org/forums/entsports for the ABA's *Entertainment and Sports Lawyer.*

- lawyers.about.com/msubentertain for Global Entertainment Law Resource Center.
- hollywoodnetwork.com/law for the Hollywood Law Cybercenter.
- www.wiredlaw.com for WiredLaw: Law for Technology and New Media.

Appendix G

WELL-KNOWN TALENT/ENTERTAINMENT INDUSTRY ORGANIZATIONS, SHOWCASES, SEMINARS, AND CONVENTIONS

1. Music

A. Organizations

- *AFM (American Federation of Musicians),* trade union that represents professional U.S. and Canadian musicians in bargaining and contract negotiations in all aspects of the entertainment industry. Also publishes *The International Musician.* In New York at 322 W. 48th Street, New York, NY, 10036. Phone (212)245-4802. Fax (212)245-6255. In Los Angeles at 817 N. Vine Street, Hollywood, CA 90028. Phone (323)462-2161. Fax (323)461-3090. Or (800)762-3444.
Web site: afm.org
- *AFIM (Association for Independent Music),* membership organization of independent record companies and wholesalers that provides resources, meetings, information, and legal assistance and acts as a go-between with major retail record chains and music unions. AFIM also sponsors the Indie Awards. P.O. Box 988, Whitesberg, KY 41858. Phone (606)633-0946. Fax (606)633-1160. Web site: afim.org
- *AFTRA (American Federation of Television and Radio Artists),* union that represents professional television and radio artists. 5757 Wilshire Blvd., 9th floor, Los Angeles, CA 90036. Phone (323)634-8100. Fax (323)634-8246.
Web site: www.aftra.org
- *AGVA (American Guild of Variety Artists),* in New York at 184 5th Ave., 6th floor, New York, New York, 10010. Phone (212)675-1003. Fax (212)633-0097. Located in Los Angeles at 4741 Laurel Canyon Blvd., Suite 208, North Hollywood, CA 91607. Phone (818)508-9984. Fax (818)508-3029.

- *AMC (American Music Conference),* service organization that distributes music industry information to amateur musicians and encourages their participation in various musical activities. Located at 5760 Armada Drive, Carlsbad, CA 92008-4391. Phone (760)431-9124.
- *ASCAP (The American Society of Composers, Authors, and Publishers),* performing rights society designed to represent songwriters and publishers, Los Angeles, New York, Chicago, Nashville, and London. Phone (800)852-7227. ASCAP also publishes a quarterly magazine, *Playback,* containing general information for members and anyone wanting to know more about the society and performing rights.
Web site: ascap.com
- *Music Publishers' Association of the United States,* in Los Angeles at P.O. Box 1561, Burbank, CA 91507. Phone/fax (818)842-6257. In New York at 1562 First Avenue, New York, NY 10028. Phone/fax (212)327-4044. Web site: mpa.org
- *BMI (Broadcast Music, Inc.),* performing rights society designed to represent songwriters and publishers. In Los Angeles at 8730 Sunset Blvd., 3d floor West, West Hollywood, CA 90069. Phone (310)659-9109. In New York, phone (212)586-2000, Nashville (615)401-2000, London (011)441-71-486-2036. For national information, phone (800)292-4779.
Web site: bmi.com
- *CMA (Country Music Association),* international organization dedicated to the preservation, development, and promotion of country music. 1 Music Circle South, Nashville, TN 37203. Phone (615)244-2840. Fax (615)726-0314.
Web site: countrymusic.org
- *GMA (Gospel Music Association),* international service organization whose purpose is to preserve and promote gospel music. 1205 Division Street, Nashville, TN 37203. Phone (615)242-0303. Fax (615)254-9755.
Web site: gospelmusic.org
- *NARAS (The National Academy of Recording Arts & Sciences, Inc.),* dedicated to improving the quality of life and cultural

conditions for music and its makers. Internationally known for the Grammy Awards. 3402 Pico Blvd., Santa Monica, CA 90405. Phone (310)392-3777. Fax (310)392-2778.

- *RIAA (Recording Industry Association of America),* trade group whose member companies create, manufacture, and/or distribute more than 90 percent of all legitimate sound recordings sold and produced in the United States. 1330 Connecticut Avenue NW, Suite 300, Washington, DC 20036. Phone (202)775-0101. Fax (202)775-7253. Web site: riaa.com
- *RMA (The Recording Musicians Association),* member association dedicated to guaranteeing effective representation in AFM contract negotiations and other affairs affecting the livelihoods of professional recording musicians. Also publishes the Recording Musicians Association Directory. 817 Vine Street, Suite 209, Los Angeles, CA 90038-3715. Phone (323)462-4762. Fax (323)462-4762. Web site: rmaweb.org
- *SESAC,* performing rights society designed to represent songwriters and publishers. 55 Music Square East, Nashville, TN 37203. Phone (615)320-0055. Fax (615)329-9627 or (800)826-9996. Web site: sesac.com

B. Showcases

- *Musician's Resource: Getting Your Act Together: The Watson-Guptill Guide to Workshops, Conferences, Artist's Colonies and Academic Programs,* Gwendolyn Freed, Watson-Guptill Publications, 1997.
- ASCAP and BMI put on regular showcases and workshops for songwriters in New York, Los Angeles, and Nashville.
- *Billboard* also sponsors regular events.
- *The Extravaganza,* Nashville Entertainment Association (non-country) three-day event in January showcasing new bands. 1014 18th Avenue South, Nashville, TN 37212. Phone (615)327-3208.

- *NACA (National Association for Campus Activities),* national and regional showcases in Nashville and Columbia, South Carolina. Phone (803)732-6222.
- *Primary clubs to network.* In Los Angeles/Hollywood: *The Viper Room* at 8852 Sunset Blvd., West Hollywood. Phone (310)358-1880. Web site: viperroom.com. *The Troubador* at 9081 Santa Monica Blvd., Hollywood. Phone (310)276-6168. Web site: troubadour.com. *The Whiskey* at 8901 Sunset Blvd., Los Angeles. Phone (310)652-4202. Web site: whiskeyagogo .com. *The Roxy* at 9009 West Sunset Blvd., West Hollywood. Phone (310)276-2222. *The Coconut Teaser* at 8117 Sunset Blvd., Los Angeles. Phone (323)654-4773. In New York, *Brownies* at 169 Avenue A Frnt., NYC. Phone (212) 420-8392. Web site: panix.com/CLUBS. *The Bottom Line* at 15 West 4th Street, NYC. Phone (212)228-6300. Web site: panix.com/ CLUBS. *The Mercury Lounge* at 217 E. Houston St., NYC. Phone (212)260-4700. In Nashville, *The Blue Bird* at 4104 Hillsboro Pike, Nashville. Phone (615)383-1461. Web site: nashville.citysearch.com. *Douglas Corner* at 2106 8th Avenue South, Nashville. Phone (615)298-1688. Web site: nashville.citysearch.com.

C. Conventions and Seminars (which may include showcasing)

- *The A & R Registry* (see Appendix E), prints a yearly list of music conferences. Contact Music Business Registry, Inc. Phone (818)769-2722. Fax (818)769-9818.
  Web site: musicregistry.com
- *In the City* (Manchester, England). Phone (011)44-161-839-3930. Fax (011)44-161-839-3940.
  Web site: inthecity@u-net.com.
- *MIDEM,* International music marketplace held annually in Cannes, France, in January. The Marketplace, The Spanish House, Turfpoortstraat 27, N1-1411 ED Naarden, The

Netherlands. Phone (011)31-3-5695-0196. Fax (011)31-3-5695-0449. U.S. contact phone number (212)689-4220. Web site: www.midem.com

- *North by Northwest (N×NW) and South by Southwest (S×SW),* annual music conventions featuring panels and new artist showcases. Both are sponsored by S×SW. S×SW is held in Austin, Texas, in March and N×NW is held in Portland, Oregon, in August. P.O. Box 4999, Austin, TX 78765. Phone (512)467-7979. There is also a North by Northeast (N×NE) in Toronto. Phone (416)469-0986
- *Gavin,* annual music convention. Contact address is 140 Second Street, Suite 200, San Francisco, CA 94105. Phone (415)495-1990.
- *BRE (Black Radio Exclusive),* 15030 Ventura Blvd., Suite 864, Sherman Oaks, CA 91403. Phone (818)907-9959. Web site: bremagazin@aol.com
- *NAMM,* annual trade show convention. 5790 Armada Drive, Carlsbad, CA 92008. Phone (760)438-8001. Web site: www.namm.com
- *Academy of Gospel Music Arts.* Phone (800)462-3211. Web site: gospelmusic.org
- *MOBfest,* Chicago. Phone (773)327-2529. Web site: mobfest.com
- *NARM (National Association of Recording Merchandisers),* 9 Evos Drive, Suite 120, Marlton, New Jersey 08053. Phone (856)596-2221. Fax (856)596-3268. Web site: narm.com
- *R & R (Radio & Records),* 10100 Santa Monica Blvd., 5th floor, Los Angeles, CA 90067. Phone (310)553-4330. Fax (310)203-9763. Web site: rronline.com
- *Country Radio Seminar,* seminars held in the first week of June. 819 18th Avenue South, Nashville, TN 37203. Phone (615)327-4487. Fax (615)329-4942. Web site: countrycharts.com

- *City of Dreams.* Phone (212)613-5758. Fax (212)391-5755. Web site: blacktalentnetwork.com or www.cityofdreams.com
- *Fan Fair* showcases in June sponsored by Country Music Association. 1 Music Circle South, Nashville, TN 37203. Phone (615)244-2840. Fax (615)726-0314. Web site: countrycharts.com
- *Country Music Awards (SRO) Standing Room Only,* a convention for country booking agents and talent buyers. Sponsored by Country Music Association. Web site: countrymusicawards.com
- *Country Music Expo* sponsors yearly seminars and showcases. P.O. Box 41489, Nashville, TN 37212. Web site: www.countrymusicexpo.com
- *Music Row Panel* sponsors industry seminars. 1231 17th Avenue South, Nashville, TN 37212. Phone (615)321-3617. Fax (615)329-0852. Web site: musicrow.com
- *TJ Martel fundraiser events in LA and Nashville,* fashion show, golf, tennis, and bowling events. 1707 Division Street, Nashville, TN 37203. Phone (615)256-2002.
- *Music City Tennis Invitational,* benefiting children's hospital in Nashville. Held in the spring. BMI major sponsor. 10 Music Square East, Nashville, TN 37203. Phone (615)322-7450. Web site: musiccitytennis.com
- *Tin Pan South*—NSAI—Nashville songwriting convention. Festival for songwriters. 15 Music Square West, Nashville, TN 37203. Phone (615)256-3354. Web site: bmi.com/musicworld
- *Songwriter's Guild* in Nashville sponsors the "Ask a Pro" session and many other events. 1222 16th Avenue South, Suite 25, Nashville, TN 37212. Phone (615)329-1782. Fax (615)329-2623. In Los Angeles, 6430 Sunset Blvd., Hollywood, CA 90028. Phone (323)462-1108. Fax (323)462-5430. Web site: songwriters.org

- *Winter Music Conference,* held in Fort Lauderdale, Florida, 3450 NE 12th Terrace, Fort Lauderdale, Florida 33334. Phone (954)563-4444. Fax (954)563-6889. Web site: wmcconfab@aol.com
- *VIBE Music Conference,* New York. Phone (212)448-7300. Fax (212)448-7400. Web site: vibe.com

2. Film/Television

A. Organizations

- *SAG (Screen Actors Guild),* organization that represents actors in various screen mediums. 5757 Wilshire Blvd., Los Angeles, CA 90036-3600. Phone (323)954-1600. Fax (323) 549-6603. Web site: sag.com
- *WGA (Writers Guild of America),* organization that represents writers in various mediums. 7000 West 3d Street, Los Angeles, CA 90048-4329. Phone (323)782-4500 or (800)548-4532. Web site: wga.org
- *DGA (Directors Guild of America),* an organization that represents directors in various mediums. 7920 Sunset Blvd., Los Angeles, CA 90046. Phone (310)289-2000. Fax (310)289-2029. Web site: dga.org
- *MPAA (Motion Picture Association of America),* trade organization representing the American motion picture, home video, and television industries. In Washington, DC, at 1600 I St. NW, Washington, DC 20006. Phone (202)293-1966. Fax (202)785-3026. Web site: mpaa.org
- *AMPAS (Academy of Motion Picture Arts & Sciences),* organization that develops and aids filmmakers. 8949 Wilshire Blvd., Beverly Hills, CA 90211-1972. Phone (310)247-3000. Fax (310)859-9351 or (310)859-9619. Web site: ampas@oscars.org
- *The American Film Institute,* national arts organization dedicated to preserving the heritage of film and television,

identifying and training new talent, and increasing the recognition of the moving image as an art form. Located at 2021 N. Western Avenue, Los Angeles, CA 90027. Phone (323)856-7600. Fax (323)467-4578. Web site: afionline.org

- *American Film Market Association,* trade association of 130 motion picture and television production and distribution companies. Phone (916)961-3784. Fax (508)546-6363. Web site: afma.com
- *Filmmakers Foundation,* nonprofit resource and career center that provides training and outreach programs, information and referral services, and hands-on production experience. Founding organization of the Los Angeles Independent Film Festival. 5820 Wilshire Blvd., Suite 503, Los Angeles, CA 90036. Phone (323)937-9137.
- *IMAGE Film & Video Center,* nonprofit Atlanta-based organization that promotes the production and exhibition of independent media arts in Atlanta and Southeast. 75 Bennett St., NW, Suite N-1, Atlanta, GA 30309. Phone (404)352-4225. Fax (404)352-0173. Web site: imagefv.org
- *ITVS (Independent Television Service),* information site on ITVS, including their full text *Study of the Field of Independent Distribution.* P.O. Box 78008, San Francisco, CA 94107. Phone (415)356-8383. Fax (415)356-8391. Web site: itvs.org
- *Association of Independent Video and Filmmakers,* also publishes a magazine called *The Independent,* which lists festivals and contact information. 304 Hudson St., 6th floor, New York, NY 10013. Phone (212)807-1400. Fax (212)463-8519. Web site: aivf.org
- *National Alliance of Media Arts and Culture,* nonprofit membership organization of over 300 independent film, video, and multimedia centers nationwide. 1551 K St. NW, Suite 518, Washington, DC 20005. Phone (202)658-2620. Fax (202) 628-2554. Web site: namac.org
- *Women in Film,* aims to "recognize, develop, and actively promote the unique visions of women" in the industry.

Features articles, interviews, and events calendar. A professional forum for the advancement and celebration of women working in the industry. 6464 Sunset Blvd., Suite 1080, Hollywood, CA 90028. Phone (323)463-6040. Fax (323) 463-0963. Web site: wif.org

B. Showcases, Seminars, and Conventions

- *Sundance Film Festival,* the preeminent showcase for the exhibition of independent cinema and the discovery of new filmmaking talent. The program includes the American Independent Dramatic and Documentary Competition, premieres, short films, and sidebar screenings, celebrating innovative filmmakers from around the world. The Sundance Institute in Utah also offers *The Feature Film Program,* which supports emerging filmmakers to develop and refine new work, and *The Sundance Theater,* dedicated to commissioning, developing, and producing new stage and screen plays and various international programs that are committed to supporting international filmmakers and film cultures. Held annually in January at 307 West 200 South, Suite 5002, Salt Lake City, UT 84101. Phone (801)328-3456. Fax (801)575-5175. Web site: sundance@xmission.com
- *Cannes International Film Festival,* held in Cannes, France, May 13–24 at 99 Boulevard Malesherbes, F-75008 Paris, France. Phone (011)33-1-4561-6600. Fax (011)33-1-4561-9760. Web site: festival@cannes.bull.net
- *Telluride Film Festival,* held annually in August in the mountain town of Telluride, Colorado. For 25 years, the Telluride Film Festival has brought the world's best films to the public in a program of premieres, revivals, and cinematic tributes. Located at 119 West Colorado Avenue, Telluride, CO. Phone (800)525-3455. Fax (970)728-6475. Web site: tellurideinfo.org

Appendix H

ENTERTAINMENT LAW PUBLICATIONS

1. General

- *Entertainment and Sports Lawyer,* a quarterly publication of the American Bar Association Forum on the Entertainment and Sports Industries, edited by David Given. 750 North Lake Shore Drive, Chicago, IL 60611. Phone (312) 988-5500. Fax (312)988-5528.
  Web site: www.abanet.org/forums/entsports/
- *Entertainment Law & Finance,* a monthly newsletter focusing on developments and analysis of the field, offering tips, etc. 345 Park Avenue South, 8th floor, New York, NY 10010. Phone (212)313-9115. Fax (212)481-8161.
  Web site: brummel@aol.com
- *The Entertainment Law Reporter by Lon Sobel,* a monthly newsletter with articles and case analysis, with a list of educational programs and publications. 2118 Wilshire Blvd., Suite 311, Santa Monica, CA 90403. Phone (310)829-9335. Web site: entertainmentlawreporter.com
- *Comment Law Journal,* Hastings Law School, quarterly. 200 McAllister Street, San Francisco, CA 94102-4978. Phone (415)551-4170.
  Web site: entertainmentandsportslawjournals.com
- *Journal of Internet Law,* Aspen Law and Business. Phone (800)638-8437. Web site: aspenpublishers.com
- *IPL Newsletter by the American Bar Association on Intellectual Property,* see www.abanet.org/abapubs/periodicals/intelprop.html for information.
- *Los Angeles County Bar Association,* publishes a yearly issue on entertainment law. 261 South Figueroa, Los Angeles, CA 90012. Phone (213)896-6560. Fax (213) 896-6585. Web site: lacba.org

- *Beverly Hills Bar Association,* has a variety of publications on entertainment law. 300 S. Beverly Drive, Suite 201, P.O. Box 7277, Beverly Hills, CA 90212. Phone (310)553-6644. Fax (310)284-8290. Web site: bhba.org
- *Various publications by The West Group,* P.O. Box 64833, St. Paul, MN 55164-0833. Phone (800)328-9352. Fax (651)687-7302. Web site: westgroup.com

  Publications include:

  A. *Lindey on Entertainment Publishing and the Arts,* by Alexander Lindey, 1963. Updated by Michael Landau, 1998.
  B. *Entertainment, Publishing, and the Arts Handbook,* annual series, edited by Robert Thorne and John David Viera, 1994.
  C. *Entertainment Law,* by Robert Fremlin, 1990. Updated by Michael Landau, 1999.
- *Clearance & Copyright: Everything the Independent Filmmaker Needs to Know,* Michael G. Donaldson, Silman-James Press, 1996.
- *Law and Business of the Entertainment Industries,* Donald E. Biederman et al., Greenwood Publishing Group, 1996.
- *Entertainment Law: Document Supplement,* Melvin Semensky & Thomas Selz, 1998.
- *Matthew Bender Books.* Phone (800)833-9844. Fax (518)487-3584. Web site: www. bender.com.

  Publications include:

  A. *The Law of Advertising,* by George Eric Rosden and Peter E. Rosden, 1993.
  B. *California Intellectual Property Laws,* by Sheldon & Mak, 1998.
  C. *Copyright Law,* by Peter Jaszi, Craig Joyce, Marshall A. Leaffer, and William Patry, 1998.
  D. *Intellectual Property Primary Law Sourcebook,* by Matthew Bender, 1999.
  E. *Nimmer on Copyright,* by David Nimmer (originally by Melville B. Nimmer), 1998.

F. *Understanding Copyright Law, Second Edition,* by Marshall A. Leaffer, 1999.

G. *Understanding Intellectual Property Law,* by Donald Chisum and Michael A. Jacobs, 1998.

H. *Entertainment Industry Contracts: Negotiating and Drafting Guide,* Donald Farber, 1986. Also updated on CD-ROM, 1999.

- *Clark Boardman Callaghan Books (now part of West Group),* has several publications. Phone (800)344-5008 or (651)687-7921. Web site: westgroup.com

  Publications include:

  A. *Boorstyn on Copyright,* by Neil Boorstyn, 1994.

  B. *Copyright Law in Business and Practice,* by John W. Hazard Jr., 1989.

  C. *Forms & Agreements on Intellectual Property & International Licensing,* by L. W. Melville, 1979.

  D. *Intellectual Property Law for Business Lawyers,* by Kinney, 1996.

  E. *Intellectual Property Law Review,* by Karen B. Tripp, 1999.

  F. *Law of Copyright,* by Howard E. Abrams, 1991.

2. Music

- *Everything You Need to Know About the Music Business,* Donald Passman, 2d ed., Simon & Schuster, 1997.
- *Get It in Writing: The Musician's Guide to the Music Business,* Brian McPherson, Hal Leonard Publishing, 1999.
- *The Musician's Business and Legal Guide,* Mark Halloran, Prentice-Hall, 1992.
- *Music, Money, and Success: The Insider's Guide to the Music Industry,* Jeffrey Brabec and Todd Brabec, Macmillan Library Reference, 1994.
- *This Business of Music,* Sidney Shemel & M. William Krasilovsky, Watson-Guptill Publications, 1995. Also updated with CD, 2000.

- *More about This Business of Music*, Sidney Shemel and M. William Krasilovsky, Watson-Guptill Publications, 1994.

3. Film/Television

- *Dealmaking in the Film and Television Industry,* Mark Litwak, Silman-James Press, 1993.
- *Litwak's MULTIMEDIA Producer's Handbook: A Legal and Distribution Guide,* Mark Litwak, Silman-James Press, 1997.
- *Film Finance & Distribution, A Dictionary of Terms,* John W. Cones, Silman-James Press, 1992.
- *The Business of Television,* Howard J. Blumenthal and Oliver R. Goodenough, Watson-Guptill Publications, 1998.

Appendix I

SAMPLE OFFICE CONFIGURATION

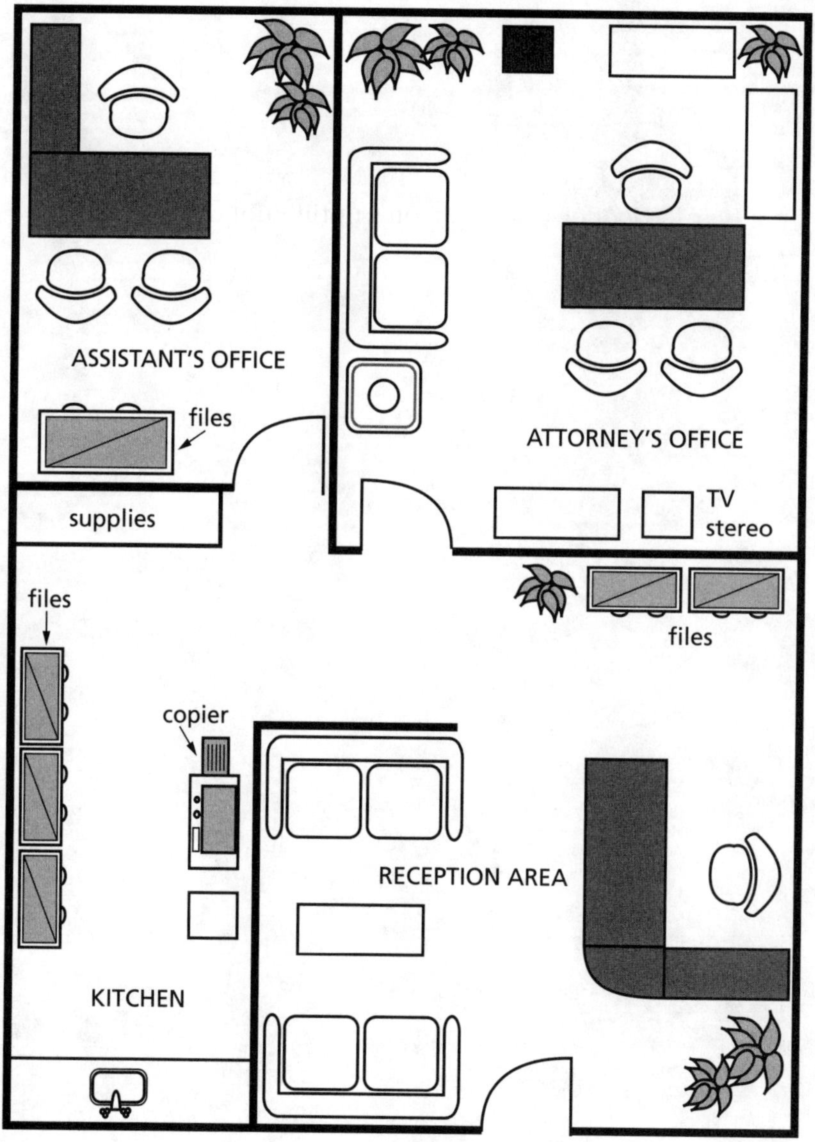

Appendix J

LETTER OF DIRECTION FOR PAYMENT OF LEGAL FEES

(Client)

____

____

Date: ____

(Company—Payer)

____

____

Gentlemen:

The undersigned hereby requests and irrevocably authorizes you to pay (Lawyer) the sum of $_____ of the next monies payable to the undersigned pursuant to the _________ Agreement dated as of _____ 20__ , including without limitation, advances and royalties payable to us. The foregoing payment shall be deducted from the otherwise applicable amount payable to us pursuant to the ____ Agreement, and shall be recoupable as set forth in the _________ Agreement. Please remit the foregoing payment to (Lawyer) at ________________ . SS#:_______________ or Fed ID#:_____________.

We understand that your compliance with this authorization constitutes an accommodation to us alone, and that our attorney is not a beneficiary of it. All payments under this authorization will constitute payment to us and you will have no liability by reason of any erroneous payment or failure to comply with this authorization. We agree to indemnify and hold you harmless against any claims asserted against you and damages, losses, or expenses you incur by reason of any such payment or otherwise in connection with this authorization.

Best regards,

(Client)

____

Appendix K

RETAINER LETTERS

Appendix K-1

HOURLY BILLING RETAINER LETTER

Date: ________

(Client)

____

____

Dear ________ :

In accordance with applicable law regulating my conduct as an attorney, I am required to have a written fee letter stating the general nature of the services I render and the fees for those services. Accordingly, you hereby agree and understand that I am in the business of giving legal advice and preparing and negotiating legal documents in the field of entertainment, and it is on this basis that you have engaged my services. I do not provide advice in other areas, such as litigation or tax.

This letter hereby confirms the rates and fees agreed upon between you and me for the rendering of legal services:

(Lawyer) hourly rate. . . . . $________

Furthermore, all long-distance telephone charges will be billed to you demonstrating the amount of the phone call, as will all mailing and delivery charges. Faxes are charged at __ per page, and copies at __ per page.

All bills will be rendered on a monthly basis at the end of every month and will clearly state the basis for all included charges.

Payment is due within ten (10) days of your receipt of the bill and is not contingent upon successful completion of any project. In the event any monthly statement rendered to you is not paid within thirty (30) days of the date it is sent, interest at the rate of __% per annum shall accrue on the amount then due until it is paid, and I shall be relieved of the responsibility of performing further work on your behalf as permitted by the applicable law regulating my conduct as an attorney. Without limiting the foregoing, I reserve the right to refer any bill that remains unpaid for more than ninety (90) days to a collection agency, in which event the amount of any collection fees shall be added to your bill and I disclaim any damages that may result to your credit. Of course, you may terminate this agreement for any reason at any time by written instruction, in which event you will remain responsible for the payment of all fees and expenses incurred on account of my representation prior to my receipt of such notice.

In the event you become dissatisfied for any reason with the fees charged or the services rendered, I encourage you to bring that to my attention immediately. It is my belief that most such problems can be resolved by good-faith discussion between us.

This agreement will not take effect, and I will have no obligation to provide legal services to you, until you return a signed copy of this agreement, but the effective date of this agreement will be retroactive to the date I first provided legal services to you. Even if this agreement is not executed and returned by you, you will be obligated to pay the reasonable value of any services I may have performed for you at your direction.

You understand that agreements entered into by you with third parties may require you to give notice, exercise your rights, or make other decisions within certain time periods (for example, granting an approval or consent). You understand and agree that I will not be responsible for monitoring those time periods, or any dates or calendar items, on your behalf.

You acknowledge that you have obtained, or knowingly waived the right to obtain, independent legal advice regarding this agreement, and that this agreement was signed after a full and fair opportunity to negotiate its terms. The provisions of this agreement are severable to the extent reasonably necessary to effectuate our intent in the event any provision is held invalid. This letter sets forth our entire agreement, and no other promises, conditions, or warranties have been made. Our agreement may be modified only in writing, signed by both of us.

If the foregoing conforms to your understanding, please so indicate by signing in the space provided for below and returning this letter to me.

For your convenience, I have enclosed a self-addressed, stamped envelope.

Sincerely yours,

(Lawyer)

AGREED TO AND ACCEPTED:

By: (Client)
Date:______________________

Appendix K-2

PERCENTAGE BILLING RETAINER LETTER

Date: ________

(Client)

____

____

Gentlemen:

I am pleased that you desire to have me represent you in connection with your activities in the entertainment business.

Percentage Fee Arrangement. This letter confirms your and my agreement that the fee for my services will be a percentage fee equal to:

(a) __% of the gross compensation paid to you or on your behalf while I represent you; and

(b) __% of the gross compensation paid to you or on your behalf at any time after you or I terminate my representation of you if such compensation is earned by you (i) while I represent you or (ii) within ___ (_) year(s) after the termination of my representation under agreements negotiated or entered into during the time I represent you.

"Gross compensation" means all income of any kind derived from any of your activities in the entertainment business (whether under agreements made during or prior to my representation of you), without the deduction of any cost or expense incurred by you.

Exclusions from Gross Compensation. Notwithstanding the foregoing:

(a) "Gross compensation" will exclude production costs of your projects.

(b) As to monies from live appearances (but not related income such as tour merchandising, broadcast rights, etc.), "gross compensation" will exclude your direct, out-of-pocket expenses for all items, other than commissions to personal managers, business managers, and agents, and the first $_______ of gross compensation received by you each year.

(c) "Gross compensation" will exclude monies paid by you to producers, and will exclude investment income and other non-entertainment income.

Calculation of Fee. My fee will apply to monies earned by you or by any corporate or other entity through which you may operate. For entertainment-related activities that you perform as a member of a group, my fee will be based on the gross compensation of the group (and I will not be entitled to a fee based on your individual share of the group's earnings).

Payment. While I will bill you for my expenses (as described below), I will not ordinarily bill you for my percentage compensation. Rather, I will rely on you to pay my percentage fee promptly after your receipt of compensation without my invoicing you. In this regard, I would like to discuss with you arranging for payment directly from your business manager.

Costs and Standard Charges. I will bill you separately for my out-of-pocket costs and expenses as they are incurred (including long-distance telephone, air-freight and express mail, messengers, and travel expenses outside the ___________ area if I travel at your request or with your consent), and office services (such as photocopying, secretarial overtime, etc.) at standard rates adopted by me from time to time.

Calendar Items. You understand that agreements entered into by you with third parties may require you to give notice, exercise your rights, or make other decisions within certain time periods (for example, granting an approval or consent). You understand and agree that I will not be responsible for monitoring those time periods, or any dates or calendar items, on your behalf.

Excluded Services. My firm is not responsible for and will not render legal services with respect to taxes, copyright and trademark work, securities work, divorce, criminal matters, or other matters that are outside my areas of expertise. At your request, I will recommend other counsel to advise you with respect to any such matter. In addition, you understand and agree that probate, litigation, arbitration, and similar proceedings are not included within the percentage fee arrangement described above; I will discuss with you an appropriate fee for any such matter if ever relevant.

Termination. Either you or I may terminate this agreement at any time, subject to your obligation to pay my fees as described above. However, if you desire me to do so, I will continue my services with regard to any matter as to which my compensation continues.

Fee Disputes. Any dispute that arises under this agreement shall be submitted for binding arbitration in accordance with the procedures of the ________ County Bar Association, or, if that organization declines to arbitrate the dispute, before the State Bar of ______.

Start Date. This fee arrangement will be effective as of ______.

If you are agreeable to my fee arrangement, please sign and return a copy of this letter to me in the envelope provided for your convenience.

If you have any questions or comments, please contact me as soon as possible.

IN SIGNING THIS AGREEMENT YOU ACKNOWLEDGE THAT YOU HAVE BEEN ADVISED TO SEEK INDEPENDENT LEGAL AND BUSINESS ADVICE WITH RESPECT TO THIS AGREEMENT AND THAT YOU HAVE EITHER SOUGHT AND OBTAINED SUCH ADVICE OR DELIBERATELY REFRAINED FROM DOING SO.

I look forward to working with you.

Best regards,

By: (Lawyer)
Date: ______________

ACCEPTED AND AGREED TO:

By: (Client)
Date: ______________________

Appendix L

CONFLICT-OF-INTEREST ARTICLES

Appendix L-1

"Conflicts in the Entertainment Industry? . . . Not!"

By Edwin F. McPherson*

SO WHAT'S ALL THIS about "conflicts of interest" in the entertainment industry? Just a few years ago the only conflict in this industry was when an actor on a series couldn't do a feature because of his series commitments or when a lead singer-turned-solo artist couldn't do a tour with the band because of his or her solo commitments.

Today, it's different; and it's all coming down on lawyers. One entertainment attorney, who requested anonymity, was recently quoted in the *Hollywood Reporter* as claiming that the only reason for which many potential clients come to the more established entertainment firms is *because* of the firm's inherent conflicts (and therefore connections), not in spite of them.

For instance, a hypothetical, prominent entertainment lawyer represents a powerful, successful producer. He also represents a powerful, successful actor and a powerful, successful actress. He puts them together, like an agent would package a deal, and the combination ensures a sure-fire, blockbuster hit, thus making the producer, the actor, the actress, and of course the attorney even more powerful and successful. It is a formula that is destined for success.

Even more obvious is the motivation behind the less powerful, less successful client, who also wants to be with our hypothetical lawyer. He could go with a younger, hungrier attorney, who would probably try a little harder and pay a little more attention to him—the lawyer would work with the agent, and negotiate the best deals

---

*Mr. McPherson is a partner at Los Angeles, California's McPherson & Kalmansohn.

he could for the actor—or he could go with our first lawyer, who has the right producer or the right director, and who can package an entire film just with his own clients.

Certainly, there is a risk that, at least for a small, less powerful artist, a lawyer who is tied to a studio or a label will not use his clout with the label to promote that particular artist but will reserve his heavy ammunition for his better-known artists. However, this is going to be a problem whether or not the attorney also represents the label or merely has a relationship with one. Moreover, the artist (or certainly the artist's personal manager) is aware of this potential problem but presumably goes with the lawyer because he or she is still perceived as the best lawyer for that particular artist's career.

Oddly enough, nobody has complained about these "conflicts" until very recently. Only now, in a time when the answer to everyone's recession woes seems to be "let's sue the lawyers" (after they try the more common solution of "let's not pay the lawyers"), do they even think of the word "conflict." Unfortunately, they usually do not even understand the significance of the word until they see another lawyer—usually not associated with the entertainment industry—who generally sees these issues as black and white, and who has no real concept of the realities of this industry.

Don't get me wrong; as a litigator I am acutely aware of conflicts of interest and the potential effects that such conflicts may have on the outcome of a case. Insurance litigators have to deal with *Cumis,*[1] under which insurance companies have to hire counsel of the insured's choice because the carrier's panel counsel might sell the insured client down the river because of his allegiances to the insurance company—and this *does* make sense (until it gets abusive *à la* Lynn Boyd Stites and the other Alliance indictments).

1. *San Diego Federal Credit Union v. Cumis Insurance Society, Inc.*, 162 Cal. App. 3d 358, 208 Cal. Rptr. 494 (Cal. 1984).

Also as a litigator, I have *never* represented both sides of a lawsuit, and I suspect that I never will. Why? Because I would hear confidential, privileged communications from each that the law (and the Code of Professional Responsibility) presumes I would use against one client for the benefit of the other, as in the aforementioned insurance situation. But, more important, because I cannot then effectively represent either side *against* the other.

But the key word here is "against." In an entertainment context is the entertainment attorney (who, unlike a litigator, is acting much less as *legal* counsel and much more as a negotiator) really representing an actor "against" a producer or a recording artist "against" a label? Is there really a conflict of interest in representing both? I am not so sure. An entertainment attorney *negotiates* on behalf of an actor-client presumably aiming for the amount of money, percentage of profits, and the like, that the client wants. He or she is a deal maker.

The entertainment attorney who represents both sides is not generally going to receive confidential information from the client that could benefit his or her other client. In addition, as a general rule, whether the attorney represents just the actor or both the actor and the producer, the producer is not going to pay the actor any more than the producer feels that he or she can afford or any more than the producer feels the actor is worth in terms of box office draw. Similarly, the actor is not going to accept less than he (or his agent) thinks he is worth.

Moreover, in many cases, when the attorney represents both the studio and the actor or both the label and the artist, the attorney will negotiate essentially on behalf of the actor or artist, and a business affairs representative or higher-ranking representative will negotiate on behalf of the studio or label. In fact, the client himself or his agent may negotiate the major deal points and leave only the paperwork to the attorney.

I was involved in one case last year in which a *major* entertainment firm was sued by the former wife of the line producer of several late seventies and early eighties blockbuster movies. One of the primary allegations of the complaint was that the firm had represented both her former husband and the production entity of the films, which allegedly constituted a conflict of interest. In truth, the firm did represent both parties, but the fact was that the two clients entirely negotiated their own deal, which the firm merely papered, and both clients made millions.

This year, another major entertainment firm got sued by a former client for representing both sides of a particular deal. Only months later, the same firm was sued by a former partner of the firm, who claims that he was terminated from the firm because he objected to the firm's practice of packaging television shows representing many sides of a deal.

In his recent suit against New York attorney Allen Grubman, Billy Joel alleges that Grubman never told him that he (Grubman) also represented CBS Records, Joel's record company, at the same time he was representing Joel. The suit has received tremendous media attention, particularly in the *Hollywood Reporter.* At least according to Grubman's attorneys in the case, however, this supposed conflict affected Joel. It got guarantees totaling $50 million for Joel, a huge amount of money even for the music industry and a sum about which most clients would not generally complain.

Grubman's response has been essentially that the suit merely exemplifies the proclivity of lawyer-bashing that is going around which is often employed to cover up other people's mistakes (in this case, Joel's personal manager). Grubman's attorneys go on to state that not only did Grubman not start representing CBS until long after he commenced representation of Joel and, in fact, long after Grubman negotiated Joel's recording agreement—and therefore there was no conflict at all—but also that Grubman only represented two divisions of CBS: manufacturing and the record club, neither of which, according to Grubman, had any potential or actual impact whatsoever on Joel or his recording agreements.

Clients like Billy Joel like to hold their entertainment lawyers to the same conflict standards as litigation lawyers and other lawyers but expect their lawyers to play a much greater role than would other lawyers. For instance, one of the allegations in the Joel–Grubman suit is that Grubman should have somehow realized that Joel's then personal manager and brother-in-law, Frank Weber, was stealing money from him and then had some duty to disclose this suspicion to Joel because Joel, at one point, allegedly could not afford to purchase a second house on Long Island. It is difficult to imagine that a non-entertainment attorney would be charged with the responsibility of investigating the reasons for which his or her client was broke or somehow ensuring that the client would not go broke.

I do not intend to imply that there is no room for abuse. In another case in which I was involved, Brian Wilson, who penned most of the Beach Boys' tremendous hits in the 1960s, sued his former publishing company and his music lawyer, alleging that his father had sold all of his (Wilson's) publishing to the publisher for a ridiculously low amount, which was then squandered by the father.

Wilson also alleged that his and other Beach Boys' signatures were forged on the deal and that he knew nothing about the sale until years later, when his attorney told him that it was a "done deal," that there was nothing to worry about, and that there was nothing that he could do about the sale anyway. Wilson also alleged that the same attorney had represented both Wilson *and* the publishing company in the deal, without bothering to mention to Wilson that the sale was taking place or that he was representing both sides. The case was reportedly settled prior to trial for an eight-figure amount.

Although clients most certainly must be protected from such gross abuses of the attorney-client relationship, no such protection is necessary or even warranted in the normal entertainment transaction. One of my problems with holding entertainment transactional attorneys to litigation standards is that disgruntled clients (and now, apparently, disgruntled former partners) fail to realize, oftentimes, a better deal can be negotiated *because* of the attorney's relationship with the label or the studio. Another problem is that, in many cases, requiring a firm to send a conflict letter to both clients is clearly form over substance because, in general, a firm's representation of a particular studio, or production company, or record label is rarely a big secret.

For instance, it is certainly no secret in the industry that Mickey Rudin represents the Warner labels, or that Payson Wolf represents Capitol, or that Skip Brittenham represents Ted Field and Interscope, or that Peter Dekom represented M.C.E.G., or that Henry Holmes represents New Line, or that a Manatt, Phelps senior music partner now heads Hollywood Records, or that a Bloom, Dekom founding partner now heads Universal, or that a former Ziffren music partner just moved to Epic.

I will posit one final thought with respect to conflicts of interest with entertainment attorneys. What is the logical extension of some of these conflict malpractice cases? Where are we going with this? If an attorney's representation of both talent and studio/label is a conflict of interest, what else might be? Representation of two actors in a picture? What if one actor is a gross profit participant, which, by definition, will take money from the second actor, who might be only a net participant?

What about representing both an artist and her record producer? What about representing all of the members of a band? Do these situations really present a conflict? The entertainment industry is far too small to expect entertainment transactional attorneys not to represent more than one participant in a film, more than one member of a band, or more than one participant on an album.

Another major concern: If the simultaneous representation of a studio or a label and an actor or a musician is a conflict of interest, what about a situation in which the attorney who represents the artist does not represent the label but would like to? One could argue that this presents a greater conflict of interest since a hungry lawyer may do more to bend over backwards for a *potential* label client than for a label that is already a client. In this case, must the attorney send a conflict letter to the client stating that he or she *would like* to represent the label, or *might* represent the label in the future, and therefore sell them out?

Perhaps the scariest prospect of all—to entertainment lawyers and other practitioners alike—is the recent discussion indicating that a written conflict waiver may not be sufficient to insulate an attorney from liability for such a conflict of interest. With the foregoing potential conflicts in mind, such a standard could virtually eliminate the entire legal/entertainment industry, requiring each entertainment attorney essentially to choose one client and only one client—a ridiculous prospect at best.

Again, this all presupposes that there are no present disputes between the two clients, in which case an actual conflict does arise. In that event, the entertainment attorney—and many of the more powerful ones do not have litigation departments (perhaps for this very reason)—should advise each client separately to consult a litigator, who will only represent one of them and therefore not have the same conflict problems.

Appendix L-2

"Serving Two Masters May Jeopardize Client Interests"

By Owen J. Sloane*

PRACTITIONERS often raise the serious question of whether traditional conflict-of-interest rules are appropriate to the entertainment bar and whether entertainment lawyers should be treated differently than other lawyers for ethical purposes.

The search for a resolution of these issues begins with a distinction between direct and indirect conflicts of interest. A direct conflict of interest occurs when a lawyer is engaged to represent clients in the same transaction in which their interests are adverse—when the interests of one client actually conflict with those of the other.

An indirect conflict of interest occurs when a lawyer does not represent another party in the same transaction but has—or had—a legal, business, financial, professional or personal relationship with that party or a party who would be affected substantially by that matter or has some other interest in the subject matter of the representation.

Although this is not covered by the Rules of Professional Conduct, an indirect conflict of interest also can occur when a lawyer seeks to develop a future relationship with a party in a transaction whom the lawyer is not representing. For instance, when a lawyer hopes to receive significant and lucrative referrals from the party on the other side of a negotiation, an indirect conflict of interest arises in that the lawyer may not be willing to explore all options or "go to the mat" for the current client.

---

*Mr. Sloane is a partner at Marina Del Rey, California's Berger, Kahn, Shafton, Moss, Figler, Simon & Gladstone.

In the direct conflict-of-interest situation the lawyer owes an obligation to two or more clients. In an indirect conflict, the lawyer owes an obligation only to his or her client in that matter, but the lawyer's judgment and willingness to pursue certain courses may be impaired or affected by his or her relationship—real or potential—to the other party.

A California appeals court has stated, "The duty of loyalty is at the core of conflict-of-interest rules and analysis."[1] The issue in a conflict-of-interest analysis is whether the conflict will "materially interfere with the lawyer's professional judgment in considering alternatives or foreclosure courses of action that reasonably should be pursued on behalf of the client."[2] Direct and indirect conflicts thus raise professional concerns because they both affect the lawyer's judgment and pursuits of reasonable strategies.

Entertainment lawyers frequently are prized more for their contacts and ability to put deals together than for their legal skills. Many clients believe that lawyers, and their drafting talents, are fungible. To these clients, a lawyer's most valuable asset is his or her ability to reach the people who can make transactions happen. Potential conflicts, in this view, are really potential contacts.

Clients need lawyers to make the best possible deal, devoting all of their expertise and energies to that end. Conflicts prevent lawyers from carrying out this duty. In effect, the role of the lawyer in this situation is transformed from that of the traditional advocate to that of a mediator. A lawyer's obligation, however, is to be an advocate for his or her client—not an independent, impartial third party. When lawyers owe a duty to more than one client to represent their interests, the lawyers cannot—ethically or practically—remain independent or impartial.

Indirect Conflicts

Indirect conflicts of interest are by far the more numerous and insidious of the conflicts found in the entertainment industry,

1. *Jeffrey v. Pounds,* 67 Cal. App. 6 (1977).
2. Comment b, Model Rule 1.7, ABA Model Rules of Professional Conduct.

although most of the recent high-profile cases filed by clients against their lawyers have been of the direct-conflict variety. Indirect conflicts are treacherous because they may be totally hidden or, even if disclosed, are viewed as assets. While it may be impossible to overcome the lay client's doubts as to the loyalty of a lawyer who represents both the client and the client's adversary in the same negotiation, no such doubts usually exist in indirect-conflict situations.

The sales pitch to a potential client may elevate the indirect conflict of interest to a benefit. The lawyer could convince the client that he or she should be represented by that lawyer because the lawyer has an excellent relationship with the other side or is a personal friend or business associate of the chief executive or principals of the other party. The other party may in fact have even recommended the lawyer to the client, which the client takes as an endorsement of the lawyer or as an implied or actual threat that to failure to engage that lawyer will result in the client's getting a less desirable deal from the other party.

As reported in the December issue of *Vanity Fair,*[3] the case of well-known singer-songwriter Billy Joel is a graphic example of this scenario. Walter Yetnikoff—then president of CBS Records Inc., Mr. Joel's record company—not only steered Mr. Joel to his friend and CBS's lawyer, Allan Grubman, for legal representation, as he had done for others, because Mr. Yetnikoff "could count on Grubman to keep the artists in line," but also "muscled" Mr. Joel to accept Mr. Grubman as his attorney. Mr. Yetnikoff apparently did so, as *Vanity Fair* reports, by telling Mr. Joel he would not deal with his current lawyer and would give him anything he reasonably wanted if he switched to Mr. Grubman, and by giving him Mr. Grubman's business card.

Besides being patently false, none of these arguments can justify representing a client when the lawyer's relationship with the other party would interfere with the lawyer's professional judgment or would "foreclose courses of action that should be pursued on behalf of the client," as stated in the Comment to Model Rule

3. Robert Sam Anson, "Tommy," *Vanity Fair,* December 1996, at 288.

1.7 of the American Bar Association's Model Rules of Professional Conduct.

Shortchanging Clients

Regardless of the justifications for representing clients when the lawyer is in an indirect conflict of interest, the fundamental fact remains that if the lawyer's relationship to the other party influences or tempers his or her judgment or representation of the client, the client will be shortchanged in the same manner as in a direct conflict because the lawyer will have failed to commit to protect the client and to devote his or her best judgment and talent to the client's interest.

By no means are all conflicts of interest harmful to the client's interests. For example, a lawyer's professional judgment or ability to pursue all courses of action may not be compromised in situations in which one or more equally sophisticated clients are looking to the lawyer either to act as the scrivener of an agreement the parties have reached themselves or to present the various options from which the parties can choose. The formation of a partnership is a good example of the latter situation.

Although there may be a loss of the attorney–client privilege, the lawyer is not compromised because these types of transactions are not usually all that adversarial. The rules on informed consent would apply to protect all parties.

Disastrous Consequences

In the negotiation of a complex contract, however, when one or both clients are looking to the lawyer to advise them as to the best deal they can make and to fight for their interests, a conflict of interest can be disastrous. This is especially true when one party is less sophisticated than the other and is relying totally on the lawyer's advice. Most of the transactional situations that arise in the entertainment industry involve the latter situation, not the former.

If practitioners reject the arguments that conflicts of interest in the entertainment industry are good for clients, the current Rules of Professional Conduct must be examined closely to determine how their proscriptions apply to the entertainment industry and whether they are adequate. Rule 3-310 of the California Rules of Professional Conduct applies to conflicts of interest.

For direct conflicts of interest, the California Rules of Professional Conduct do not require the lawyer to withdraw. The rules do require the informed written consent of the clients to enable the lawyer to continue to represent clients in conflict.

Rule 3-310(A)(2) defines "informed written consent" as "the client's or former client's written agreement to the representation following written disclosure." "Disclosure" is defined in Subsec. (1) as "informing the client or former client of the relevant circumstances and of the actual and reasonably foreseeable adverse consequences to the client or former client."

Obtaining Consent

Accordingly, in order to comply with Rule 310(c) of the Rules of Professional Conduct, lawyers may represent conflicting interests if they secure the informed, written consent of the clients involved. Depending on the extent of the disclosure required to satisfy the informed-consent rule, the sophistication of the clients, and the nature of the transaction involved, this general rule has some applicability to the entertainment industry.

When one client is unsophisticated, the extent of the disclosure must be more extensive than in other cases, especially if the transaction in question is complex and beyond the general experience of the client. For example, a lawyer should be required to disclose in such situations that he or she would be acting more as a mediator than as an advocate and that the client would be receiving the benefit of the independent advice. The client also should be given enough information about the lawyer's relationship to the other client to form a considered judgment on the likely chances of being favored or disfavored.

Notwithstanding such consent, however, there are certain situations in which the lawyer should be required to decline or withdraw from representation. California courts have consistently held in cases of dual representation of conflicting interests in conjunction with a trial hearing that, for nondisciplinary purposes, informed consent is not sufficient and the lawyer must withdraw.[4]

In cases in which one or both clients are unsophisticated and need to rely on the lawyer's judgment and advice in reaching an agreement on complex business and legal issues beyond their expertise, the contract negotiation should be treated for ethical purposes as if it were akin to a contested hearing, and the lawyer should be required to withdraw. In fact, it is even more compelling to require such withdrawal in negotiations because there is no judge or third party to protect the client's interest as there would be in a trial or contested hearing.

Rule 310(B) addresses indirect conflicts. A lawyer with an indirect conflict still may accept or continue representation of a client without the client's consent as long as the lawyer makes a written disclosure. Since the client most likely has sought out the lawyer in the first place because the client believes the lawyer's contacts will be beneficial, it is hard to imagine how disclosure will protect the client.

For example, if the party on the other side is not a client of the lawyer but is the source of numerous financially lucrative referrals to the lawyer, written disclosure under Rule 310(B) would be required because the referrals would constitute a business, financial, professional or personal relationship. This disclosure to a potential client, especially an unsophisticated one, however, would probably have little effect on the client's decision to engage that lawyer. In fact, it probably would reinforce the client's decision to select that lawyer.

The client may believe that the other party refers clients to the lawyer because the lawyer is effective. While in some cases this may be true, it is more likely that the referring party likes doing business with the lawyer because the referring party gets a better deal when the other party is represented by that lawyer, or the lawyer will be less vigorous in pursuing the client's interest for fear of jeopardizing future referrals.

---

4. *Tsakos Shipping & Trading v. Juniper Garden,* 12 Cal. App. 4th 74, 15 Cal. Reptr. 2d 585 (1993).

Moreover, when the indirect conflict involves a party whom the lawyer has never represented or has no current relationship with, but with whom the lawyer desires a future relationship, the Rules of Professional Conduct do not even require disclosure. Consequently, implied or express threats by the other party to the lawyer to "go easy" in this negotiation need not even be disclosed to the current client.

Because of these inadequate protections for entertainment industry clients—particularly creative individuals—Rule 3-310 should be modified.

Appendix M

CONFLICT-OF-INTEREST WAIVER

As of ____ , ____

(Client #1)

____

____

(Client #2)

____

____

Re: Legal Representation

Dear ____ and ____:

Each of you has requested that I represent each of you in connection with, among other matters, the negotiation of agreements (the "Agreements") between you.

The State Bar of _____ requires that both of you be informed of any situation where a conflict of interest may exist and the adverse effects that it may have upon you. I am also required to give you the opportunity to consult independent legal counsel of your own choosing before deciding whether or not to permit my concurrent representation of each of you in connection with the Agreement and, if you decide to permit such representation, to obtain written consent to such decision from each of you.

There may arise one or more conflicts between you during my concurrent representation. In such event, my duty of loyalty to and obligation to render independent professional judgment on behalf of each of you, respectively, would possibly be influenced by my representation of the other.

My concurrent representation of you also raises the possibility that I will be unable to guarantee the confidentiality of communications between each respective party and this firm. If you agree to concurrent representation as set forth herein, each acknowledges and agrees that its confidential communications may be disclosed to the other.

If any dispute develops between you, you will endeavor to resolve the dispute between yourselves, and I will proceed based upon your joint advice as to the resolution thereof. Should I not receive such joint advice, or should any such dispute not be resolved (whether or not such dispute gives rise to litigation) or should I decide in my sole judgment that the representation of any party should not continue, I shall have the right to resign my representation of either or both of you.

By signing this letter, each of you agrees for itself and for its partners, officers, directors, shareholders, agents, employees, representatives, affiliates, successors, and assigns, and each of them, to waive any claims now existing or arising in the future that you may have by virtue of the conflict of interest that arises out of or in connection with my concurrent representation of the two of you. You also agree that such representation will not derogate from the binding nature of the Agreement nor be deemed as a breach of any fiduciary relationship or fee agreement between me and either of you.

If you agree to my representation under the terms and conditions of this letter, please sign one copy of this letter in the space indicated and return it to me. This letter may be executed in counterparts and all such counterparts taken together shall be deemed to constitute a single agreement. If you have any questions regarding anything contained herein, please feel free to contact me.

Yours very truly,

(Lawyer)

ACCEPTED AND AGREED:

____

(Client #1)

____

(Client #2)

Appendix N

TRANSACTION FORMS

General Form:	N-1	Personal Management Agreement
Music Forms:	N-2	Artist Recording Agreement
	N-3	Songwriter Agreement
	N-4	Music Producer Agreement
Film/TV Forms:	N-5	Loan-Out Actor Agreement
	N-6	Screenwriter Agreement
	N-7	Film Producer Agreement

Appendix N-1

PERSONAL MANAGEMENT AGREEMENT

AGREEMENT made and entered into this ___ day of ____, ____, by and between _____ ("Manager"), on the one hand, and _____ ("Artist"), on the other hand.

1. <u>ENGAGEMENT AND TERM</u>

1.1 Artist hereby engages Manager as Artist's exclusive personal manager for an initial period of ____ (__) years commencing on the date hereof.

1.2 Manager shall have ____ separate options, each to extend the term of this Agreement for _____ (___) additional period(s) of _____ (___) years each (the "option periods"). Such option periods shall commence automatically upon the expiration of the immediately preceding contract period of this Agreement unless Manager gives Artist notice to the contrary in writing at any time prior to the end of any such contract period of his or her desire to terminate the term of this Agreement. Any reference to the "term" of this Agreement shall include the initial period and any option periods, if applicable.

2. <u>MANAGER'S SERVICES</u>

2.1 During the term hereof, Manager agrees to use all reasonable efforts to promote, develop, and advance Artist's professional career and to advise and counsel Artist with respect to all phases of Artist's career in the entertainment industry, including the following:

2.1.1 Advise and counsel in the selection of literary, artistic, and musical material;

2.1.2 Advise and counsel in any and all matters pertaining to publicity, public relations, and advertising;

2.1.3 Advise and counsel with relation to the adoption of a proper format for presentation of Artist's talents and in the determination of proper style, mood, setting talents, and characterizations in keeping with Artist's talents;

2.1.4 Advise, counsel, and direct in the selection of artistic talent to assist, accompany, or embellish Artist's artistic presentation;

2.1.5 Advise and counsel with regard to general practices in the entertainment industries and with respect to such matters of which Manager may have knowledge concerning compensation and privileges for similar artistic values;

2.1.6 Advise and counsel concerning the selection of talent agencies and any other Persons who may be engaged to counsel and advise Artist and to seek and procure contracts of employment and engagements for Artist (collectively, "Agents");

2.1.7 To the extent allowed by law, advise and counsel in connection with the negotiations of all agreements affecting Artist's career; and

2.1.8 At Manager's discretion and only to the extent permitted by law, seek to obtain employment for Artist as a recording artist in the recording industry, provided, however, that Manager shall not be obligated to seek, obtain, or procure any other employment or engagements for Artist.

2.2 Manager shall be required to render all reasonable services called for by this Agreement and customarily performed by personal managers in the entertainment industries as and when reasonably required. Manager shall not, however, be required to travel to meet with Artist at any particular place outside of the ____ metropolitan area, except in Manager's discretion and subject to satisfactory arrangements for payment or reimbursement of the reasonable costs and expenses of such travel.

3. <u>NONEXCLUSIVITY.</u> Manager's services hereunder are nonexclusive and Manager shall at all times be free to perform the same or similar services for others, as well as to engage in any and all other business activities.

4. <u>MANAGER'S AUTHORITY</u>

4.1 At Manager's discretion, Manager is authorized and empowered for Artist and on Artist's behalf to do the following:

4.1.1 Approve and permit, with Artist's consent, any and all publicity and advertising;

4.1.2 Approve and permit, with Artist's consent, the use of Artist's name, photograph, likeness, voice, sound effects, caricatures, literary, and artistic and musical materials for purposes of advertising and publicity and in the promotion and advertising of any and all products and services;

4.1.3 Execute for Artist, in Artist's name and/or on Artist's behalf, any and all agreements, documents, and contracts for Artist's services, as Artist's true and lawful attorney-in-fact, such power of attorney being irrevocable during the term hereof and coupled with an interest, provided that Manager shall not exercise said power of attorney in executing any such agreements without first obtaining Artist's consent in each instance;

4.1.4 Collect and receive all monies on behalf of Artist, endorse Artist's name upon and deposit or cash any and all checks payable to Artist for Artist's services, talents, and literary and artistic materials, and to retain therefrom all sums owing to Manager hereunder, provided Manager promptly remits the balance to Artist in accordance with Artist's instructions. Notwithstanding the foregoing or anything to the contrary in this Agreement, Artist shall have the right, at any time, by notice to Manager to engage an accountant/business manager ("Accountant") to collect and receive all such monies, and endorse and deposit checks in accordance with the foregoing, provided that in such event, Artist agrees to direct Accountant to account to and pay all monies due and owing to Manager hereunder directly to manager within two (2) weeks after receipt thereof.

4.1.5 Engage, as well as discharge and/or direct for Artist and in Artist's name, with Artist's approval, all Agents.

4.2 Artist shall instruct and direct any Agent to remit to Manager any monies that may become due Artist received by any such Agent.

5. <u>OFFERS OF EMPLOYMENT.</u> Artist shall advise Manager of all offers of employment submitted to Artist and will refer any inquiries concerning Artist's services to Manager, for Manager's advice and approval and in order that Manager may determine whether the same are compatible with and in the best interests of Artist's career.

6. LOANS, ADVANCES, AND EXPENSES

6.1 Manager is not required to make any loans of advances to or for the account of Artist, but in the event Manager does so at Artist's request, Artist shall repay such loans or advances immediately after Manager's request therefor. In addition, Artist authorizes Manager to deduct and retain the amount of any such loans or advances from any sums Manager may receive for Artist's account hereunder.

6.2 All expenses, other than Manager's normal overhead expenses, incurred by Manager on Artist's behalf and otherwise in connection with the rendition of Manager's services hereunder, including, but not limited to, long-distance telephone calls, messenger, Federal Express, and other similar document transmittal fees, travel costs and expenses, promotion and publicity expenses, and any other similar disbursements directly attributable to Artist hereunder, shall be paid by Artist and/or reimbursed if Manager initially advances the funds for said expenses. If after consultation with Artist, Manager's presence is required outside of the ________ metropolitan area, Artist agrees that Artist will pay and/or reimburse Manager for Manager's reasonable expenses, including hotel, round-trip airfare, and living costs. Upon Artist's request, Manager will furnish to Artist invoices and/or itemized expense statements with respect to Manager's expenses hereunder. In addition, Artist authorizes and empowers Manager to deduct and retain the amounts of such expenses/costs hereunder from any monies which Manager may receive for Artist's account hereunder.

7. ARTIST'S DUTIES. Artist agrees at all times during the term hereof to diligently attend to Artist's career to the best of Artist's ability and to do all things reasonably requested by Manager and which are otherwise necessary and desirable to promote Artist's career and to maximize earnings therefrom. Artist shall only engage and utilize qualified and competent Agents to obtain employment for Artist.

8. EXCLUDED SERVICES. Even though Manager is a licensed "Talent Agent," Manager is under no obligation to procure employment for Artist. Manager has made no representations to Artist, either oral or written, to the contrary. Artist acknowledges that

Manager has not offered to, attempted to, or promised to obtain, seek, or procure employment or engagements for Artist, and that Manager is not obligated to do so.

9. RELATIONSHIP OF THE PARTIES. This Agreement shall not be construed to create a partnership between Manager and Artist. It is specifically understood that Manager is acting hereunder as an independent contractor and Manager may appoint or engage other persons, firms, and corporations, in Manager's discretion, to perform services that Manager has agreed to perform hereunder at Manager's sole expense.

10. COMMISSIONS

10.1 In consideration of Manager's services hereunder, Artist agrees to pay to Manager, as and when received by Artist, for the term hereof, a sum equal to __ percent (__%) of any and all "gross monies or other considerations" that Artist may receive as a result of Artist's activities in and throughout the entertainment, amusement, motion picture, television, music, and recording industries, including all of the results and proceeds thereof. Without in any manner limiting the foregoing, the matters upon which Manager's compensation shall be computed shall include any and all of Artist's activities in connection with: motion pictures; television; radio; music; records and recordings; literary publications; theater; personal and public appearances; and the use of Artist's name, voice, likeness, and other talents for purposes of merchandising; advertising; endorsements and trade.

10.2 The term "gross monies or other considerations" shall include, but not be limited to, salaries, earnings, fees, royalties, gifts, bonuses, shares of profit, shares of stock, partnership interests, percentages of the amount paid for any entertainment package (such as television or radio programs, live or recorded, or motion pictures) earned or received directly or indirectly by Artist or Artist's heirs, executors, administrators, or assignees, or by any other Person on Artist's behalf. If Artist receives, as all or part of Artist's compensation for activities covered hereunder, stock or the right to buy stock in any corporation, or if Artist becomes the packager, owner, or other interest holder of all or part of an entertainment property, whether as individual proprietor, stockholder, partner, joint venturer, or otherwise, Manager's commission shall apply thereto and Manager shall be entitled to Manager's commission hereunder. Should Artist be required to make any payment for such interest, Manager will pay Manager's percentage share thereof as well, unless Manager elects not to participate therein.

11. CONTINUING COMMISSIONS. Artist agrees to pay Manager a commission at the following rates instead of the rate provided herein following the expiration of the term hereof upon and with respect to any and all engagements, contracts, and agreements entered into during the term hereof relating to any of Artist's activities set forth herein, and upon any and all extensions, renewals, and substitutions thereof that were contemplated at the time the original agreement was entered into, and upon resumptions of such engagements, contracts, and agreements that may have been discontinued during the term and resumed within one (1) year thereafter:

a. First post-term year: ____ (__) percent
b. Second post-term year: ____ (__) percent
c. Third post-term year: ____ (__) percent

12. ASSIGNMENT. Manager shall have the right to assign this Agreement to any third party associated or affiliated with Manager or in which Manager has a direct or indirect interest, provided that no such assignment shall relieve Manager of Manager's obligations hereunder without Artist's consent, and further provided that _______ shall remain personally and primarily responsible for the rendition of Manager's services hereunder.

13. CONFLICTING INTERESTS. From time to time during the term hereof, Manager may, either alone or in association with others, employ Artist as a songwriter, composer, arranger, producer, performer, or otherwise in connection with the creation of literary or musical works, or Manager may acquire rights therein. Artist acknowledges that such activity shall be for the mutual best interests of Manager and Artist and that such activity shall not be deemed to be a breach of Manager's fiduciary obligations or other duties to Artist hereunder.

14. INDEMNITY. If either Artist or Manager does not fulfill or cause to be fulfilled any agreement or obligation undertaken by

either Artist or Manager hereunder, Artist and Manager agree to indemnify and hold each other harmless from any claims, demands, or actions against the other in connection with such non-fulfillment that are reduced to final judgment in a court of competent jurisdiction, or are settled with the other's reasonable consent. It is agreed that Manager will not be held liable or responsible for any breach or contract or act or omission on the part of any Person with respect to any engagement or agreement concerning Artist's services.

15. NOTICES. All notices hereunder shall be delivered by personal service or sent by prepaid telegram or cablegram, or by certified or registered mail, return receipt requested, postage prepaid, as follows: if to Manager, at ______, with a copy to ________ at ________; and if to Artist at ____________, unless either party notifies the other as provided herein that notices should be sent to a different address. The date of mailing or telecopying, or in the case of personal service, the date of delivery, shall be deemed the date of the giving of said notice, except for notice of a change of address, which shall be effective only upon actual receipt.

16. MISCELLANEOUS PROVISIONS

16.1 This Agreement shall be deemed to have been executed in and shall be construed in accordance with the laws of the State of _____. If any provision hereof shall for any reason be illegal or unenforceable, such unenforceability shall not affect the validity of the remaining portion of the provisions hereof.

16.2 This Agreement is the only agreement of the parties and there is no other agreement, oral or written, between the parties relating to the subject matter hereof. Specifically, but without limiting the generality of the foregoing, this agreement is intended to supersede any prior management agreement between Artist and Manager.

16.3 Manager shall not be deemed to be in breach of any of Manager's obligations hereunder unless and until Artist shall have first given Manager specific written notice by certified or registered mail, return receipt requested, of the nature of such alleged breach and Manager shall have failed to cure such alleged breach within thirty (30) days after written notice, or if the alleged breach is not capable of being cured within such period, Manager shall have such additional time as is reasonably necessary to complete such cure.

16.4 The term "Artist" as used herein shall refer to ______ , individually and doing business as any entity furnishing his/her services or owned or controlled by him/her, including any publishing companies. The term "Person" as used herein shall mean a person, firm, partnership, corporation, business association, joint venture, or other entity.

IN WITNESS WHEREOF, the parties hereto have executed this Agreement as of the date first above written.

By:_________________________ By:___________________________

(Manager) (Artist)

Appendix N-2

ARTIST RECORDING AGREEMENT

Agreement made and entered into as of this ___ day of ____ , ____ , by and between _____ , whose address is _____________ ("Company"), on the one hand, and _____ p/k/a "_______" ("Artist"), on the other hand, whose address is c/o ___________ .

1. (a) Company hereby engages Artist's exclusive personal services as a recording artist in connection with the production of records and Artist hereby accepts such engagement and agrees to exclusively render such services for Company during the term hereof and all extensions and renewals.

(b) The rights herein granted to Company and the obligations of Artist shall be for _______ ("Territory").

2. (a) The term of this Agreement shall be for an initial period commencing on the date hereof and continuing until the last day of the ninth (9th) full month following the release of the first album, or the twelfth (12th) full month following the month during which Artist shall have delivered and Company shall have accepted as technically and commercially satisfactory for the production and exploitation of records the final masters required to be delivered during said period ("Initial Period"). Artist hereby grants to Company __ (_) consecutive separate options to extend the term for further periods ("Option Periods"), each upon the same terms and conditions applicable to the Initial Period, except as otherwise hereinafter set forth. Each Option Period for which Company has exercised its option shall commence upon the expiration of the immediately preceding Period and shall continue until the last day of the ninth (9th) full month following the release of the applicable album hereunder, or the twelfth (12th) full month following the month during which Artist shall have delivered and Company shall have accepted the final masters required to be

delivered ("minimum recording commitment") during the applicable Option Period. The Initial Period and every Option Period for which Company has exercised its option are hereinafter sometimes referred to together as the "Term." Each option shall be deemed exercised, if at all, unless Company sends notice to Artist to the contrary at any time prior to the date the Term would otherwise expire.

(b) If Artist is a California resident, Company guarantees that, as of the end of each of the first seven Contract Years of this agreement, Artist will have received Compensation (as defined below) of not less than the following amounts:

First Contract Year: Nine Thousand Dollars ($9,000);
Second Contract Year: Twelve Thousand Dollars ($12,000);
Third Contract Year: Fifteen Thousand Dollars ($15,000);

and

Each Subsequent Contract Year: Fifteen Thousand Dollars ($15,000).

In the event the Compensation paid to Artist is below the amount described above as of thirty (30) days prior to the end of the applicable Contract Year, Artist will give Company written notice containing specific reference to this paragraph and specifying such deficiency. Such notice may be given no earlier than thirty (30) days nor later than fifteen (15) days prior to the expiration of the Contract Year concerned. Promptly after its receipt of such notice, during the term of this agreement, Company will pay the actual amount of any such deficiency, which payment shall be a prepayment of any monies due hereunder (other than Mechanical Royalties). Any failure by Company to make such payment will not constitute a material breach of this agreement. As used in this paragraph Contract Year means the annual period beginning on the first day of the term hereof and each subsequent annual period during the continuance of the term and Compensation means all monies paid by Company to Artist (including, but not limited to, Advances and Record royalties, but not including Mechanical Royalties).

3. (a) During the Initial Period, Artist shall record and deliver to Company masters the equivalent in playing time of one (1) Album ("minimum recording commitment").

(b) During each Option Period, Artist shall record and deliver to Company masters the equivalent in playing time of one (1) Album ("minimum recording commitment").

(c) The masters recorded hereunder by Artist shall be recorded in a recording studio mutually selected or approved by Company and Artist at such times (subject to Artist's bona fide prior professional commitments) as Company and Artist may designate or approve. Each master delivered hereunder shall consist of Artist's newly recorded studio performances of material selected or approved by Company and not previously released by Artist. Each master shall be subject to Company's approval as commercially satisfactory in Company's reasonable, good-faith judgment. Artist shall deliver to Company a two-track stereo tape for each master. Each master shall be delivered to Company in the form of a completed, fully edited, mixed, leadered, and equalized 1630 tape for each configuration (e.g., compact-disc, analog cassette), and otherwise in the proper form for the production of the parts necessary for the manufacture of commercial records. Upon the reasonable request of Company, Artist shall rerecord any selection until a commercially satisfactory master shall have been obtained. Only masters delivered in compliance with the provisions of this subparagraph shall be applied in fulfillment of Artist's recording and delivery obligation, unless otherwise accepted by Company. Each master shall be delivered to Company at Company's address first set forth above, or such other place as Company may notify Artist in writing.

(d) The first Album required to be delivered during the Initial Period or any Option Period shall be delivered to Company within four (4) months following commencement of the applicable Period.

4. Artist warrants and agrees that:

(a) During the Term, Artist shall not perform for the purpose of making records for anyone other than Company and shall not authorize the use of Artist's name, likeness, or other identification for the purpose of distributing, selling, advertising, or exploiting records in the Territory for anyone other than Company.

(b) Artist shall not perform any selection recorded hereunder for anyone other than Company for use in the Territory for a period of (i) five (5) years after the initial date of release of the respective record containing such selection or (ii) two (2) years after the expiration or other termination of this Agreement, whichever is later ("Re-recording Restriction").

5. All masters recorded by Artist during the Term from the inception of the recording thereof and all reproductions derived therefrom, together with the performances embodied thereon, shall be the property of Company for the Territory free from any claims whatsoever by Artist or any person deriving any rights or interests from Artist. Without limiting the generality of the foregoing, Company and its designee(s) shall have the exclusive and unlimited right to all the results and proceeds of Artist's recording services hereunder rendered during the Term, including, but not limited to, the exclusive, unlimited, and perpetual rights throughout the Territory:

(a) To manufacture, advertise, sell, lease, license, distribute, or otherwise use or dispose of, in any or all fields of use by any method now or hereafter known, records embodying the masters subject hereto, all upon such terms and conditions as Company may elect, or at its discretion, to refrain therefrom;

(b) To use and publish, and to permit others to use and publish, Artist's name (including any professional name heretofore or hereafter adopted by Artist), photographs, portrait, likeness, and biographical material concerning Artist for advertising and trade purposes in connection with all masters recorded by Artist and all Videos produced during the Term, including, but not limited to, in the marketing, sale, or other exploitation of records;

(c) To obtain copyrights and renewals thereof in sound recordings (as distinguished from the musical compositions embodied thereon) recorded by Artist during the Term, in Company's name as owner and employer-for-hire of such sound recordings;

(d) To release records embodying the performances to be recorded hereunder under any name, trademark, or label that Company or its subsidiaries, affiliates, or licensees may from time to time elect;

(e) To perform the records publicly and to permit public performances thereof by means of radio broadcast, television, or any other method now or hereafter known, it being agreed that if Company receives royalties solely attributable to the public performance of Masters hereunder, Artist's account shall be credited with a proportionate share thereof (i.e., in the same proportion as Artist's basic royalty in the territory concerned hereunder bears to the corresponding amount received by Company from its distributors therefor).

6. Artist acknowledges that the sale of records is speculative and agrees that Company may exercise its reasonable commercial judgment with regard to any matter affecting the sale, distribution, and exploitation of such records. Nothing contained in this Agreement shall obligate Company to make, sell, license, or distribute records manufactured from masters subject hereto.

7. Company shall pay to Artist the following sums, which shall be Advances (exclusive of recording costs) against and recoupable by Company out of all royalties becoming payable to Artist pursuant to this or any other agreement:

(a) (i) With respect to the First Album, the Advance shall be ______ Dollars ($____). (ii) With respect to all subsequent Albums, the minimum Advance shall be ____ Dollars ($____). For convenience, the foregoing minimum Album Advances shall hereinafter be referred to as the "Base Advances."

(b) (i) With respect to each subsequent Album required to be recorded and delivered hereunder after the First Album, the Advance shall be the greater of:

(1) the applicable Base Advances set forth in subparagraph 7(a) hereof, or:

(2) an amount that is the equivalent of the lesser of (A) _______ (___%) percent of the net earned royalties in respect of sales of royalty bearing units through normal retailer channels

in the United States of the immediately preceding Album required to be recorded and delivered hereunder or (B) _______ (__%) percent of the average of the net earned royalties in respect of sales of royalty bearing units through normal retailer channels in the United States of the two (2) immediately preceding Albums required to be recorded and delivered hereunder, less the greater of (A) the recording costs for the immediately preceding Album required to be recorded and delivered hereunder or (B) the average recording costs of the two (2) immediately preceding Albums to be recorded and delivered hereunder.

(ii) For the purposes of making the computations under subparagraph 7(b)(i), Company shall refer to accounting statements rendered to Artist through the end of the accounting period following the earlier of (A) the date twelve (12) months following Company's initial release of each applicable Album or (B) the date upon which the Album for which the Advance is being determined is delivered. It is understood that in no event shall any Advance exceed _______ Dollars ($____).

(iii) No payments will be made hereunder until this agreement is fully executed.

(iv) (A) With respect to the First Album, the Advance shall be payable as follows:

(1) _______ Dollars ($____), promptly following the complete execution hereof.

(2) _______ Dollars ($____), within ten (10) business days following Artist's written notice to Company that recording of the First Album has commenced and is scheduled to proceed without interruption to completion. Such notice shall also, to the extent then known, (1) set forth the name of the producer engaged in accordance with this Agreement, (2) set forth the dates and places of all studio time scheduled in connection with the applicable Album, and (3) set forth the selections to be recorded; and

(3) _______ Dollars ($____) promptly following the complete delivery and acceptance by Company of the completed First Album.

(B) With respect to the Second Album and each subsequent Album required to be recorded and delivered hereunder each applicable Advance shall be payable as follows:

(1) ______ (__%) percent of the Base Advance within ten (10) business days following Artist's written notice to Company that recording of the masters comprising the applicable Album required to be recorded and delivered hereunder has commenced, and is scheduled to proceed without interruption to completion. Such notice shall also, to the extent then known, (1) set forth the name of the producer engaged in accordance with this Agreement, (2) set forth the dates and places of all studio time scheduled in connection with the applicable Album, and (3) set forth the selections to be recorded; and

(2) The balance of the applicable Advance within ten (10) business days following Artist's delivery to and Company's acceptance of the completed Album.

(c) In the event Company requests Artist to record and deliver masters (and Artist consents) consisting of less than an Album, the advance otherwise payable for such masters shall be computed by multiplying the applicable advance for the applicable Contract Period by a fraction, the numerator of which is the number of masters that Company requests and the denominator of which is ten (10).

(d) All monies paid to Artist or on behalf of Artist or to or on behalf of any person, firm, or corporation representing Artist at Artist's request, other than royalties payable pursuant to Paragraphs 10, 14, and 20 of this Agreement, shall constitute advances recoupable from any monies (excluding mechanical royalties) payable under this or any other agreement, unless Company shall otherwise consent in writing.

8. (a) Prior to any recording session for any master(s) hereunder, Company and Artist shall in good faith mutually determine the following: (i) the producer(s); (ii) selection of material, including the number of compositions to be recorded; (iii) specification of accompaniment, arrangement, and copying services, (iv) recording fees or arranging fees that will exceed union scale and the

proposed recipient thereof, and (v) the dates of recording and mixing and studios where recording and mixing are to take place, including the cost of each recording session. Company shall determine the budget for all costs to be incurred in each and every recording session and all studio time. Upon approval of all elements of each recording proposal, Artist shall commence such session(s).

(b) Company shall pay all recording costs up to the amount of the written recording budget approved by Company. Artist shall be solely responsible for and shall pay all recording costs incurred in the production of masters subject to this Agreement in excess of the written recording budget approved by Company to the extent caused by Artist. In the event Company elects to pay any excess recording costs (for which Artist is responsible pursuant to the preceding sentence), all such costs paid by Company shall be deducted from any and all monies becoming payable to Artist under this or any other agreement.

(c) It is of the essence of this Agreement that Artist obtain prior to each applicable recording session and deliver to Company within forty-eight (48) hours following each such recording session, a duly completed and executed Form I-9 (or such similar or other form(s) as may be prescribed by the United States Immigration and Naturalization Service or other government agency regarding citizenship, permanent residency, or so-called documented worker status) in respect of each individual employed to render services in the recording of masters hereunder. Artist shall simultaneously obtain and deliver to Company true and complete copies of all evidentiary documents relating to the contents or subject matter of said form(s). In the event Artist fails to comply with any of the foregoing requirements, subject to a reasonable notice and cure, Company may deduct any resulting penalty payments from any and all monies due under this or any other agreement.

(d) Company shall pay all monies becoming payable to all third parties engaged by Company and included in the written recording budget approved by Company. Artist shall be solely responsible for and shall pay all monies becoming payable to all third parties rendering services or otherwise in respect of sales of recordings derived from masters subject to this Agreement not engaged by Company or included in the written recording budget approved by Company. In the event Company pays any such approved monies, all such monies shall be deducted from any and all applicable monies becoming payable to Artist hereunder. Company shall only recoup ____ % of the cost of independent radio promotion hereunder.

(e) All recording sessions hereunder shall be held under Company's license and, if required, Artist shall notify the appropriate local of the American Federation of Musicians in advance of each recording session. Artist warrants and represents that Artist is a party to all applicable agreements with all applicable unions and guilds. At Company's request, Artist shall furnish Company with appropriate documentation confirming the foregoing. The amount of studio and other costs charged for recording done at studios owned by Company shall be at the most favorable rates then being charged to third parties at the time of such recording for the use of such studio facilities.

9. Each master subject hereto shall be produced and/or mixed/remixed by producers mutually selected or approved by Company. Company shall be solely responsible for engaging such producers and shall pay all monies becoming payable to such producers. At Artist's request, Company will furnish Artist with a copy of all such producer agreements. All such sums so paid by Company shall be deducted from the applicable written recording budget approved by Company. Artist understands that producers selected by Company may include Company's staff producers. With respect to the services of those staff producers, the producer fees and royalties charged hereunder shall be at the most favorable rates then being charged for comparable services to third parties by such producers at the time.

10. Conditioned upon Artist's full and faithful performance of each and all of the terms hereof, Company shall pay Artist the following royalties in respect of records subject to this Agreement:

(a) (i) (A) A royalty of __ (__%) percent in respect of retail sales in the United States of Singles and Maxi-singles derived from masters recorded and delivered during the Term;

(B) The royalty rate hereinabove set forth in subparagraph 10(a)(i)(A) shall be hereinafter referred to as the "Basic U.S. Singles Rate."

(ii) (A) A royalty of __ (__%) percent in respect of retail sales in the United States of Albums derived from masters recorded and delivered during the Term;

(B) The royalty rate hereinabove set forth in subparagraph 10(a)(ii)(A) shall be hereinafter referred to as a "Basic U.S. Album Rate."

(iii) (A) With respect to retail sales in the United States of EPs derived from masters recorded and delivered during the Term, the royalty rate shall be three-fourths (3/4) of the applicable Basic U.S. Album Rate.

(B) The royalty rate hereinabove set forth in subparagraph 10(a)(iii)(A) shall be hereinafter referred to as the "Basic U.S. EP Rate."

(b) (i) (A) With respect to retail sales of Singles and Maxi-singles in Canada, the royalty rate shall be ________ (___%) percent of the Basic U.S. Singles Rate.

(B) With respect to retail sales of Singles and Maxi-singles in the United Kingdom, France, Germany, Belgium, the Netherlands, Luxembourg, Spain, Greece, Denmark, Italy, Japan, Australia, and New Zealand, the royalty rate shall be ________ (___%) percent of the Basic U.S. Singles Rate.

(C) With respect to retail sales of Singles and Maxi-singles outside the United States, Canada, and those territories referred to in subparagraph 10(b)(i)(B) above, the royalty rate shall be ________ (___%) of the Basic U.S. Singles Rate.

(D) The royalty rates hereinabove set forth in subparagraphs 10(b)(i)(A) to (C) shall each be hereinafter referred to as a "Basic Foreign Singles Rate."

(ii) (A) With respect to retail sales of Albums in Canada, the royalty rate shall be _______ (___%) percent of the Basic U.S. Album Rate.

(B) With respect to retail sales of Albums in the United Kingdom, France, Germany, Belgium, the Netherlands, Luxembourg, Spain, Greece, Denmark, Italy, Japan, Australia, and New

Zealand, the royalty rate shall be ________ (___%) percent of the Basic U.S. Album Rate.

(C) With respect to retail sales of Albums outside the United States and outside those territories referred to in subparagraph 10(b)(ii)(B) above, the royalty rate shall be __________ (___%) percent of the Basic U.S. Album Rate.

(D) The royalty rates hereinabove set forth in subparagraphs 10(b)(ii)(A) to (C) shall each be hereinafter referred to as a "Basic Foreign Album Rate."

(iii) (A) With respect to retail sales of EPs outside the United States, the royalty rate shall be three-fourths (3/4) of the applicable Basic Foreign Album Rate.

(B) The royalty rate hereinabove set forth in subparagraph 10(b)(iii)(A) shall be hereinafter referred to as the "Basic Foreign EP Rate."

(iv) (A) Notwithstanding anything to the contrary contained herein, with respect to records sold in India, Kenya, Zambia, Zimbabwe, Nigeria, and any other territory in which governmental or other authorities place limits on the royalty rates permissible for remittances to the United States in respect of records sold in such territory(ies), the royalty rate payable to Artist hereunder in respect of sales of records in such territory(ies) shall equal the lesser of (1) the applicable Basic Foreign Singles Rate, applicable Basic Foreign EP Rate, or applicable Basic Foreign Album Rate, as the case may be or (2) the effective royalty rate permitted by such governmental or other authority for remittances to the United States *less* a royalty equivalent to ____ (__%) percent of the retail list price and such monies as Company or its licensees shall be required to pay to all applicable union funds in respect of said sales.

(B) Royalties in respect of sales of records outside the United States shall be computed in the same national currency as Company is accounted to by its licensees and shall be paid to Artist at the same rate of exchange as Company is paid. It is understood that such royalties will not be due and payable until payment thereof is received by Company in the United States of America. In the event Company is unable to receive payment in

United States dollars in the United States due to governmental regulations, royalties therefor shall not be credited to Artist's account during the continuance of such inability except that (1) if any accounting rendered to Artist hereunder during the continuance of such inability shows Artist's account to be in a credit position, Company will, after Artist's request and at Artist's expense, if Company is able to do so, deposit such royalties to Artist's credit in the applicable foreign currency in a foreign depository, or (2) if the royalties not credited to Artist's account exceed the amount, if any, by which Artist's account is in a debit position, then Company will, after Artist's request and at Artist's expense, and if Company is able to do so, deposit such excess royalties to Artist's credit in the applicable foreign currency in a foreign depository. Deposit as aforesaid shall fulfill Company's obligations under this Agreement as to record sales to which such royalty payments are applicable.

(c) With respect to records sold (i) through any direct mail or mail-order distribution method or any direct-to-consumer method, including, without limitation, record club distribution, whether or not such record club is affiliated with Company, (ii) by distribution through retail outlets in conjunction with special advertisements on radio or television, or (iii) by any combination of the methods set forth above, the royalty payable in connection therewith shall be one-half (1/2) of Company's net earned royalty receipts in respect of reported sales through such channels. No royalties shall be payable with respect to records given away as "bonus" or "free" records as a result of joining a record club or plan or of purchasing a required number of records or with respect to records received by members of any such club operation either in an introductory offer in connection with joining such club or upon recommending that another join such club operation.

(d) With respect to mid-priced records, the royalty rate shall be two-thirds (2/3) of the applicable royalty rate payable in respect of full-priced records in the same configuration or format.

(e) With respect to budget records, the royalty rate shall be one-half (1/2) of the applicable royalty rate payable in respect of full-priced records in the same configuration or format.

(f) Notwithstanding anything to the contrary contained in this Agreement, in the event that Company (or its licensee(s)) shall in any country(ies) of the Territory adopt a policy applicable to the majority of Albums in Company's (or its licensee(s)') then current catalog pursuant to which the retail list price of an Album is reduced subsequent to its initial release, then the royalty rates otherwise payable to Artist under this Agreement shall be reduced in the proportion that such reduced retail list price of the applicable Album bears to the retail list price of such Album as initially released in the applicable country.

(g) Notwithstanding anything to the contrary contained herein:

(i) with respect to records in compact-disc form, the royalty rate payable shall be ________ (___%) percent of the Basic U.S. Singles Rate, applicable Basic U.S. Album Rate, applicable Basic U.S. EP Rate, applicable Basic Foreign Singles Rate, applicable Basic Foreign Album Rate, or applicable Basic Foreign EP Rate, as the case may be; and

(ii) with respect to records in digital audiotape form, the royalty rate payable shall be ________ (___%) percent of the Basic U.S. Singles Rate, applicable Basic U.S. Album Rate, applicable Basic U.S. EP Rate, applicable Basic Foreign Singles Rate, applicable Basic Foreign Album Rate, or applicable Basic Foreign EP Rate, as the case may be; and

(iii) With respect to records in any form, configuration, format, or technology not herein described that is now known but not widely distributed or hereafter becomes known ("New Technology Configurations"), the royalty rate payable shall be ________ (___%) percent of the Basic U.S. Singles Rate, applicable Basic U.S. Album Rate, applicable Basic U.S. EP Rate, applicable Basic Foreign Singles Rate, applicable Basic Foreign Album Rate, or applicable Basic Foreign EP Rate, as the case may be.

(h) In the event that Company shall sell or license third parties to sell "records" via telephone, satellite, cable, or other direct transmission to the consumer over wire or through the air ("Satellite Sales"), Artist shall be paid royalties with respect thereto at the Basic U.S. Singles Rate, applicable Basic U.S. Album Rate, applicable Basic U.S. EP Rate, applicable Basic Foreign Singles Rate, applicable Basic Foreign Album Rate, or applicable Basic Foreign EP Rate, as the case may be as if such sales were New Technology

Configurations. For purposes of calculating royalties payable in connection with such sales, the retail list price of such "records" shall be deemed to be the then current retail list price of analog tape copies of such records (but in the United States, _______ (___%) percent of the then current retail list price of such analog tape copies).

(i) The royalty rate payable for records sold to the United States government, its subdivisions, departments, and agencies, and to educational institutions and libraries shall be _______ (__%) percent of the otherwise applicable basic U.S. rate and shall be based upon the retail list price (Post Exchange list price where applicable) of such records.

(j) The royalty rate payable for records sold as "premiums" shall be _______ (__%) percent of the otherwise applicable royalty rate, and the retail list price for such records shall be deemed to be Company's actual sales price.

(k) Company shall have the right to license the masters to third parties for record use and/or all other types of use on a flat-fee or royalty basis. With respect to masters licensed on a flat-fee basis, Company shall credit Artist's royalty account with ______ (___%) percent of the net amount received by Company under each such license. With respect to masters licensed on a royalty basis, Company shall credit Artist's royalty account with _____ (___%) percent of Company's net earned royalty receipts under each such license. For the purposes of this subparagraph 10(k), the term "net amount" or "net earned royalty receipts" shall mean the amount received by Company less all copyright, union fund payments, including so-called "re-use" payments, producer, collection, and all other applicable third-party payments.

(l) As to records not consisting entirely of masters recorded and delivered hereunder, the royalty rate otherwise payable to Artist hereunder with respect to sales of any such record shall be prorated by multiplying such royalty rate by a fraction, the numerator of which is the number of masters recorded and delivered hereunder embodied on such record and the denominator of which is the total number of masters embodied thereon.

(m) As to masters embodying performances of Artist together with the performances of another artist or artists, the royalty rate otherwise payable hereunder with respect to sales of any record derived from any such master and the recording costs and/or advances otherwise payable by Company hereunder with respect to any such master shall be prorated by multiplying such royalty rate or recording costs and/or advances by a fraction, the numerator of which is one and the denominator of which is the total number of artists whose performances are embodied on such master.

(n) Company shall have the right to include or to license others to include any one or more of the masters in promotional records on which such masters and other recordings are included, which promotional records are designed for sale at a substantially lower price than the regular price of Company's Albums. No royalties shall be payable on sales of such promotional records.

(o) No royalties shall be payable in respect of: (i) records given away or furnished on a "no-charge" basis to "one-stops," rack jobbers, distributors, or dealers, whether or not affiliated with Company; (ii) records given away or sold at below stated wholesale prices for promotional purposes to disc jockeys, record reviewers, radio and television stations and networks, motion picture companies, music publishers, Company's employees, Artist, or other customary recipients of promotional records or for use on transportation facilities; (iii) records sold as scrap, salvage, overstock, or "cut-outs"; (iv) records sold below cost; (v) "sampler" records in tape form intended for free distribution to automobile purchasers and containing not more than two (2) masters delivered hereunder. No royalties shall be payable on any sales by Company's licensees until payment has been received by Company in the United States.

(p) As to records sold at a discount to "one-stops," rack jobbers, distributors, or dealers, whether or not affiliated with Company, in lieu of the records given away or furnished on a "no-charge" basis as provided in subparagraph 10(o)(i) above, the applicable royalty rate otherwise payable hereunder with respect to such records shall be reduced in the proportion that said discount wholesale price bears to the usual stated wholesale price.

(q) The royalty rates provided for in this Paragraph 10 shall be applied against the retail list price (less Company's container deductions, excise taxes, duties, and other applicable taxes) for records sold that are paid for and not returned. The term "retail list price" as used in this Agreement shall mean (i) for records sold in the United States, the manufacturer's suggested retail price in the United States and (ii) for records sold outside the United States, the manufacturer's suggested retail price in the country of manufacture or sale, as Company is paid. In those countries where a manufacturer's suggested retail price is not utilized, the generally accepted retail price shall be utilized. Notwithstanding the foregoing, (A) with respect to sales in the United States, the retail list price for a "Maxi-single" shall be deemed to be the lesser of (1) ________ (___%) percent of the retail list price of a Single or (2) the actual retail list price of such "Maxi-single" and (B) with respect to sales outside the United States, the retail list price for a "Maxi-single" shall be deemed to be the retail list price of a Single. In computing sales, Company shall have the right to deduct all returns made at any time and for any reason.

(r) Company's container deductions shall be a sum equal to: (i) _______ (___%) percent of the retail list price for records in disc form (other than compact-disc records), (ii) ________ (___%) percent of the retail list price for records in disc form (other than compact-disc records) in "double-fold" jackets or covers or in jackets that contain an insert or any other special elements, (iii) _______ (___%) percent of the retail list price for records in analog prerecorded tape form, and (iv) _______ (___%) percent of the retail list price for Satellite Sales, New Technology Configurations, compact-disc records, records in digital audiotape form, and any other form or configuration of record or form of package, container, or box other than as described herein.

(s) The monies payable to Artist hereunder shall be inclusive of all monies, if any, required to be paid to the A.F. of M. Music Performance Trust Fund, Phonograph Record Manufacturers Special Payments Fund, AFTRA Pension and Welfare Fund, and all other union funds with respect to the manufacture, distribution, and sale of records hereunder. In the event that any monies shall become due to any such union funds, Company shall deduct such monies from any and all monies payable to Artist under this or any other agreement and shall pay same directly to such union funds.

(t) The royalties set forth herein represent the total royalties payable to the Artist, the producers, mixers, and any other parties rendering services in connection with masters recorded hereunder. If Company pays any such royalties directly to anyone other than Artist, such royalty payments shall be deducted from Artist's royalties hereunder, provided that if Company pays any such royalties at a time when Artist's account is not recouped hereunder, such payments shall be deemed to be additional advances to Artist hereunder.

11. Statements as to royalties payable hereunder shall be sent by Company to Artist within ___ (__) days after the expiration of each semiannual calendar period for the preceding semiannual period. Concurrently with the rendition of each statement, Company shall pay Artist all royalties shown to be due by such statement, after deducting all recording costs paid by Company, all payments made on behalf of Artist, and all advances made to Artist prior to the rendition of the statement. For purposes of the prior sentence, "advances" shall mean advances previously paid to Artist, all artist advances payable pursuant to paragraph 7 above, as well as all costs of marketing, promotion, publicity, tour support, rehearsal and showcasing expenses, wardrobe, travel, and any other amounts paid to Artist or on Artist's behalf with Artist's consent or at Artist's request, subject only to any specific limitations otherwise set forth herein. No statements need be rendered by Company for any such period after the expiration of the Term hereof for which there are no sales of records derived from masters hereunder. All payments shall be made to the order of Artist and shall be sent to Artist at Artist's address first above written. Company shall be entitled to maintain a single account with respect to all recordings subject to this or any other agreement. Company may maintain reasonable reserves. Artist shall be deemed to have consented to all accountings rendered by Company hereunder, and said accountings shall be binding upon Artist and shall not be subject to any objection by Artist for any reason unless specific objection, in writing, stating the basis thereof, is given to Company

within ______ (__) months/years after the date rendered, and after such written objection, unless suit is instituted within ___ (_) months/years after the date upon which Company notifies Artist that it denies the validity of the objection.

12. (a) Artist shall have the right at Artist's sole cost and expense to appoint a Certified Public Accountant who is not then currently engaged in an outstanding audit of Company to examine Company's books and records as same pertain to sales of records subject hereto as to which royalties are payable hereunder, provided that any such examination shall be for a reasonable duration and shall take place at Company's offices during normal business hours on reasonable prior written notice and shall not occur more than once in any calendar year.

(b) Artist shall not have the right to examine any distributor statements in Company's possession.

13. (a) All notices to Artist may be served upon Artist personally, by prepaid telegram, or by depositing the same, postage prepaid, in any mailbox, chute, or other receptacle authorized by the United States Postal Service for mail, addressed to Artist at Artist's address first above written. A copy of all notices to Artist shall be simultaneously sent to _________ at _________.

(b) All notices to Company shall be in writing and shall be sent postage prepaid by registered or certified mail, return receipt requested, addressed to Company's address first above written. A copy of all notices to Company shall be simultaneously sent to ________ at __________.

14. (a) All musical compositions or material recorded pursuant to this Agreement that are written or composed, in whole or in part, by Artist or any individual member of Artist or any producer of the masters subject hereto, or are owned or controlled, directly or indirectly, in whole or in part, by Artist or any producer of the masters subject hereto (herein called "Controlled Compositions") shall be and are hereby licensed to Company:

(i) For the United States, at a royalty per selection equal to _________ (___%) percent of the minimum statutory per selection rate (without regard to playing time) effective on the earlier of the date of delivery of the masters concerned to Company hereunder, or the date such masters were required to be delivered to Company hereunder. The aforesaid ________ (___%) percent per selection rate shall hereinafter sometimes be referred to as the "U.S. Per Selection Rate"; and

(ii) For Canada, at a royalty per selection equal to ________ (__%) percent of the statutory per selection rate (without regard to playing time) effective on the earlier of the date of delivery of the masters concerned to Company hereunder, or the date such masters were required to be delivered to Company hereunder, or, if there is no statutory rate in Canada on such date, _________ (___%) percent of the per selection rate (without regard to playing time) then generally utilized by major record companies in Canada. The applicable aforesaid per selection rate shall hereinafter sometimes be referred to as the "Canadian Per Selection Rate."

(b) Notwithstanding the foregoing, the maximum aggregate mechanical royalty rate that Company shall be required to pay in respect of any Single, Maxi-single, EP, or Album hereunder, regardless of the total number of compositions contained therein, shall not exceed the following: (i) Singles—____ (__) times, (ii) Maxi-Singles—____ (__) times, (iii) EP—the number of compositions contained thereon, and (iv) Albums—____ (__) times the applicable U.S. Per Selection Rate or Canadian Per Selection Rate, respectively.

(c) It is specifically understood that in the event that any Single, Maxi-single, EP, or Album contains other compositions in addition to the Controlled Compositions and the aggregate mechanical royalty rate for said Single, Maxi-single, EP, or Album shall exceed the applicable rate provided in subparagraph 14(b), the aggregate rate for the Controlled Compositions contained thereon shall be reduced by the aforesaid excess over said applicable rate. Additionally, Company shall have the right with respect to any Single, Maxi-single, EP, or Album, the aggregate mechanical royalty rate for which exceeds the applicable rate provided in subparagraph 14(b) to deduct such excess payable thereon from any and all monies payable to Artist pursuant to this or any other agreement. All mechanical royalties payable hereunder shall be paid on the basis of net records sold hereunder for which royalties are payable to Artist pursuant to this Agreement. Company may maintain reserves with respect to payment of mechanical royalties. If Company makes an overpayment of mechanical royalties in respect of compositions recorded under this Agreement, Artist will reimburse Company for same, failing which Company may recoup any such overpayment from any monies becoming payable to Artist pursuant to this or any other agreement. Mechanical royalty payments on records subsequently returned are considered overpayments. Notwithstanding anything to the contrary contained herein, mechanical royalties payable in respect of Controlled Compositions for sales of records for any use other than as described in subparagraphs 10(a), (b), and (g) hereof shall be ________ (___%) percent of the otherwise applicable U.S. Per Selection Rate or Canadian Per Selection Rate, as the case may be. Controlled Compositions that are arranged versions of any musical compositions in the public domain, when furnished by Artist for recording hereunder, shall be paid in the same proportion as the appropriate performing rights society grants performing credits to the publisher of such composition, provided Artist has furnished Company with a copy of the letter from such performing rights society setting forth the percentage of the otherwise applicable credit that the publisher will receive. Any assignment of the ownership or administration of copyright in any Controlled Composition shall be made subject to the provisions hereof and any inconsistencies between the terms of this Agreement and mechanical licenses issued to and accepted by Company shall be determined by the terms of this Agreement. If any Single, Maxi-single, EP, or Album contains compositions that are not Controlled Compositions, Artist will obtain for Company's benefit mechanical licenses covering such compositions on the same terms and conditions applicable to Controlled Compositions pursuant to this Paragraph 14.

(d) In respect of all Controlled Compositions performed in Videos, Company is hereby granted an irrevocable perpetual worldwide license to record and reproduce such Compositions in such Videos and to distribute and perform such Videos including, but not limited to, all Videoshows thereof, and to authorize others to do so. Company will not be required to make any payment in connection with those uses, and that license shall apply whether or not Company receives any payment in connection with those Videos. Simultaneously with Artist's submission to Company of the information required pursuant to subparagraph 20(c)(i) hereof, Artist shall furnish Company with a written acknowledgment from the person(s) or entity(ies) controlling the copyright in each non-Controlled Composition to be embodied on any Video confirming the terms upon which said person(s) or entity(ies) shall issue licenses in respect thereof. Upon Company's request therefor, Artist shall cause said person(s) or entity(ies) to forthwith issue to Company (and its designees) licenses containing said terms and such other terms and conditions as Company (or its designees) may require. Royalties in connection with licenses for the use of non-Controlled Compositions pertaining to Videos and Videoshows are included in the royalties set forth in subparagraph 20(d) hereof, as described in subparagraph 20(d)(ii). If the copyright in any Controlled Composition is owned or controlled by anyone else, Artist will cause that person, firm, or corporation to grant Company the same rights described in this Paragraph 14, on the same terms.

(e) Notwithstanding anything in the foregoing provisions of this Paragraph 14 to the contrary, if a particular selection recorded hereunder is embodied more than once on a particular record, Company shall pay mechanical royalties in connection therewith at the applicable rate for such composition as though the selection were embodied thereon only once.

(f) Artist understands that it shall be Artist's responsibility to cause Artist's publishers to comply with the provisions of this paragraph 14 with respect to all Controlled Compositions.

15. (a) In the event that Artist for any reason other than as a result of Company's actions or omissions fails to timely fulfill all of Artist's recording and delivery commitments hereunder in accordance with all of the terms and conditions of this Agreement, then, in addition to any other rights or remedies Company may have, Company shall have the right, upon written notice to Artist at any time prior to the expiration of the then current Period, (i) to

terminate this Agreement without further obligation to Artist as to unrecorded or undelivered masters or (ii) to reduce the minimum number of masters required to be recorded and delivered during the then current Period to the number that have been timely recorded and delivered during such Period. It is specifically understood that Company may exercise any or all of its rights pursuant to subparagraphs 15(a)(i) and (ii) at any time(s) prior to the date the Term would otherwise expire. Company's obligations hereunder shall be suspended for the duration of any such default, and Company will use reasonable efforts to notify Artist of such suspension.

(b) Nothing herein contained shall obligate Company to permit Artist to record the minimum number of masters specified herein to be recorded during each period of the term hereof, it being understood that if Artist is ready, willing, and able to fulfill Artist's recording obligations hereunder, and Company refuses, without cause, to allow Artist to do so for a period in excess of ___ (_) months, Artist may notify Company of Artist's desire to terminate the term of this agreement if Company does not allow Artist to complete such recording obligation within ___ (__) days thereafter. In the event of any such termination, all parties will be deemed to have fulfilled their obligations hereunder, except those obligations that typically survive the end of the term (e.g., warranties, rerecording restrictions, and obligation to pay royalties on previously delivered product hereunder).

(c) Company reserves the right, at its election, to suspend the operation of this Agreement for the duration of any of the following contingencies, if by reason of any such contingency, it is materially hampered in the performance of its obligations under this Agreement or its normal business operations are delayed or become impossible or commercially impracticable: Act of God, fire, catastrophe, labor disagreement, acts of government, its agencies, or officers, any order, regulation, ruling, or action of any labor union or association of artists, musicians, composers, or employees affecting Company or the industry in which it is engaged, delays in the delivery of materials and supplies, or any other cause beyond Company's control.

(d) If Artist's voice should be materially or permanently impaired, then in addition to any other rights or remedies that Company may have, Company shall have the right, upon written notice to Artist, to terminate this Agreement and shall thereby be relieved of any liability in connection with unrecorded masters.

16. Artist expressly acknowledges that Artist's services hereunder are of a special, unique, and intellectual character that gives them peculiar value, and that in the event of a breach or threatened breach by Artist of any term, condition, or covenant hereof, Company may be caused irreparable injury. Artist expressly agrees that Company shall be entitled to seek injunctive and other equitable relief, as permitted by law, to prevent a breach or threatened breach of this Agreement, or any portion thereof, by Artist, which relief shall be in addition to any other rights or remedies, for damages or otherwise, available to Company.

17. (a) Artist warrants and represents that Artist is under no disability, restriction, or prohibition, whether contractual or otherwise, with respect to Artist's right to execute this Agreement and perform its terms and conditions. Without limiting the foregoing, Artist specifically warrants and represents that no prior obligations, contracts, or agreements of any kind undertaken or entered into by Artist will interfere in any manner with the complete performance of this Agreement by Artist or with Artist's right to record any and all selections hereunder. Artist warrants and represents that there are now in existence no prior unreleased masters embodying Artist's performances. Artist further warrants and represents that Company shall not be required to make any payments of any nature for, or in connection with, the rendition of Artist's services or the acquisition, exercise, or exploitation of rights by Company pursuant to this Agreement, except as specifically provided hereinabove.

(b) Artist warrants and represents that no materials, or any use thereof, will violate any law or infringe upon or violate the rights of any third party. "Materials," as used in this subparagraph 17(b), shall include: (i) all musical compositions and other material contained on masters subject hereto to the extent of Artist's creative contributions thereto, (ii) each name used by Artist, in connection with masters recorded hereunder, and (iii) all other materials, ideas, other intellectual properties or elements furnished or selected by Artist and contained in or used in connection with any masters recorded hereunder or the packaging, sale, distribution, advertising, publicizing, or other exploitation thereof.

(c) Artist agrees to and does hereby indemnify, save, and hold Company harmless from any and all loss and damage (including court costs and reasonable attorneys' fees) arising out of, connected with, or as a result of any inconsistency with, failure of, or breach or threatened breach by Artist of any warranty, representation, agreement, undertaking, or covenant contained in this Agreement including, without limitation, any claim by any third party in connection with the foregoing. In addition to any other rights or remedies Company may have by reason of any such inconsistency, failure, breach, threatened breach, or claim, Artist shall reimburse Company, on demand, for any payment made by Company at any time after the date hereof with respect to any loss, damage, or liability resulting therefrom and in addition thereto Company shall have the right to deduct from any and all monies otherwise payable to Artist under this or any other agreement a sum(s) equal to such loss, damage, and liability (including anticipated and actual court costs and reasonable attorneys' fees). Pending the determination of any such claim, Company may withhold payment of all monies under this agreement in a reasonable amount consistent with such claim, provided that if litigation has not been commenced within ___ (__) months of such claim first being made, Company will pay such withheld monies to Artist. However, such payment to Artist shall not limit Company's right to withhold sums at a later date if litigation based on such claim is thereafter commenced.

18. Wherever in this Agreement approval or consent is required, such approval or consent shall not be unreasonably withheld by either party. Company may require Artist to formally give or withhold such approval or consent by giving Artist written notice requesting same and by furnishing Artist with the information or material in respect of which such approval or consent is sought. Artist shall give Company written notice of approval or dis-

approval within ____ (__) days after such notice. Neither Artist nor Company shall hinder or delay the scheduled release of any record hereunder. In the event of disapproval or no consent, the reasons therefor shall be stated. Failure to give such notice to Company as aforesaid shall be deemed to be consent or approval.

19. During the Term, to the extent necessary, Artist shall become and remain a member in good standing of any labor unions with which Company may at any time have agreements lawfully requiring such union membership, including, but not limited to, the American Federation of Musicians and the American Federation of Television and Radio Artists. All masters subject hereto shall be produced in accordance with the rules and regulations of all unions having jurisdiction.

20. (a) In addition to Artist's recording and delivery commitments as set forth in Paragraph 3 of this Agreement, Artist shall comply with requests, if any, made by Company in connection with the production of Videos. In this connection, subject to Artist's bona fide prior professional commitments, Artist shall appear on dates and at places requested by Company for the filming, taping, or other fixation of audiovisual recordings. Artist shall perform services with respect thereto as Company deems desirable in a timely and first-class manner. Artist acknowledges that the production of Videos involves matters of judgment with respect to art and taste, which judgment shall be exercised by Company solely in its own discretion and that Company's decisions with respect thereto shall be final.

(b) (i) Each Video produced during the Term of the Agreement shall be owned by Company (including the worldwide copyrights therein and thereto and all extensions and renewals thereof) to the same extent as Company's rights in master recordings made under this Agreement.

(ii) Company will have the unlimited right to manufacture Videoshows of the Video and to rent, sell, distribute, transfer, sublicense, or otherwise deal in such Videoshows under any trademarks, trade names, and labels; to exploit the Video by any means now or hereafter known or developed; or to refrain from any such exploitation, throughout the world.

(c) (i) Following Company's receipt of invoices therefor, Company agrees to pay all costs actually incurred in the production of Videos made at Company's request hereunder, provided such costs have been previously approved by Company in writing. In this connection, prior to commencing production of any Video, Artist shall submit to Company, in writing, a detailed proposal for each Video. Said proposal shall include the following information: (i) the musical compositions and other material to be embodied thereon; (ii) the general concept therefor; (iii) the producer, director, and any other key personnel therefor; and (iv) the estimated costs of completing the Video. In the alternative, Company shall have the right to designate any of the foregoing elements. Following Artist's receipt of Company's approval of each element of said proposal, Artist shall commence production of the Video. All costs incurred in excess of the applicable approved budget, caused by Artist, shall be Artist's sole responsibility and Artist agrees to pay and discharge all such excess costs. In the event Company agrees to pay any excess costs (for which Artist is responsible pursuant to the preceding sentence) on Artist's behalf, Artist shall, upon demand, reimburse Company for such excess costs and/or Company may deduct such excess costs from any and all monies due to Artist pursuant to this or any other agreement. All sums paid by Company in connection with each Video shall be an advance against and recoupable by Company out of all royalties becoming payable to Artist pursuant to this or any other agreement. For clarification, no sums recoupable by Company in connection with any Video shall be recouped more than once.

(ii) Each of the following sums, if any, paid by Company in connection with each Video shall be an advance against and recoupable by Company out of all royalties (excluding mechanicals) becoming payable to Artist pursuant to this or any other agreement, provided that Company shall not recoup more than ________ (___%) percent of such sums from royalties becoming payable to Artist pursuant to Paragraph 10 hereof:

(A) All expenses incurred by Company in connection with the preparation and production of the Video and the conversion of the Video to Video Masters that are made to serve as prototypes for the duplication of the Videoshows of the Video;

(B) All of Company's direct out-of-pocket costs (such as for rights, artists (including Artist), other personnel, facilities, materials, services, and the use of equipment) in connection with all steps in the production of the Video and the process leading to and including the production of such Video Masters (including, but not limited to, packaging costs and the costs of making and delivering duplicate copies of such Video Masters); and

(C) If in connection therewith Company furnishes any of its own facilities, materials, services, or equipment for which Company has a standard rate, the amount of such standard rate or if there is no standard rate, the market value for the services or thing furnished.

(iii) All sums that Company in its sole discretion deems necessary or advisable to pay in connection with the production of Videos and the exploitation of Company's rights therein in order to clear rights or to make any contractual payments that are or may become due on the part of Company, to Artist or any other person, firm, or corporation by virtue of the exploitation of Company's rights therein, in order to avoid, satisfy, or make unnecessary any claims or demands by any person, firm, or corporation claiming the right to payment therefor, including, but not limited to, any payment to an actual or alleged copyright owner, patent owner, union, union-related trust fund, pension plan, or other entity, and any payment for an actual or alleged rerun fee, residual, royalty, license fee, or otherwise shall constitute advances against and recoupable out of all royalties becoming payable to Artist pursuant to this or any other agreement. No payment pursuant to this subparagraph 20(c)(iii) shall constitute a waiver of any of Artist's express or implied warranties and representations.

(d) Company shall pay Artist the following royalties with respect to Videos:

(i) In respect of Company's commercial exploitation, if any, of Vidcoshows solely embodying Videos subject hereto that are sold through normal retailer channels for the "home video market" (as such term is commonly understood in the music and video industry):

(A) (1) With respect to Album Videoshows sold through normal retailer channels in the United States, full priced as initially released, a royalty rate of __ (__%) percent;

(2) The royalty rate set forth in subparagraph 20(d)(i)(A)(1) is hereinafter sometimes referred to as the "Basic U.S. Home Video Rate."

(B) (1) With respect to Album Videoshows sold through normal retailer channels outside the United States, full priced as initially released, the royalty rate shall be reduced in the same percentages as Company's applicable rate is reduced;

(2) The royalty rate set forth in subparagraph 20(d)(i)(B)(1) is hereinafter sometimes referred to as the "Basic Foreign Home Video Rate."

(C) Except as otherwise set forth in this Agreement, the applicable Basic U.S. Home Video Rate and the applicable Basic Foreign Home Video Rate shall be calculated, computed, determined, prorated, reduced, adjusted (but not escalated), and paid in the same manner and at the same times (e.g., configurations other than Albums, "free goods," reserves, percentages of sales, price, number of units for which royalties are payable, etc.) as the royalties payable by Company to Artist are calculated, computed, determined, prorated, reduced, adjusted (but not escalated) pursuant to Paragraph 10 of this Agreement.

(ii) (A) The applicable Basic U.S. Home Video Rate and applicable Basic Foreign Home Video Rate shall be applied against Company's wholesale price, as hereinafter defined (less Company's container deductions, distribution fees, excise taxes, duties, and other applicable taxes) for Videoshows sold that are paid for and not returned. The term "wholesale price" as used in this Paragraph 20 shall mean the amount that Company receives from Company's distributor(s), whether or not affiliated with Company, for each such Videoshow. In computing sales, Company shall have the right to deduct all so-called free goods and all returns made at any time and for any reason. Company may maintain reasonable reserves against returns. Videoshows distributed in the United States by any of Company's affiliated branch wholesalers shall be deemed sold for the purposes of this Agreement only if sold by any such affiliated branch wholesaler to one of its independent third-party customers.

(B) Company's container deductions in respect of Videoshows shall be a sum equal to: (i) _______ (___%) percent of the wholesale price of the applicable Videoshow for Videoshows in Company's standard packaging for one cassette, disc, cartridge, or other unit, and (ii) ________ (___%) percent of the wholesale price of the applicable Videoshow for Videoshows in packaging for more than one cassette, disc, cartridge, or other unit, or packaging with special materials, components, inserts, or elements, or in any form of package, container, or box other than Company's standard packaging for one cassette, disc, cartridge, or other unit.

(iii) With respect to sales and uses of Videos hereunder other than Videoshows sold through normal retailer channels for the home video market, Company shall pay Artist royalties equal to ________ (___%) percent of Company's Video Net Receipts with respect to Company's exploitation of Videos subject to this Agreement, unless otherwise elsewhere provided to the contrary in this Agreement. Monies earned and received by Company from any licensee (rather than monies earned and received by the licensee) in respect of exploitation of Videos shall be included in the computation of Video Net Receipts.

(iv) No royalties shall be payable to Artist hereunder in respect of Videoshows comprising so-called video magazines, samplers, or other promotional formats, or in respect of Videos or Videoshows used or distributed for promotional purposes, whether or not Company receives payment therefor.

(v) The royalties provided in subparagraphs 20(d)(i) and (iii) include any royalty obligations Company may have to any other person, firm, or corporation that supplied services or rights used in connection with Videos, including, without limitation, producers, directors, extras, and music publishers, and any such royalties shall be deducted from the video royalties otherwise payable to Artist.

(vi) With respect to records embodying Videos made hereunder together with other material, royalties payable to Artist shall be computed by multiplying the royalties otherwise applicable by a fraction, the numerator of which is the amount of playing time in any such record of Videos made hereunder and the denominator of which is the total playing time of all material in any such record.

(vii) As to Videos embodying performances of Artist together with the performances of another artist or artists, the royalties otherwise payable hereunder shall be prorated by multiplying such royalties by a fraction, the numerator of which is one and the denominator of which is the total number of artists whose performances are embodied on such Videos.

(e) Company shall have the right to use and allow others to use each Video for advertising and promotional purposes with no payment to Artist.

(f) In all other respects (e.g., the times for accountings to be rendered, and warranties and representations made by Artist) Video and Video Masters shall be governed by the same terms and conditions as are applicable to masters subject to this Agreement.

21. (a) Company shall have the perpetual right, without any liability to any party, to use and to authorize others to use Artist's name and biographical material and the names (including any professional names heretofore or hereafter adopted), and any likenesses, whether or not current (including photographs, portraits, caricatures, and stills from any Videos made hereunder), and biographical material relating to Artist for purposes of advertising, promotion, and in connection with all Masters and Videos, including, without limitation, in the marketing, sale, and exploitation of records hereunder and in general goodwill advertising. Artist warrants and represents that Artist owns the exclusive right to so use such names, likenesses, and biographical materials and that the use of same will not infringe upon the rights of any third party. If any third party challenges any Artist's right to use a professional name, Company may, at its election and without limiting Company's rights, require Artist to adopt another professional name approved by Company without awaiting the determination of the validity of such challenge. During the Term, Artist will not change the name by which Artist is professionally known without Company's prior written approval. During the term of this Agreement, all photographs and biographical material concerning Artist that

Company may desire to use for the purposes herein stated shall be submitted to Artist for Artist's reasonable approval, which approval (or disapproval) shall be given to Company within ten (10) days after such materials are submitted. Artist's failure to give such notice as aforesaid shall be deemed to be approval. Promptly following the execution of this agreement, Artist may furnish Company with a reasonable number of photographs and biographical material that Artist deems approved. No inadvertent failure by Company to obtain approval pursuant to this subparagraph in any instance will be deemed to be a breach of this Agreement by Company.

(b) The merchandising rights granted to Company pursuant to subparagraph 21(a) above, include but are not limited to the exclusive right to use the names, biographical material, and likenesses described in subparagraph 21(a), alone or together with other elements: (i) in items derived from or embodying the artwork of records hereunder or other materials prepared for or paid for by Company or its distributors ("Company Materials"), (ii) articles of merchandise embodying Company Materials, such as T-shirts, hats, sweaters, posters, etc., through retail channels or at concert venues, and/or (iii) Company Materials in connection with so-called bounceback merchandising, i.e., merchandising through advertisements printed on or inserted in record packages, and/or other merchandising utilized directly in connection with the sale of records hereunder.

(c) If Company receives any payment or credit against a prior advance for any commercial use of Artist's name or likeness (other than in connection with the exploitation of records and Videos for which payment is separately provided for herein), Company will render statements to Artist as set forth in paragraph 11 hereof, and will credit Artist's royalty account hereunder with ________ (___%) percent of the net amounts received by Company directly from any such uses solely involving Artist (prorated in instances where others are involved).

22. At Artist's request, Company agrees to allow Artist the nonexclusive right to use any Company Materials in connection with articles of merchandise that Artist wishes to use for sale at

Artist's concert venues or through normal retail outlets, provided that Artist agrees to split any net amounts received by Artist directly from any such uses on a _____ basis until such time as Company has been repaid ______ of the full amount of Company's initial costs in creating such Company Materials. Thereafter Artist may retain _________ (___%) percent of such net amounts.

23. For clarification, nothing herein is intended to prohibit Artist from rendering producing and songwriter services for other persons, provided such services do not interfere with Artist's obligations hereunder, which shall be Artist's first priority.

24. Notwithstanding any provision to the contrary herein, Artist shall have the right to perform as a so-called nonfeatured backup musician, background vocalist, or sideman with featured artists for the purpose of making phonograph records for third parties only upon the following conditions:

(a) Artist's activities in this regard will not in any way interfere with the prompt and timely performance of the recording and delivery obligations provided in this Agreement;

(b) Artist shall give Company written notice thereof in advance and the compositions to be performed and recorded shall not be compositions recorded pursuant to this Agreement;

(c) Artist shall not in any manner be restricted from thereafter performing the same compositions for Company;

(d) Artist shall not receive more than twice the applicable minimum union scale payment for any such performances;

(e) If any such records are released in an album, Artist's name may only be used on the liner of such album in a size, prominence, and type style as is customary in the recording industry for the names of such nonfeatured backup musicians, background vocalists, and sidemen whose performances are used and who are given credit on such album and in the same place on the liner where all other such nonfeatured performers are listed, and Company shall be given appropriate courtesy credit in conjunction with any use of the Artist's name on the liner of such album;

(f) Artist shall not perform any step-outs, solos, or duets in connection with such master recordings;

(g) Except as otherwise provided above, Artist's name, likeness, or photograph shall not be used in any manner by any third party in connection with such Artist's performances or in any advertising thereof. Artist's visual performance may not be used in any manner in connection with "sight and sound" devices. No Singles may be released embodying such Artist's performances;

(h) Nothing contained in this Agreement shall be deemed to limit Artist from performing any producing activities for third parties, provided that such activities do not interfere with the timely performance by Artist of Artist's obligations hereunder; and

(i) At Artist's request, Company agrees to consider any side artist request that does not conform to all of the foregoing requirements, subject to the requirements of the Distributor.

25. For the purposes of this Agreement, the following definitions shall apply:

(a) "Master"—The equivalent of a recording of a single selection or medley of not less than 3-1/2 minutes of playing time intended for use in the manufacture and sale of records.

(b) "Single"—A record embodying thereon two (2) masters.

(c) "Maxi-single"—A record embodying thereon not more than four (4) masters.

(d) "EP"—A record embodying thereon either five (5) masters or six (6) masters, provided, however, that in the event that more than one (1) of such masters embody the same musical composition, such record shall be deemed to be a Maxi-single for the purposes of this Agreement.

(e) "Album"—A record of not less than 35 minutes of playing time. Multiple sets that consist of more than one (1) Album intended to be released, packaged, and sold together for a single overall price shall be deemed to be the equivalent of one (1) Album for the purposes of this Agreement, but shall not be recorded hereunder without Company's prior written consent.

(f) "Records," "phonograph records," "recordings," and "sound recordings"—All forms of recording and reproduction by which sound may be recorded now known or that may hereafter become known, manufactured, or sold primarily for home use, juke box use, or use on or in means of transportation, including, without limiting the foregoing, magnetic recording tape, film, electronic video recordings, and any other medium or device for the production of artistic performances manufactured or sold primarily for home use, juke box use, or use on or in means of transportation, whether embodying (i) sound alone or (ii) sound synchronized with visual images, e.g., "sight and sound" devices.

(g) "Delivery," "deliver," or "delivered"—The actual receipt by Company at ________ Studios of completed, fully edited, mixed, leadered, and equalized 1630 tapes for each configuration (e.g., compact-disc, analog cassette) of all the masters comprising the applicable minimum recording commitment, commercially satisfactory in Company's opinion and ready for Company's manufacture of records, together with all materials, consents, approvals, licenses, and permissions.

(h) "Recording costs"—Wages, fees, advances, and payments of any nature to or in respect of all musicians, vocalists, conductors, arrangers, orchestrators, engineers, producers, copyists, etc.; payments to a trustee or fund based on wages to the extent required by any agreement between Company and any labor organization or trustee; all studio, tape, editing, mixing, remixing, mastering (excluding the cost of manufacture of metal parts), and engineering costs; all costs of travel, per diems, rehearsal halls, non-studio facilities and equipment, dubdown, rental and transportation of instruments; all costs occasioned by the cancellation of any scheduled recording session; and all other costs and expenses incurred in producing the master recordings hereunder then customarily recognized as recording costs in the recording industry.

(i) "Mid-priced record"—A record sold by Company or its licensee(s) at a price below Company's or the applicable licensee's then prevailing top-line suggested retail list price, which price is consistently applied by Company to such records and which records are sold by Company or its licensee(s) as mid-priced records.

(j) "Budget record"—A record sold by Company or its licensee(s) at a price below Company's or the applicable licensee's then prevailing top-line suggested retail list price, which price is consistently applied by Company to such records and which records are sold by Company or its licensee(s) as budget records.

(k) "Videos"—Audiovisual works that have a soundtrack substantially featuring performances of Artist.

(l) "Videoshows"—Videocassettes, Videodiscs, or any other devices, now or hereafter known or developed, that enable the Video to be perceived visually, with or without sound, when used in combination with or as part of a piece of electronic, mechanical, or other apparatus.

(m) "Videodisc"—A disc-type Videoshow that enables the Video to be perceived visually, with or without sound, through a television-type playback system or device.

(n) "Videocassette"—A Videoshow other than a Videodisc (e.g., a Videoshow in the form of prerecorded tape).

(o) "Video Masters"—Master Videoshows.

(p) "Video Net Receipts"—Monies earned and received by Company from exploitation of Videos less (i) a gross distribution fee of (A) ________ (___%) percent in respect of broadcast, telecast, cablecast, or other exploitation (excluding the sale of Videoshows, which shall be ________ (___%) percent) within the United States, and (B) ________ (___%) percent in respect of broadcast, telecast, cablecast, or other exhibition outside the United States, and (ii) any out-of-pocket expenses, copyright, union and other third-party payments, taxes, and adjustments borne by Company in connection with exploitation and collection and receipt by Company of such monies.

(q) "or any other agreement"—Means any amendment, modification, supplement, replacement, or a renewal agreement pertaining to the recording services of Artist or recordings embodying Artist's performances. The phrase "all royalties pursuant to this or any other agreement" shall not include mechanical royalties payable in respect of mechanical reproduction of Controlled Compositions hereunder.

26. (a) Company shall have the right to assign this Agreement in whole or in part to the Distributor or any subsidiary, parent company, or affiliate, or to any third party acquiring a substantial portion of Company's assets or stock. Artist shall not have the right to assign any of Artist's rights or obligations hereunder without Company's prior written agreement.

27. This Agreement sets forth the entire agreement between the parties with respect to the subject matter hereof. Without limiting the generality of the foregoing, it is intended that this agreement will supersede all prior agreements between the parties. No modification, amendment, waiver, termination, or discharge of this Agreement shall be binding upon Company unless confirmed by a written instrument signed by an officer of Company. A waiver by Company of any term or condition of this Agreement in any instance shall not be deemed or construed as a waiver of such term or condition for the future, or of any subsequent breach thereof. All of Company's rights and remedies in this Agreement shall be cumulative and none of them shall be in limitation of any other remedy or right available to Company. Should any provision of this Agreement be adjudicated by a court of competent jurisdiction as void, invalid, or inoperative, such decision shall not affect any other provision hereof, and the remainder of this Agreement shall be effective as though such void, invalid, or inoperative provision had not been contained herein, provided that same will not defeat the purpose of this agreement. It is agreed that all accountings and payments required herein, and all grants made herein, shall survive and continue beyond the expiration or earlier termination of this Agreement. No breach of this Agreement by Company shall be deemed material unless within thirty (30) days after Artist learns of such breach, Artist serves written notice thereof on Company specifying the nature thereof and Company fails to cure such breach, if any, within sixty (60) days after receipt of such notice. No breach of this Agreement by Artist shall be deemed material unless within sixty (60) days after Company learns of such breach, Company serves written notice thereof on Artist specifying the nature thereof and Artist fails to cure such breach within thirty (30) days after receipt of such notice. The foregoing shall not be applicable to any breach, alleged breach, or threatened breach of the exclusivity provisions of this Agreement or to Artist's failure to timely deliver any recording commitment hereunder, or otherwise for which a cure period is already provided for in this Agreement, nor to the rerecording restrictions set forth herein.

28. THIS AGREEMENT SHALL BE DEEMED TO HAVE BEEN MADE IN THE STATE OF __________ AND ITS VALIDITY, CONSTRUCTION, PERFORMANCE, AND BREACH SHALL BE GOVERNED BY THE LAWS OF THE STATE OF ________ APPLICABLE TO AGREEMENTS MADE AND TO BE WHOLLY PERFORMED THEREIN. ARTIST AGREES TO SUBMIT TO THE JURISDICTION OF THE FEDERAL OR STATE COURTS LOCATED IN ________ COUNTY IN ANY ACTION WHICH MAY ARISE OUT OF THIS AGREEMENT AND SAID COURTS SHALL HAVE EXCLUSIVE JURISDICTION OVER ALL DISPUTES BETWEEN COMPANY AND ARTIST PERTAINING TO THIS AGREEMENT AND ALL MATTERS RELATED THERETO. NOTHING CONTAINED IN THIS PARAGRAPH 28 SHALL PRECLUDE COMPANY OR ARTIST FROM JOINING THE OTHER IN AN ACTION BROUGHT BY A THIRD PARTY AGAINST COMPANY IN ANY JURISDICTION, ALTHOUGH COMPANY'S OR ARTIST'S FAILURE TO JOIN THE OTHER IN ANY SUCH ACTION IN ONE INSTANCE SHALL NOT CONSTITUTE A WAIVER OF ANY OF COMPANY'S OR ARTIST'S RIGHTS WITH RESPECT THERETO, OR WITH RESPECT TO ANY SUBSEQUENT ACTION BROUGHT BY A THIRD PARTY AGAINST COMPANY. NOTHING CONTAINED HEREIN SHALL CONSTITUTE A WAIVER OF ANY OTHER REMEDIES AVAILABLE TO COMPANY OR ARTIST.

29. This Agreement shall not become effective until it is executed by all parties.

30. Artist agrees to be available from time to time, whenever the same will not unreasonably interfere with other professional activities of Artist, to appear for photography, poster, and cover art, etc., under the direction of Company or its nominees and to appear for interviews with representatives of the communications media and Company's publicity personnel and to otherwise perform all reasonable promotional services requested by Company.

31. Company and its licensees shall have the nonexclusive right, throughout the Territory, to create, maintain, and host a web page relating to Artist's recording services hereunder that is connected to Company's overall website ("our web page") (i.e., as

opposed to an entirely separate artist website) and to register and use the name "__________.com" and any mutually approved variations thereof, provided that Company shall at all times retain the exclusive right to use the Company's name in connection with websites and Artist shall at all times retain the right to use the Artist's name in connection with websites as Uniform Resource Locators (or URLs), addresses, or domain names. Notwithstanding any of the foregoing to the contrary, if Artist requests Company to pay for and/or set up a website separate and apart from our web page, and Company agrees to do so, each such website created by Company in respect of Artist including, but not limited to, our web page shall each be hereinafter referred to as an "Artist Site." Each Artist Site and all rights thereto and derived therefrom shall be Company's property throughout the Territory and in perpetuity. Any Record sold via an Artist Site and not returned shall be deemed to be a New Technology Sale for purposes of calculating royalties hereunder for that sale. Company's rights in operating each Artist Site shall include, without limitation, the following: (i) the leasing of commercial advertising space to Persons other than Company or its licensees on an Artist Site, provided that any advertising for products other than Company's products and services shall only be with Artist's prior written consent; (ii) the placement on an Artist Site of links to so-called e-commerce websites owned or controlled by Persons other than Company or its licensees; and (c) the inclusion on Records of web browsers, software applications, utilities, or website links or Persons other than Company or its licensees. For clarification, Artist shall not offer for sale or authorize other Persons to offer for sale any Records on any websites owned, operated, or authorized by Artist, but shall link to Company's authorized agents for fulfillment of any such sales.

IN WITNESS WHEREOF, the parties hereto have executed this Agreement on the day and year first above written.

(Company)

By:______________________________

An Authorized Signatory

AGREED AND ACCEPTED BY:

By: (Artist)
An Authorized Signatory
SSN/ID#:_____-____-______

Appendix N-3

SONGWRITER AGREEMENT

*NOTE: THIS IS A SINGLE SONG FORM. IF MULTIPLE SONGS ARE INCLUDED, ATTACH A SCHEDULE. IF A WRITER IS BEING ENGAGED TO PERFORM FUTURE SERVICES, A WRITING COMMITMENT AND OTHER PROVISIONS MUST BE ADDED THAT WILL BE SIMILAR TO THOSE CONTAINED IN THE ARTIST RECORDING AGREEMENT IN APPENDIX N-2.

Dated:__________________

AGREEMENT made as of ______________ ,____ , between _______ (Writer), on the one part (hereinafter "you," below), and ________ (Publisher) (hereinafter "___" below).

1. SUBJECT MUSICAL COMPOSITION

You warrant and represent that the musical composition entitled "___________" (the "Composition") was written by you in the following percentage: __% by you ("Your Creative Share").

2. GRANT OF RIGHTS

2.01. Assignment of Copyrights. You hereby sell, transfer, and assign to _____ , its successors and assigns, an undivided ______ percent (___%) of your interest in the Composition, including without limitation, the copyrights therein and any and all renewals and/or extensions thereof throughout the Territory, and all claims and causes of action related to the Composition accruing at any time and all other rights of whatsoever nature in the Composition, including without limitation, the titles, words, and music of the Composition and each and every arrangement, adaptation, and version thereof. You will execute and deliver to _____ such instruments of transfer and other documents regarding the rights of ____ in the Composition as ______ may reasonably request to carry out the purposes of this agreement (including, without limitation, the Exhibits and Schedules annexed hereto), and ____ may sign such documents in your name and make appropriate disposition of them.

2.02. Administration. ____ and its licensees will have the sole and exclusive right in perpetuity throughout the Universe, to:

(a) License and cause others to license the exploitation of the Composition, including, without limitation, the right to license broadcast and other public performances, sound synchronization in audiovisual works, and the right to license the manufacture, distribution, and sale of Phonograph Records embodying the Composition.

(b) Administer and grant rights in the Composition and the copyrights therein.

(c) Print, publish, and sell printed editions of the Composition.

(d) Collect all monies payable at any time with respect to the Composition, in addition to all monies due prior to the date hereof, and all performance royalties payable to you with respect to the Composition by the American Society of Composers, Authors, and Publishers (ASCAP), Broadcast Music, Inc. (BMI), or any other applicable performing rights society (hereinafter collectively the "Societies"), but excluding any songwriter share of public performance income. If a Society in any territory does not license any particular public performance use of the Composition, it is understood ____ may license that use directly and all income received by ____ in connection with such licenses shall be deemed Gross Receipts subject to accounting hereunder.

(e) Make arrangements, or otherwise adapt or change the Composition in any manner.

(f) Otherwise administer the Composition and the copyright therein and act as the publisher thereof and exercise all of such rights as the sole and exclusive owner of the Composition.

2.03. Power of Attorney. You hereby irrevocably authorize, empower, and appoint ____ your true and lawful attorney, for the term of the copyright in the Composition and any renewals or extensions thereof, to secure and renew the copyright in the Composition for the initial and any renewal periods for ____'s benefit, to initiate and compromise any claim or action with respect to the Composition including any claim or action against infringers of ____'s or your rights in the Composition, and to execute in your name any and all documents and/or instruments necessary or desirable to accomplish the foregoing and/or to evidence ___'s ownership of the copyright and/or to effectuate ____'s rights hereunder. The power granted herein is coupled with an interest and is irrevocable. ____ will cause the copyright in the Composition to be registered or reregistered in the name of ___.

2.04. Names and Likenesses. _____ and any Licensee of ______ each shall have the right and may grant to others the right to reproduce, print, publish, or disseminate in any medium your name, portraits, pictures, and likenesses (including, without limitation, all professional, group, and other assumed or fictitious names used by you), and biographical material concerning you, as news or information, for the purposes of trade, or for advertising purposes in connection with the exploitation of the Composition, institutional advertising for ____, and other marketing.

2.05. Without limitation of anything contained in this Article 2, for the countries of Australia and New Zealand, you grant to ___ the exclusive right to make and manufacture and to grant to others the right to make and manufacture mechanical and electrical transcriptions of the Composition. The parties hereby agree and acknowledge that this paragraph operates to grant to ____ an exclusive license within the meaning of the Australian Copyright Act 1968, as amended, and the Copyright Act 1962 of New Zealand, as such acts may be further amended.

2.06. Without limitation of anything contained in this Article 2, for the country of Brazil, you grant to ____ the exclusive right in respect to mechanical and electrical reproduction of the Composition on Phonograph Records and the exclusive collection of the sub-publishing rights (including performance and mechanical rights) in accordance with local representation by ____________ at ________________ (or any successor organizations), to whom all necessary powers are granted for the collection and administration of the Composition for which __________ agrees to undertake all necessary proceedings to execute the requirements of this agreement.

2.07. You will not grant to any French TV broadcasters for TV performances (or performances by any other similar means) or films and TV series from your catalog(s), mechanical reproduction rights relating to the Composition, with or without lyrics, included in such films and series, these rights having previously been granted to ________ and you shall indemnify Société des Auteurs, Compositeurs, et Editeurs de Musique (SACEM) against any claim which may be brought by TV broadcasters by reason of, and, limited to, the amounts paid by SACEM.

3. <u>COLLECTION AND DIVISION OF INCOME</u>

3.01. Royalties

3.01.1. ____ shall pay you Your Creative Share of songwriter royalties with respect to monies received by ____ from ____'s exploitation of the Composition in accordance with the annexed Schedule "A," all such royalties (except for royalties with respect to printed editions) to be based upon "Net Income" (as defined below). NOTE: IF LESS THAN 100% OF A COMPOSITION IS BEING ASSIGNED, ROYALTIES WILL INCLUDE AN ADDITIONAL SHARE OF NET INCOME.

3.01.2. As used herein, "Gross Receipts" shall include the following:

(A) Except with respect to printed editions, amounts received by ___ in the United States (or credited to ____'s account in reduction of any advance previously received by ___ in the United States) in respect of the use or exploitation of the Composition.

(B) With respect to printed editions manufactured and sold by ___ or by ____'s subsidiaries or affiliates in the United States and/or Canada, the percentages on Exhibit "A," based on copies sold and not returned for which payment is received ("net paid sales"), prorated based only on Your Creative Share of the Composition and also prorated where any edition does not consist solely of the Composition (such prorating to be based upon the number of copyrighted, royalty-bearing compositions included therein).

3.01.3. "Net Income" is hereby defined as Gross Receipts less:

(A) Copyright registration fees, the costs of preparing lead sheets, and other direct administration expenses;

(B) All audit, litigation, and other collection expenses;

(C) An administration fee to _____ of ___ percent (__%) of Gross Receipts.

(D) Costs of translating and rearranging the Composition; and

(E) All other expenses incurred by _________ in connection with the Composition and the exploitation thereof.

3.02. You shall not be entitled to participate in any advances or guarantees paid to ____ by any of ____'s licensees.

4. <u>ACCOUNTING AND PAYMENT</u>

4.01. ____ will account to you (and make payment where appropriate) within 90 days following the end of each semiannual calendar period. The exchange rates used by third parties in accounting to ______ shall be used by _____ in accountings hereunder.

4.02. ___ will only be required to account and pay with respect to amounts actually received by ___ in the U.S. (or credited to ___ account in reduction of a previous advance received by ___ in the U.S.).

4.03.1. You (or a certified public accountant on your behalf) shall have the right to audit ___'s books and records as to each statement for a period of 1 year after such statement is received (or deemed received as provided below). Legal action with respect to a specific accounting statement or the accounting period to which such statement relates shall be barred if not commenced in a court of competent jurisdiction within 2 years after such statement is received (or deemed received as provided below).

4.03.2. For the purposes of calculating such time periods, you shall be deemed to have received a statement when due unless _____ receives notice of nonreceipt from you (in the manner prescribed below) within 30 days thereafter. However, your failure to give such notice shall not affect your right to receive such statement (and, if applicable, your royalty and/or net income payment) after such 30-day period.

4.03.3. You shall have no right to audit any of ____'s licensees.

4.04. In "blocked currency" situations, ___ shall not be required to pay you until the blockage shall have been removed, but if requested to do so, ___ shall use responsible efforts to deposit blocked currency royalties in the local currency in a depository of your choice.

4.05. All payments hereunder shall be subject to all applicable taxation statutes, regulations, and treaties.

4.06. ___ may retain reserves for income derived from print income as it deems reasonable.

5. WARRANTIES AND REPRESENTATIONS

5.1. By your signature below, you warrant and represent (1) that you have the unrestricted right to grant the rights granted herein; (2) that the Composition, and the use of your name and likeness, does not infringe any third party's right or violate any applicable statute, including but not limited to such third party's copyright, trademark, servicemark, or right of privacy or publicity; (3) that the Composition is not defamatory, and contains no third-party copyrighted material; (4) that you are and will remain affiliated with ASCAP, BMI, or another recognized performing rights society (and in the event of your failure to so affiliate and for the purpose of preventing loss of income due to such failure, ____ shall be entitled to claim 100% of the writer's share with the performing rights society and account to you for income derived therefrom until such time as you formally affiliate and notify ____ of such affiliation); and (5) there are no other writers who collaborated with you in the creation of the Composition, nor any persons who could claim to be entitled to any compensation as a result of ___'s exercise of the rights acquired hereunder.

5.2. Neither you nor your music publishing designee, nor anyone acting on your and/or your music publishing designee's behalf or deriving rights from or through you or your music publishing designee (A) has received or will receive an advance, loan, or other payment from a performing rights society, company, or other third party that is or may be recoupable from (or otherwise subject to offset against) monies that would otherwise be collectible by ____ hereunder, or (B) is presently subject to any agreement that would allow a company to charge any amount against royalties.

6. INDEMNITIES; CURE OF BREACHES; WAIVER

6.1. You will indemnify ____ and ____'s licensees against any loss or damage (including court costs and reasonable attorneys' fees) due to a breach of this Agreement by you. You shall give ____ prompt notice of any third-party claim that you receive in respect of the Composition. ___ shall have the sole right to control the defense of any claim respecting the Composition, provided that __________w will use reasonable efforts to give you the opportunity to participate in the defense thereof by counsel of your choice, at your sole cost and expense.

6.2. If a claim is made against ___, ____ may withhold a reasonable amount from monies due or to become due to you until that claim is resolved.

6.3. ____ will not be deemed to be in breach hereunder unless you give _____ notice and _____ fails to cure within 30 days after receiving notice; *provided,* that if the alleged breach is of such a nature that it cannot be completely cured within 30 days, ____ will not be deemed to be in breach if the notified party commences the curing of the alleged breach within such 30-day period and proceeds to complete the curing thereof with due diligence within a reasonable time thereafter. All payments required to be made by ___ hereunder shall be subject to any rights and/or remedies that may otherwise be available to ___ in the event of a breach of this Agreement on your part not cured in the manner prescribed above, and to any withholding that may be required by the rules and regulations of any taxing jurisdiction having authority.

6.4. The waiver of the applicability of any provision of this Agreement or of any default hereunder by ______ in a specific instance shall not affect _____'s rights thereafter to enforce such provisions or to exercise any right or remedy in the event of any other default, whether or not similar.

7. NOTICES/STATEMENTS/CONSENTS

7.1. Notices shall be sent by certified (return receipt requested) or registered mail to you and to _____ at the addresses first set forth above, or to such other addresses as the parties may designate from time to time by notice in like manner.

7.2. Statements (and payments, if applicable) shall be sent by ordinary mail to you.

8. LAW AND FORUM

8.1. This agreement has been entered into in, and is to be interpreted in accordance with the laws of, the State of ________. All actions or proceedings seeking the interpretation and/or enforcement of this agreement shall be brought only in the State or Federal Courts located in _____ County, all parties hereby submitting themselves to the jurisdiction of such courts for such purpose. In the event of any action arising hereunder between the parties hereto, the prevailing party in any such action shall be entitled to recover its reasonable attorneys' fees and costs in connection with such action.

8.2. Service of Process

8.2.1. Service of process in any action between the parties may be made by registered or certified mail addressed to the parties' then current addresses for notice as prescribed herein.

8.2.2. Service shall become effective 30 days following receipt by the party served (unless delivery is refused, in which event service shall become effective 30 days following the date of such refusal).

8.3. Representation

8.3.1. You hereby represent that you have read and understand this agreement, and have had the opportunity to seek the advice of counsel in connection herewith, and have either engaged such counsel or have elected not to do so voluntarily.

9. ASSIGNMENTS

_____ shall have the unrestricted right to assign any and all of its rights hereunder to any party at any time in its sole discretion. You shall not have the right to assign any portion of this agreement.

IN WITNESS WHEREOF, the parties hereto have agreed to the terms of this agreement by their signature below.

AGREED AND ACCEPTED BY:

(Publisher)

____

(Writer)

____

SS/ID#: ____________________

Schedule "A"

WRITER ROYALTIES

(1) U.S. and Canada
Print: (all on net paid sales):

Piano/vocal sheet: ___ cents

Folios (other than "fake books" or "educational editions"): ___% of wholesale (prorated in the case of "mixed" folios to reflect the number of royalty-bearing compositions);

"Educational editions" and "fake books": ___% of wholesale (subject to same proration);

(2) Mechanical Royalties: ___% of Net Income

(3) Performance Royalties: If collected directly by ____ and not through a society: ___% of Net Income

(4) Foreign Income: ___% of Net Income

(5) Other Income: ___% of Net Income; *provided*, that you shall not be entitled to receive any portion of any amount received by ____ from a source that pays you an equivalent amount directly (including but not limited to distributions from a performing rights society and direct payments of portions of any blank tape tax or charge that may be enacted by Congress if writers and publishers are paid separately).

(6) Demo costs: To the extent approved by both parties in writing in advance, ____ shall pay for the cost of making demonstration records. ______ (___) of a pro rata share corresponding to your percentage of such total costs shall be deemed additional advances to you hereunder.

Above royalties to be prorated where only part of a composition is subject to this Agreement.

Dated:________________

TO WHOM IT MAY CONCERN:

This is to advise that we have entered into an exclusive administration agreement dated as of __________ with (Publisher) ("Administrator") for the ownership and administration of the musical composition entitled "________________" for the territory of the Universe, in perpetuity.

You are hereby authorized and directed to address all correspondence, inquiries, royalty statements, and royalty payments (regardless of when earned) to Administrator at the address it directs you.

Any such payments made by you pursuant to this authorization shall discharge you of any obligation to make any such payments to the undersigned.

The foregoing authorization shall remain in full force and effect until modified or terminated by both the undersigned and Administrator.

Very truly yours,

(Writer)

ASSIGNMENT

ASSIGNOR: (Writer)____________________

ASSIGNEE: (Publisher)__________________

PORTION
CONVEYED: ____________________

For valuable consideration, Assignor hereby assigns, transfers, sets over, and conveys to Assignees and their respective successors and assigns ____% of Assignor's interest in all right, title, and interest in and to the following musical composition(s):

[Name(s) of composition(s)]

including the copyrights and proprietary rights therein and in any and all versions of said musical composition(s), and any renewals and extensions thereof (whether available or subsequently available as the result of intervening legislation) in the United States of America and elsewhere throughout the world, and further including any and all causes of action for infringement of the same, past, present, and future, and all proceeds from the foregoing accrued and unpaid and hereafter accruing.

This Assignment includes the exclusive, worldwide right to administer and exploit ___% of Assignor's interest in and to said compositions in accordance with the terms and conditions of the Co-Publishing Agreement between the parties of even date herewith.

Assignor agrees to sign any and all other papers that may be required to effectuate the purpose and intent of this Assignment, and hereby irrevocably authorizes and appoints Assignee, his attorney and representative in its name or in his name as his true and lawful attorney-in-fact to take such actions and make, sign, execute, acknowledge, and deliver all such documents as may from time to time be necessary to convey to Assignee, its successors, and assigns, all rights granted herein.

IN WITNESS WHEREOF, the undersigned has executed the foregoing Assignment as of this ________ day of ______________, 20____.

By: (Writer)__________________

Appendix N-4

MUSIC PRODUCER AGREEMENT

(Company)

____
____
____

______, ____

(Producer)

____
____
____

Dear _____:

This will confirm the basic terms of the agreement between you ("Producer"), on the one hand, and us ("Company"), on the other hand, concerning Producer's being engaged to produce the artist currently professionally known as ________________ ("Artist"), as follows:

1. Company hereby engages Producer to produce __ (_) masters (the "Masters"), for Artist's ____ album (the "Album") pursuant to the respective Exclusive Recording Artist Agreement between Artist and Company (the "Recording Agreement"). It is understood that Company will not be obligated to include the Masters on the Album, nor to make any other use of Producer's services hereunder.

2. The term of this Agreement will commence as of the date hereof and shall continue until the satisfactory completion of all of Producer's services hereunder, subject to the ongoing obligations of the parties hereto that survive the expiration of the term hereof.

Producer will not commence recording until Company has approved the material to be recorded. Company's representatives will be notified of all sessions and be given the opportunity to attend. All aspects of the production, including but not limited to mixing, shall be subject to Company's approval.

3. In consideration for the satisfactory completion of all of Producer's services hereunder and for the rights granted herein, Company shall pay Producer the following compensation:

a. An "all-in" fund (i.e., inclusive of all recording costs and all fees to Producer or anyone working with Producer) of ____ Dollars ($______) for the Masters produced hereunder (the "Fund"). The Fund shall be payable one-half upon the commencement of recording of the applicable Masters, and the balance shall be paid within the later of execution of this Agreement and ten (10) business days of Producer's satisfactory delivery of the applicable fully completed, edited, and mixed Masters to and acceptance thereof by Artist and Company. For purposes of determining recoupment hereunder, _________ percent (__%) of the Fund will be deemed an advance ("Advance") fully recoupable from royalties (other than mechanical royalties) otherwise payable to Producer under this Agreement. Payment of the Fund and accounting and payment of royalties shall constitute full payment for, and to the extent applicable shall be deemed to be a prepayment for, all services rendered by Producer in connection with the Masters, including but not limited to as a musician, background vocalist, studio owner, and engineer.

b. With respect to exploitation of the Masters by Company or its licensees by means of records, Company will pay to Producer a royalty based on Net Sales of full-price Albums embodying the Masters sold for distribution through normal retail channels in the United States and not returned ("USNRC Net Sales"), determined by multiplying the suggested retail list price therefor by a royalty rate of ____ percent (_%). Producer's royalties hereunder shall be prorated based on a ratio, the numerator of which is the number of Masters produced hereunder and the denominator of which is the total number of royalty-bearing master recordings on the applicable record. Producer's royalties shall also be reduced by royalties payable to any coproducers of the Masters. With respect to all exploitations of the Masters other than in the form of USNRC Net Sales of full-priced Albums, Producer's royalties shall be calculated and adjusted (e.g., subject to the same proportionate deductions and reductions) in the same proportionate manner as Artist's corresponding royalties are calculated and adjusted under the Recording Agreement. With respect to royalties payable under the Recording Agreement that are calculated as a percentage of net receipts (e.g., flat-fee master-use licenses), Producer's royalty therefor shall be a proportionate share of such net receipts received by or credited to Artist computed according to the ratio that Producer's royalty rate hereunder bears to Artist basic U.S. royalty rate under the Recording Agreement (the "Producer's Percentage"). With respect to the commercial exploitation of audio/ visual recordings embodying any Masters produced hereunder, Producer's royalty therefor shall be an amount equal to ________ percent (__%) of the Producer's Percentage of the applicable royalty payable or credited to Artist therefor. No royalty shall be payable to Producer until such time as all Recording Costs for the Masters (as defined in the Recording Agreement) have been recouped at the so-called net artist rate (Artist's applicable basic royalty rate in the Recording Agreement, less Producer's royalty rate hereunder), at which time Producer shall receive Producer's royalties retroactive to the first record sold, subject to recoupment of the Advance at Producer's royalty rate hereunder.

c. Except as specifically defined herein, all terms used herein shall have the same meaning as set forth in the Recording Agreement. Extracts of the relevant provisions of the Recording Agreement shall be provided to Producer.

d. Company will account and pay Producer's royalties to Producer directly at the same times as Company accounts and pays Artist under the Recording Agreement. Producer shall have the right upon reasonable advance written notice to Company to inspect Company's books and records at Company's normal place of business during normal business hours, as the same may relate specifically to the royalties payable to Producer hereunder, provided that Producer shall: (i) only have the right to do so with respect to any royalty statement within __ year(s) of the date such statement was rendered, and only once with respect to any such statement, and (ii) not have the right to inspect Company's distributors' books or records. Without limiting the foregoing, if Company audits its distributors' books and records and recovers additional royalties for the Masters, Company shall promptly pay Producer Producer's share of such royalties after such recovery is received by or credited to Company, after deduction of a proportionate share of the costs of such audit.

4. Producer agrees to produce the Masters hereunder for the amount of the Fund. Accordingly, Producer shall be responsible for paying all recording costs incurred in connection with the Masters that exceed the Fund ("Overages") only if and to the extent the Overages were the fault of Producer's decisions or actions or lack thereof. Producer shall not be responsible for any Overages caused by Artist or Company's decisions or actions or lack thereof. To the extent Company pays any Overages that are Producer's responsibility, Producer agrees that Company may apply the second installment of the Fund and any record royalties payable to Producer hereunder against such repayment obligation.

5. a. Producer agrees to render all services pertaining to the production of the Masters, as and when reasonably requested by Artist and Company, and as may otherwise be necessary to produce and complete delivery of the fully completed Masters, commercially and technically satisfactory to Artist and Company, including but not limited to attending meetings, recording sessions, and all mixing and mastering sessions. Producer shall produce the Masters in all respects in accordance with the recording and delivery procedures and requirements reasonably requested by Company and otherwise as set forth in the Recording Agreement. This includes, but is not limited to, Producer's delivery of album mixes of the Masters delivered hereunder, plus clean/radio versions of each as needed, in such configurations as Company may reasonably request in the time periods set forth in the Recording Agreement.

b. Producer acknowledges that all performances rendered by Producer or anyone engaged by Producer that are embodied in the Master will be on a "work-for-hire" basis (as that term is commonly used in the music industry), and that, as between Company and Producer, the Masters shall be the sole and exclusive property of Company free from any claims by Producer or anyone deriving rights through Producer. If, for any reason, any such performances are not deemed to be work for hire, this Agreement shall operate as an irrevocable assignment of all rights thereto to Company and its licensees. Producer also hereby grants to Company and its licensees the right to use Producer's name, as well as Producer's approved likeness and approved biographical data, in connection with the exploitation of the Masters and the Album (and other records derived from the Masters).

c. Promptly after the execution hereof, Producer may provide Company with approved pictures of and biographical material concerning Producer that Producer would like used in connection with the Masters and the Album. Company shall have the right to reject said photographs and biographical material only on reasonable grounds. In the event that Company rejects the photographs and/or biographical material provided by Producer, Company may make available to Producer for Producer's approval photographs and biographical material concerning Producer to be used as set forth in this provision. Producer's approval of said materials shall not be unreasonably withheld and shall be deemed given unless Producer's disapproval is accompanied by a reasonable reason therefor, and has been received by Company within five (5) business days after such materials have been made available to Producer.

6. Producer warrants and represents that Producer has the authority and power to grant the rights granted herein, that Producer's contribution to the Masters will be entirely original, and that the use thereof shall not infringe upon the rights of any person, firm, or entity. Producer agrees to indemnify and hold Artist, Company, and their respective affiliates and assigns harmless from and against any claims that are inconsistent with the foregoing, or with any representations, obligations, or agreements in this Agreement. Without limiting the generality of the foregoing, the amount of any monies payable to Producer hereunder may be reduced by

the amount of any liability to which the foregoing indemnity relates. In addition, payment of such monies may be withheld pending the determination of any claim to which the foregoing indemnity relates, provided that the amount so withheld shall not exceed a good-faith estimate of the amount of the potential liability involved.

7. Producer agrees to promptly execute and deliver to Company at Company's sole cost any further documents that Company may reasonably request to evidence or effectuate the provisions hereof.

8. Producer agrees not to produce any Composition recorded hereunder for any other person for the purpose of making records for a period of ___ years from the date of delivery of the applicable Master hereunder.

9. Producer and Producer's publishers agree to be bound by the so-called controlled composition provisions in the Recording Agreement, and agrees to issue a mechanical license for their share of the compositions hereunder in accordance therewith, as well as free synch licenses for any promotional videos embodying the composition hereunder.

10. With respect to the Masters produced by Producer that are released on the Album (and any singles derived therefrom), Producer shall be entitled to receive appropriate credit as producer of the Masters, in substantially the following form: "Produced by ________." Such credit shall appear in the liner notes and/or back cover of the Album containing the Masters (and in singles derived therefrom if it is then Company's policy to accord producer credit on singles). Such credit shall also appear in all one-half (1/2) page or larger trade advertisements placed by Artist or Company with respect to the Album (and singles derived therefrom) embodying the Masters, subject to Company's then current policy with respect to such credit. Notwithstanding the foregoing, no inadvertent failure to provide said credit by Company shall be deemed to be a material breach of this Agreement, and Producer's sole remedy shall be to notify Company of such failure, in which event Company shall use reasonable efforts to rectify the failure on a prospective basis.

11. Company may assign all or part of this Agreement to any entity affiliated with or owned or controlled by Company or its affiliates or distributors. Producer may not assign any of Producer's obligations hereunder.

12. This Agreement is deemed to have been entered into and wholly performed in the State of ____, and its laws shall apply in its interpretation. The _____ Courts shall have sole jurisdiction over any action that either party brings against the other hereunder, and the parties hereby agree that any such action must be brought in _______ , _____ , and nowhere else. In the event of any action, suit, or proceeding by any party hereto against any other party hereto under this Agreement, the prevailing party shall be entitled to recover its attorneys' fees in addition to the cost of said action, suit, or proceeding.

13. It is currently contemplated that the parties hereto may elect to replace this Agreement at a later date with a more formal agreement embodying the foregoing terms and such other customary terms as may be agreed upon at that time. Until such time, if ever, as that more formal agreement is executed, this Agreement shall constitute the full and final expression of the agreement of the parties hereto with respect to the production of the Masters. All references to "Producer" hereunder shall refer to "_______" and to any entities entitled to furnish Producer's services.

14. Any so-called samples (i.e., third-party copyrighted material) that Producer wishes to incorporate into the Masters must be fully disclosed to Artist and Company and approved by Artist and Company in advance of any recording thereof. If such sample use is approved, Producer will not be responsible for any sample clearance fees or royalties payable to the owner of the original master recording, which shall nonetheless constitute recoupable recording costs; however, Producer shall be responsible for any fees or copyright participations to the owners of the underlying musical material. If such sample use is not approved, Producer will fully indemnify and hold Artist, Company, and their respective licensees harmless from any liability as a result of such use in accordance with paragraph 6 above.

If the foregoing reflects the understanding of the parties, please so indicate by signing in the spaces provided below.

Very truly yours,
(Company)

By: ______________________________
An Authorized Signatory

AGREED AND ACCEPTED BY:

By: (Producer)_______________
SS/ID#: ___________________

Appendix N-5

LOAN-OUT ACTOR AGREEMENT

The following agreement, dated as of ________, ____, shall constitute the terms and conditions of the agreement between _____________ ("Company") and __________________ ("Lender"), with respect to the services of ___________ ("Artist").

1. ENGAGEMENT. Company hereby engages Lender to furnish the services of Artist as an actor in the motion picture photoplay tentatively entitled "____________" ("Picture"), and Lender hereby accepts such engagement.

2. SERVICES. Lender hereby agrees to cause Artist to render all services as are required by Company hereunder and all services as are customarily rendered by actors in first-class feature-length theatrical motion pictures in the motion picture industry, as, when, and where required by Company, and to comply with all directions, requests, rules, and regulations of Company in connection therewith, whether or not the same involve matters of artistic taste or judgment.

3. TERM. Lender agrees to cause Artist to commence the rendition of Artist's services hereunder in connection with the principal photography of the Picture on a date to be designated by Company ("Start Date"), which is presently scheduled to be approximately ______, ____. Lender shall furnish the services of Artist on an exclusive basis for ______ (__) consecutive weeks thereafter ("Guaranteed Payment Period") or until completion of principal photography of the Picture, whichever shall be later.

4. COMPENSATION. On condition that Lender and Artist shall fully and faithfully perform all of the services, duties, and obligations required to be performed by Lender and Artist hereunder and that Lender and Artist are not in default hereunder, and subject to Company's rights of suspension and/or termination on account of Lender's and/or Artist's disability or default or an event of force majeure (as more particularly set forth in Exhibit "A"

attached hereto), Company agrees to pay Lender, and Lender agrees to accept, as full and complete compensation for all undertakings and services of Lender and Artist hereunder and for all of the rights granted to Company hereunder, the following:

(a) Minimum Compensation. The sum of __________ Dollars ($______) ("Minimum Compensation"), payable in approximately ____ (_) equal weekly installments (subject to Company's rights of suspension, extension, and termination hereunder), commencing on the Start Date.

(b) Overages. In the event that Company shall require Lender to cause Artist to render services in connection with the principal photography of the Picture beyond the expiration of the Guaranteed Payment Period, Company shall pay Lender the sum of ($_______) ("Overage Compensation") for each additional week of such services, prorated as hereinafter provided in the event of a partial week of service.

(c) Preproduction. Commencing on a date to be designated by Company, presently scheduled to be approximately ____, ____, Lender shall cause Artist to render exclusive services in connection with rehearsals, preproduction meetings, costume fittings, makeup, tests, publicity stills, and other customary preproduction services as, when, and where required by Company. Notwithstanding anything to the contrary contained in this Agreement, the Minimum Compensation specified in Paragraph 4(a) hereof shall also constitute full and complete consideration to Lender for all such preproduction services.

(d) Postproduction. Lender shall cause Artist to render Artist's services in connection with customary postproduction services for the Picture including, without limitation, looping, dubbing, retakes, added scenes, and reshooting for the Picture as, when, and where required by Company. If Artist shall be required to render postproduction services subsequent to the completion of Artist's services in connection with principal photography of the Picture or the expiration of the Guaranteed Payment Period, whichever is later, such services shall be subject to Artist's prior conflicting professional commitments, and Company shall pay the Overage Compensation to Lender for such services. Notwithstanding anything to the contrary contained herein, the Minimum Compensation specified in Paragraph 4(a) hereof shall also constitute full and complete consideration to Lender for the first three (3) days (consecutive or nonconsecutive, at Company's option) of Artist's looping and dubbing services.

(e) Nights, Sundays, Holidays, Work Time. No increased or additional compensation shall accrue or be payable to Lender by reason of the fact that any of Artist's services are rendered at night or on Sundays or holidays, or after the expiration of any particular number of hours of service in any period.

(f) Proration and Application of Compensation. For purposes of computing compensation hereunder for fractional weeks of service, the Overage Compensation shall be prorated on the basis of a five (5) day week with respect to services rendered at a studio or in the vicinity of ______ , ________ , and a six (6) day week with respect to services rendered on location. If Company is required, under any applicable collective bargaining agreement, to pay Lender compensation in addition to that provided in this Agreement, then such compensation shall be paid to Lender at the minimum applicable rates specified in such collective bargaining agreement. Notwithstanding anything to the contrary contained in this Agreement, to the extent permitted by any collective bargaining agreement, Company may apply any payments in excess of the minimum compensation required to be paid pursuant to said collective bargaining agreement against and in reduction of any additional payments that Company shall be required to make to Lender pursuant to any such collective bargaining agreement, and may likewise apply any such additional payments against such excess compensation.

(g) Agency Payment. All payments to Lender hereunder shall be paid to Lender in care of __________ , __________ , Attn: _____ , and Lender hereby authorizes Company to make all such payments as aforesaid.

(h) Contingent Compensation. Upon condition that Artist shall appear recognizably in the Picture as released in the role for which Artist is engaged hereunder, Lender shall be entitled to receive:

(i) A contingent deferment ("Deferment") in the amount of _________________ Dollars ($_____), payable, if at all, out of the first sums that would otherwise constitute "net profits" of the Picture (as "net profits" are hereinafter defined). The Deferment shall be payable pro rata with all other contingent deferments payable out of the first sums that would otherwise constitute "net profits" of the Picture.

(ii) An amount equal to ________ percent (_%) of one hundred percent (100%) of the "net profits" of the Picture.

Lender acknowledges that Company has granted to ____ Pictures ("_______") the right to distribute the Picture in any and all media throughout the universe, in perpetuity. "Net profits" shall be defined, computed, accounted for, and paid in accordance with ____'s standard definition of net profits. Company shall cause _____ to pay all sums due Lender pursuant to this Paragraph 4(e) directly to Lender. Company makes no representation that the Picture will generate any net profits, or any particular amount of net profits.

5. TRAVEL AND EXPENSES. If Company shall require Artist to render services hereunder at a location more than fifty (50) miles from Artist's principal residence ("Location"), Company shall provide Artist with the following:

(a) Transportation. One (1) round-trip air transportation, first-class if available and if used, between Artist's principal residence and the Location.

(b) Expenses. Reasonable living expenses not to exceed the sum of ________ Dollars ($_____) per week, prorated on the basis of a seven (7) day week, commencing on the date of Artist's arrival at the Location and continuing until Company advises Lender or Artist that it no longer requires Artist's services at the Location. Lender hereby authorizes Company to pay the foregoing expense allowance directly to Artist.

6. CREDIT. Upon condition that Lender and Artist shall fully and faithfully perform all of the services and obligations required to be performed by each of them hereunder, that Lender and Artist are not in default hereunder, and that Artist shall appear recognizably in the Picture as released, Artist shall receive credit:

(a) On Screen. On screen on a separate card and in no less than _____ position of all cast members.

(b) Paid Advertising. Subject to the customary exclusions and practices of Company, ____ and/or any third-party distributor(s) of the Picture, in paid advertising under the control of Company, in no less than _____ position of all cast members.

All other matters with respect to Artist's credit hereunder shall be determined in Company's sole discretion. Company shall have the right, but not the obligation, to accord Artist more prominent credit than that provided for herein. All references herein to the title of the Picture shall be deemed to mean the "regular" title unless reference is specifically made to the "artwork" title. No casual or inadvertent failure of Company to comply with the provisions of this paragraph, nor any failure by third parties to comply with their agreements with Company, shall constitute a breach of this Agreement by Company.

7. GRANT OF RIGHTS. Lender hereby grants to Company all rights of every kind and nature in, to, and with respect to, the results and proceeds of Lender's and Artist's services hereunder. Lender acknowledges that Company shall be the sole and exclusive owner of all rights in and to the Picture, including, without limitation, the copyright therein, and of all the results and proceeds of Lender's and Artist's services hereunder and shall have the right to use, exploit, advertise, exhibit, and otherwise turn to account any or all of the foregoing in any manner and in any media, whether now known or hereafter devised, throughout the world, in perpetuity, in all languages, as Company, in its sole and unfettered discretion, shall determine. Any materials written or contributed by Lender or Artist are intended by Lender, Artist, and Company to be a "work-made-for-hire" by Artist pursuant to Section 201 of Title 17 of the United States Code.

8. NAME AND LIKENESS. Lender hereby grants to Company the right to use Artist's name, likeness, and/or biography in connection with the production, exhibition, advertising, and other exploitation of the Picture and all subsidiary and ancillary rights therein, in any and all media, including, but not limited to, recordings (in any configuration) containing any material derived from the Picture, including, without limitation, all or any part of the soundtrack of the Picture, publications, merchandising, and commercial tie-ups;

provided, however, that in no event shall Artist be depicted as using or endorsing any product, commodity, or service without Artist's prior consent.

9. BREACH OF AGREEMENT. No act or omission of Company hereunder shall constitute an event of default or breach of this Agreement unless Lender shall first notify Company in writing setting forth such alleged breach or default and Company shall not cure the same within thirty (30) days after receipt of such notice. In the event of any breach by Company of this Agreement, Lender and Artist shall be limited to their remedy at law for damages, if any, and shall not have the right to terminate or rescind this Agreement or to enjoin or restrain in any way the production, distribution, advertising, or exploitation of the Picture, or any parts or elements thereof.

10. STANDARD TERMS. All other terms and conditions of Lender's engagement and Artist's services hereunder are set forth in the Standard Terms and Conditions attached hereto as Exhibit "A," which Standard Terms and Conditions are by this reference incorporated herein and made a part of this Agreement.

11. INSURANCE. Company shall have the right to apply for and take out, at Company's expense, life, health, accident, cast, or other insurance covering Artist, in any amount Company deems necessary to protect Company's interest hereunder. Artist shall assist Company in obtaining such insurance by submitting to usual and customary medical and other examinations, and by signing such applications, statements, and other instruments as may be reasonably required by any insurance company. In the event Artist fails or is unable to qualify for such insurance at customary rates, Company shall have the right to terminate this Agreement.

IN WITNESS WHEREOF, the parties hereto have executed this Agreement the day and year first above written.

"COMPANY"

By:______________________________

Its:______________________________

"LENDER"

By:______________________________
Its:______________________________

I have read and understand the foregoing agreement and confirm the authority of Lender to grant the rights granted therein and to furnish my services thereunder. As a material inducement to _________, I agree to abide and be personally bound by all of the terms and conditions thereof as though I were a direct party thereto. I shall look solely to Lender for the payment of any compensation that may be due me in connection with my services or grant of rights thereunder.

____

____
[name]

Exhibit "A"

STANDARD TERMS AND CONDITIONS

These Standard Terms and Conditions shall constitute a part of that certain agreement ("Underlying Agreement") dated as of ____, between ________________ ("Company") and ("Lender") relating to the services of ____________ ("Artist") in connection with the motion picture presently entitled "__________" ("Picture"). These Standard Terms and Conditions shall be deemed fully incorporated in said Underlying Agreement and these Standard Terms and Conditions and said Underlying Agreement shall hereinafter be collectively referred to as the "Agreement". All terms used in these Standard Terms and Conditions shall, unless expressly provided to the contrary herein, have the same respective meanings as set forth in the Underlying Agreement. Unless expressly provided to the contrary herein, to the extent that any provision of Standard Terms and Conditions conflicts with any provision of the Underlying Agreement, the Underlying Agreement shall control.

A-1. Default. Upon any breach by Lender or Artist of any of the provisions of this Agreement, Company shall immediately have the right, exercisable at any time after becoming aware of such breach, to suspend Lender's engagement hereunder and/or to terminate this Agreement by so notifying Lender in writing. Company's election to suspend this Agreement shall not affect its right thereafter to terminate this Agreement.

In the event of a suspension pursuant to this Paragraph A-1, Company's obligation to make the payments described in Paragraph 4 of the Underlying Agreement shall likewise be suspended. In the event of a termination pursuant to this Paragraph A-1, no further compensation shall be payable to Lender hereunder. The foregoing shall in no way limit any other remedy that Company may have against Lender, including, without limitation, the right to recover all monies theretofore paid to Lender.

A-2. Force Majeure. If the preparation or production of the Picture is hampered, interrupted, or prevented due to an event of force majeure (as that term is customarily defined in the motion picture and television industries), including, without limitation, an Act of God, war (whether declared or undeclared), riot, civil commotion, fire, casualty, strike (including a strike by the members of any guild or labor union), boycott, labor dispute, act of any federal, state, or local authority, the death, incapacity, or default of the director, director of photography, a principal member of the cast of the Picture, or other key personnel, or for any other similar or dissimilar reason beyond Company's reasonable control, Company shall have the right to suspend this Agreement while such event continues (and for such period after its abatement as may be required for Company to resume production of the Picture) and/or to terminate this Agreement. Company's election to suspend this Agreement shall not affect its right thereafter to terminate this Agreement.

In the event of a suspension pursuant to this Paragraph A-2, Company's obligation to make the payments described in Paragraph 4 of the Underlying Agreement shall likewise be suspended. In the event of a termination pursuant to this Paragraph A-2, Company and Lender shall each be released from all of their respective executory obligations hereunder and the Minimum Compensation, if any, theretofore accrued to Lender hereunder, when paid, shall be deemed payment in full of the compensation payable to Lender hereunder.

A-3. Disability. If Artist shall die or shall suffer any mental and/or physical injury, impairment, sickness, or other incapacity, or any physical disfigurement or any change (including, without limitation, any anticipated change) in voice or appearance (any of the foregoing being referred to as a "disability") that may or does detract from Lender's ability to furnish Artist's services to the full extent required by Company hereunder or Artist's performance of his or her services to the full extent required by Company hereunder, Company shall have the right to suspend this Agreement while such disability continues. In the event such suspension shall last longer than four (4) consecutive days or eight (8) days in the aggregate, Company shall have the right to terminate this Agreement. Company's election to suspend this Agreement shall not affect its right thereafter to terminate this Agreement.

In the event of a suspension pursuant to this Paragraph A-3, Company's obligations to make the payments described in Paragraph 4 of the Underlying Agreement shall likewise be suspended. In the event of a termination pursuant to this Paragraph A-3, Company and Lender shall each be released from all of their executory obligations hereunder and the Minimum Compensation, if any, theretofore accrued to Lender, when paid, shall be deemed payment in full of the compensation payable to Lender hereunder.

A-4. Postponement of Start Date. If any event of default, force majeure, or disability shall occur before the Start Date, the Start Date may be postponed for a period equal to the continuance of said event plus the period commencing upon the occurrence of such event and ending on the Start Date; provided, however, that Company shall have the right to reduce the period of postponement, in its sole and complete discretion, by giving Lender written notice of its election so to do.

A-5. Promotional Services. Lender shall cause Artist to be available, as, when, and where Company shall require, to participate in such publicity and promotional tours and activities, photo sessions, interviews, personal appearances, premieres, and the like (collectively, "Promotional Services") as Company may request and the Minimum Compensation specified in Paragraph 4(a) of the Underlying Agreement shall constitute full and complete consideration to Lender for such Promotional Services. The provisions of Paragraph 5 of the Underlying Agreement shall be applicable with respect to any services required of Artist pursuant to this Paragraph A-5.

A-6. No Obligation to Proceed. Nothing herein contained shall in any way obligate Company to use Lender's or Artist's services hereunder or to include the results and proceeds of Artist's services in the Picture or to produce, exhibit, advertise, or distribute the Picture; provided that nothing contained in this paragraph shall relieve Company of its obligation to pay Lender the amount of

Minimum Compensation specified in Paragraph 4(a) of the Underlying Agreement at the times and in the manner and subject to the conditions and contingencies described herein, and Company's obligations to Lender and Artist hereunder shall be deemed fully performed by payment to Lender of said amount.

A-7. Injunctive Relief. Lender acknowledges and agrees that the services to be rendered by Artist hereunder are of a special, unique, unusual, extraordinary, and intellectual character, making them difficult to replace and giving them a peculiar value, the loss of which cannot be reasonably compensated in damages in an action at law; that if Lender or Artist breaches any provision of this Agreement, Company will be caused irreparable damage; and that, therefore, Company shall be entitled, as a matter of right, at its election, to enforce this Agreement and all of the provisions hereof by injunction or other equitable relief.

A-8. Notices. All notices required hereunder shall be in writing and shall be given either by personal delivery, telegram, or telefax (toll prepaid) or by registered or certified mail (postage prepaid), and shall be deemed given hereunder on the date delivered, telegraphed, or telefaxed or a date forty-eight (48) hours after the date mailed. Until further notice, the addresses of the parties shall be as follows:

LENDER	COMPANY
____________________	____________________
____________________	____________________
____________________	____________________
With a Copy to	With a Copy to
____________________	____________________
____________________	____________________
____________________	____________________

A-9. Assignment. Company shall have the right to assign this Agreement, in whole or in part, in any manner and to any person, firm, or corporation that Company shall determine, and Company shall be relieved of its obligations to Lender and Artist hereunder by reason of such assignment. Lender shall not have the right to assign this Agreement.

A-10. Indemnification. Lender agrees at all times to defend, indemnify, and hold Company and __________, its and their parents, subsidiaries, affiliates, constituent corporations, and its and their employees, officers, agents, successors, licensees, and assigns, harmless from and against any and all liabilities, losses, claims, demands, costs, and expenses (including reasonable attorneys' fees and legal costs, whether or not litigation is actually commenced) arising out of any breach or alleged breach of any representation, warranty, or agreement made by Lender or Artist under this Agreement. Lender agrees that Company shall have the sole right to control litigation, including the right to select counsel of its choice and to compromise or settle any such claims, demands, or litigation.

A-11. Publicity. Lender and Artist warrant and agree that neither of them shall authorize the publication of any news story, magazine article, or other publicity or information of any kind or nature relating to the Picture or Artist's services hereunder or to Company or to any exhibitor or any distributor of the Picture without the prior written consent of Company in each instance; provided, however, that Lender may issue personal publicity concerning Artist in which the Picture is mentioned incidentally, so long as such references to the Picture are not derogatory.

A-12. Commitments to Others. Lender and Artist shall have no right or authority to and shall not employ any person in any capacity, nor contract for the purchase or rental of any article or material, or make any commitment, agreement, or obligation whereby Company shall be required to pay any monies or other consideration without Company's prior written consent in each instance.

A-13. Right to Withhold. Company shall have the right to deduct and withhold from any sums payable to Lender hereunder any amounts required to be deducted and withheld by Company pursuant to any present or future law, ordinance, or regulation of the United States of America, or of any state thereof or any subdivision of any state thereof, or of any other country, including, without limitation, any country wherein Artist performs any services hereunder, or pursuant to any present or future rule or regulation of any union or guild (if any) having jurisdiction over the services to be performed by Artist hereunder.

A-14. Lender's Agreement with Artist. Lender hereby represents and warrants that Lender is a duly organized and existing corporation and is presently in good standing under the laws of the state of its incorporation, that Lender has a valid, binding, and subsisting agreement with Artist pursuant to which Artist is obligated to render services exclusively to Lender for at least full term of this Agreement and that, by the terms of such agreement, Lender has the right to enter into this Agreement with Company for the furnishing of Artist's services hereunder and to grant to Company any and all of the services and rights herein set forth. Company shall pay directly to Lender all of the compensation that would have been payable to Artist had Artist rendered services directly to Company in the first instance, and Company shall not be obligated to make any payments of any nature whatsoever to Artist. In no event shall Lender's failure to pay any amounts to Artist be deemed to constitute a breach of this Agreement by Company.

Artist's services hereunder shall be rendered as Lender's employee, and Lender hereby agrees that Lender will fully perform and discharge, and that Company shall have no responsibility or liability on account of, any and all obligations of an employer with respect to Artist and Artist's services hereunder, including, but not limited to, the withholding and/or payment of any sums required to be withheld and/or paid by such employer to any governmental authority, or pursuant to any guild or union health, welfare, or pension plan, or on account of any other so-called fringe benefits, based on or resulting from the services rendered by Artist hereunder or the compensation paid to Lender for such services, and Lender agrees to and does hereby indemnify and hold Company harmless from and against any such liability or obligation.

A-15. Union Agreement and Membership. To the extent that any provisions of this Agreement conflict with the mandatory provisions of any collective bargaining agreement applicable to and binding upon Company in connection with the rendition of Artist's services hereunder ("Union Agreement"), the Union Agreement shall prevail; provided, however, that in such event the provision(s) of this Agreement so affected shall be curtailed and limited only to the extent necessary to permit compliance with the minimum mandatory terms and conditions of the Union Agreement. Company shall have the full benefit of all rights accorded employers under the Union Agreement. To the extent and during such period as it may be lawful for Company to require Artist to do so, Lender shall cause Artist to become and remain a member in good standing of any appropriate union(s), including, without limitation, the Screen Actors Guild. If Artist fails, neglects, or refuses to become a member in good standing of any such union(s), Company shall have the right at Company's sole election (in addition to its other rights and remedies hereunder) to terminate this Agreement or to pay on Artist's behalf any required dues, fees, or other payments to such union(s) and in the event of any such payment, Company may deduct the amounts paid by Company from any compensation otherwise payable to Lender hereunder. Company shall acquire the maximum rights permitted to be acquired by an employer pursuant to the Union Agreement. Artist agrees to the content of any and all waivers that Company may obtain from any relevant union.

A-16. Public Opinion. Lender warrants that Artist has conducted and will conduct himself or herself with due regard to public conventions and morals and has not done and will not do anything that will degrade him or her in society or bring him or her into public disrepute, contempt, scorn, or ridicule or that will shock, insult, or offend the community, public morals, or decency or prejudice Company or the motion picture industry in general. In the event of any breach of the terms of this Paragraph, Company may terminate this Agreement by written notice to Lender and thereupon be released of all further obligations hereunder.

A-17. Insurance. Company shall have the right to apply for and take out, at Company's expense, life, health, accident, cast, or other insurance covering Artist, in any amount Company deems necessary to protect Company's interest hereunder. Neither Lender nor Artist shall have any right, title, or interest in or to such insurance. Artist shall assist Company in obtaining such insurance by submitting to usual and customary medical and other examinations, and by signing such applications, statements, and other instruments as may be reasonably required by any insurance company. In the event Artist fails or is unable to qualify for such insurance at customary rates, Company shall have the right to terminate this Agreement. During the term of this Agreement, Artist shall not travel on any chartered or unscheduled airline or plane, unless requested to do so by Company, or engage in any conduct prohibited by any policy of insurance obtained by Company in accordance with this Paragraph A-17.

A-18. Effect of Expiration or Termination. Notwithstanding anything to the contrary contained in this Agreement, neither the expiration nor the termination of this Agreement for any reason shall affect the ownership by Company of the results and proceeds of the services rendered by Artist hereunder, or alter any of the rights or privileges of Company or any warranty, representation, covenant, or undertaking on the part of Lender or Artist hereunder.

A-19. Remedies. The remedies herein provided shall be deemed cumulative and the exercise of one shall not preclude the exercise of any other. Lender and Artist specifically agree that Company may recover by appropriate action the amount of the actual damage caused by Company by any failure, refusal, or neglect of Lender or Artist to keep and perform their agreements and warranties herein contained. No waiver by either of the parties hereto of any failure by the other party to keep or perform any covenant or condition of this Agreement shall be deemed to be a waiver of any preceding or succeeding breach of the same, or any other, covenant or condition.

A-20. Miscellaneous. This Agreement constitutes the entire agreement of the parties hereto with respect to the subject matter hereof and shall not be modified except by a written document executed by all parties. This Agreement shall be governed by and construed pursuant to the laws of the State of _______ applicable to agreements executed and to be performed entirely therein. Paragraph headings are for the convenience of the parties only and shall have no legal effect or validity.

Appendix N-6

SCREENWRITER AGREEMENT

<u>"Company"</u>

____

____

____

As of __________

<u>"Lender"</u>

____

____

____

Attention: __________

Re: _______________

Gentlemen:

This will confirm the agreement between _________ ("___") and _________ ("Lender") with respect to the writing services of _______________ ("Employee") in connection with a proposed motion picture tentatively entitled "_____________" ("Picture"), as follows:

A. <u>Condition Precedent:</u> All of _____'s obligations under this Agreement are conditioned upon ________________.

1. <u>Services</u>

(a) <u>Initial Commitment.</u> Lender shall cause Employee to write an [*original] first draft screenplay ("First Draft") and a set of revisions thereto ("Revisions") [*based upon assigned material in the form _______].

---

*As applicable.

(b) <u>Option.</u> At _______'s option, exercisable in its sole discretion ("Option"), Lender shall cause Employee to write a second draft of the screenplay ("Second Draft") and a complete polish ("Polish") thereof. ____ may exercise the Option at any time, provided that if ____ exercises the Option after expiration of the Option Period set forth in Paragraph 3 below, Employee's obligations under this subparagraph (b) shall be subject to Employee's professional availability.

2. <u>Compensation.</u> In full and complete consideration for all of Lender's and Employee's services hereunder and for all rights granted to ______ hereunder, and subject to _______'s rights of suspension and/or termination in the event of force majeure, disability, or default, Lender shall be entitled to the following compensation:

(a) <u>Fixed</u>

(i) For the First Draft and Revisions, __________ Dollars ($_____), payable as follows:

(A) $_____ on the later of Employee's commencement of writing services on the First Draft upon ______'s instruction to do so, and ______'s receipt of both an executed copy of this letter agreement and an executed copy of the Certificate of Authorship attached hereto;

(B) $_____ on delivery of the First Draft;

(C) $_____ on start of the Revisions; and

(D) $_____ on delivery of the Revisions.

(ii) If ______ exercises the Option, __________ Dollars ($_____), payable as follows:

(A) $_____ on start of the Second Draft;

(B) $_____ on delivery of the Second Draft;

(C) $_____ on start of the Polish; and

(D) $_____ on delivery of the Polish.

If ______ does not require a specific item of nonoptional material to be written hereunder (e.g., the Revisions, or the Polish if ______ has exercised the Option), payment for such item shall be made upon expiration of the immediately preceding reading period, provided that at any time thereafter, upon _______'s instruction Employee shall write and deliver said material to _______ within the applicable writing period thereafter, subject only to Employee's professional availability.

(b) Contingent

(i) Sole Writing Credit. If the Picture is produced and Employee receives sole "screenplay by" or sole "written by" credit in connection therewith in accordance with a final determination of credits under the applicable WGA Basic Agreement (other than pursuant to Paragraph 7 Theatrical Schedule A thereof) ("screenplay credit"), Lender shall be entitled to the following:

(A) An amount ("Sole Credit Bonus") equal to _________ Dollars ($_____) *less* all amounts previously paid to Lender for Employee's services; and

(B) An amount ("Sole Participation") equal to _____ percent (___ % of 100% of the net profits derived from the Picture.

(ii) Shared Writing Credit. If the Picture is produced and Employee received shared screenplay credit in connection therewith, Lender shall be entitled to the following:

(A) An amount ("Shared Credit Bonus") equal to ___________ (___) of the Sole Credit Bonus; and

(B) An amount ("Shared Participation") equal to ________ percent (__%) of 100% of the net profits derived from the Picture.

(c) Net Profits Definition. ________'s standard definition of net profits will apply, subject to any changes that are mutually agreed upon after good-faith negotiations.

(d) Notwithstanding anything to the contrary contained herein, to the maximum extent permitted under the WGA Agreement, all so-called residuals (e.g., for supplemental market exhibition or any other use of the Picture for which an additional payment is required pursuant to the WGA Agreement) shall be applied against and in reduction of the Sole or Shared Participation payable with respect to the Picture, and vice versa. Lender agrees that _______ shall have acquired the maximum rights permitted to be acquired by an employer pursuant to the WGA Agreement.

3. Reading and Writing Periods. The periods within which Lender shall cause Employee to deliver each item of material after ______'s instruction that Employee commence writing said material ("Writing Periods"), and ______'s reading and option periods, shall be as follows, it being agreed that Employee's services shall be exclusive to ______ during the Writing Periods and that time is of the essence with respect to Employee's delivery of the required material within the applicable Writing Period:

First Draft:	__ weeks
Reading Draft:	__ weeks
Revisions:	__ weeks
Option Period:	__ weeks
Second Draft:	__ weeks
Reading Period:	__ weeks
Polish:	__ weeks

4. Separation of Rights/Passive Payments.** If Employee is awarded sole "separation of rights" in accordance with the applicable provisions of the WGA Basic Agreement, Lender shall be entitled to the following in connection with a theatrical sequel or remake ("theatrical production"), or a U.S. network prime-time television series, MOW, or miniseries ("TV production") based upon the Picture, if and only if Employee does not render services in connection with said theatrical or TV production (the following amounts being inclusive of any amounts required to be paid pursuant to the WGA Agreement in connection with such productions):

(a) Theatrical Sequels: Amounts equal to the following:

(i) ______ (___) of the (A) applicable Fixed Compensation and (B) applicable Sole or Shared Credit Bonus; and

(ii) A percentage of the net profits (if any) of the sequel equal to ______ (___) of the applicable Sole or Shared Participation.

**If part of the deal.

(b) Theatrical Remakes: Amounts equal to the following:

(i) ______ (__) of the (A) applicable Fixed Compensation and (B) applicable Sole or Shared Credit Bonus; and

(ii) A percentage of the net profits (if any) of the remake equal to _______ (___) of the applicable Sole or Shared Participation.

(c) Network Prime-Time Television Series: For a U.S. network prime-time television series based on the Picture, the following applicable per-episode royalties, payable on a one-time basis within 10 days after telecast of the respective episode:

(i) 0-30 minutes $______

(ii) 31-60 minutes $______

(iii) over 60 minutes $______

(iv) An amount equal to ________ percent (__%) of the applicable per-episode royalty for the first five (5) reruns of each episode on U.S. prime-time network television, payable within 10 days after telecast of the respective rerun episode, such payment constituting payment in full for the sixth and all subsequent reruns of such episode.

(d) MOW or Mini-Series: For a U.S. network prime-time MOW or miniseries based on the Picture, a one-time royalty of _______ Dollars ($____) for the first two (2) hours as actually telecast and _______ Dollars ($____) for each additional hour as actually telecast (with a maximum payment for eight (8) hours), payable within 10 days after telecast of the applicable program.

(e) Novelization. If _________ desires to cause a novelization of the screenplay of the Picture to be published, ______ shall have the right to negotiate the publishing deal. If Employee is the "guild-named writer" for purposes of novelization rights pursuant to the WGA Agreement, the gross revenues received from the publisher shall be split ______ percent (__%) to ______ and ______ percent (__%) to Lender, after deducting "off-the-top" from such gross revenues all third-party payments (including without limitation payments to the novelizer and payments to any persons other than Employee entitled to separation of rights in connection with the Picture).

5. First Negotiation.** Provided that neither Lender nor Employee is in default hereunder and that Employee receives sole screenplay credit on the Picture, the following shall apply:

(a) Sequels and Remakes. If within ______ years following the initial release of the Picture, _____ elects to produce a theatrical sequel, theatrical remake, or television series pilot based upon the Picture, then, provided Employee is then active as a writer of theatrical motion pictures or television productions, as the case may be, and subject to ________'s standard terms, conditions, and contingencies (including without limitation network approval in the case of a TV series pilot), Employee shall have a right of first negotiation with respect to his/her writing services on the screenplay for the first such sequel, remake, or TV pilot, on terms not less favorable than those contained in this agreement with respect to a theatrical sequel or remake only.

(b) Surviving Obligations. If no agreement is reached under subparagraph (a) above for a given production within 10 days after negotiations with Employee begin, or if Employee is unavailable or declines to render services, ______ will have no further obligation to Employee except to the extent Employee is entitled to payments pursuant to Paragraph 4 above. In the event Employee does render services under this Paragraph 5, Employee's compensation pursuant to this paragraph shall be in lieu of the payments provided for with respect to that production pursuant to Paragraph 4 above.

6. Expenses. If _______ requires Employee to render services hereunder at a location more than 50 miles from Employee's permanent residence, Employee will be reimbursed for, or provided with, at _______'s election, first-class round-trip air transportation, if available, between Employee's permanent residence and such location, plus an allowance to cover all meals, lodging, ground transportation, and all other living expenses while at such location, in the amount of $______ per week in major metropolitan

**If part of the deal.

areas such as New York and London, $_____ per week in other major cities, and $______ per week elsewhere, prorated on the basis of a 7-day week.

7. Results and Proceeds. Lender and Employee acknowledge that all of the results and proceeds of Employee's services hereunder are and will be created by Employee as a "work-made-for-hire" specially ordered or commissioned by _____ with _____ being deemed the sole author of all such results and proceeds. Lender and Employee acknowledge that _____ is and shall be the sole and exclusive owner of all rights of every kind and nature in, to, and with respect to Employee's services hereunder and the results and proceeds thereof and that _____ shall have the right to use, refrain from using, change, modify, add to, subtract from, and exploit, advertise, exhibit, and otherwise turn to account any or all of the foregoing in any manner and in any or all media, whether now known or hereafter devised, throughout the world, in perpetuity, in all languages, as _____, in its sole discretion, shall determine. Employee hereby waives any and all so-called moral rights of authors.

8. No Injunctive Relief. In the event of a breach of this Agreement by ____, neither Lender nor Employee shall be entitled to rescind this Agreement or any of the rights granted to _____ hereunder, nor shall either of them be entitled to restrain, enjoin, or otherwise impair the exploitation of the Picture or any rights therein, Lender's and Employee's sole remedy being an action at law for damages.

9. Balance of Terms. All other terms and conditions of Employee's engagement shall be pursuant to _____'s standard terms and conditions, subject to any changes that are mutually agreed upon after good-faith negotiations. Said terms and conditions include, without limitation, grant of name and likeness rights in connection with the Picture, no obligation to proceed, WGA membership, and _______'s rights of suspension and/or termination in the event of force majeure, disability, or default. NOTE: MOST OF THE BASIC BOILERPLATE PROVISIONS FROM THE ACTOR AGREEMENT IN

APPENDIX N-5 (TO THE EXTENT NOT OTHERWISE ALREADY CONTAINED HEREIN OR OTHERWISE NOT APPLICABLE) MAY BE USED HEREIN.

Please indicate your agreement to the foregoing by executing this Agreement in the space provided below.

Very truly yours,
“ ”

By:________________________
An Authorized Signatory

ACCEPTED AND AGREED:
(“Lender”)

By:________________________

I have read and understand the foregoing agreement and confirm the authority of Lender to grant the rights granted therein and to furnish my services thereunder. As a material inducement to ________, I agree to abide and be personally bound by all of the terms and conditions thereof as though I were a direct party thereto. I shall look solely to Lender for the payment of any compensation that may be due me in connection with my services or grant of rights thereunder.

____

____
[name]

Appendix N-7

FILM PRODUCER AGREEMENT

The following Agreement, dated as of ________, ____, shall constitute the terms and conditions of the agreement between __________ ("Company") and ___________ ("Employee") in connection with that certain feature-length theatrical motion picture currently entitled _______________ ("Picture").

1. Employment: Company hereby employs Employee as a producer of the Picture pursuant to the terms and conditions hereof and Employee hereby accepts such employment.

2. Services: Employee shall render all services as are required by Company hereunder and all services as are customarily rendered by producers of first-class feature-length theatrical motion pictures in the motion picture industry, as, when, and where required by Company, and shall comply with all directions, requests, rules, and regulations of Company in connection therewith, whether or not the same involve matters of artistic taste or judgment. Employee shall use Employee's best efforts to cause the Picture to be produced in accordance with the approved budgets and production schedule for the Picture.

3. Term: The term of this Agreement shall commence as of the date hereof, and shall continue until the full and satisfactory completion of all services to be rendered by Employee hereunder or the earlier termination hereof, if any, by Company (as herein provided). Employee shall render services hereunder on an exclusive basis during the period commencing ___ (_) weeks prior to the scheduled date for commencement of principal photography for the Picture and continuing through the complete delivery of the Picture to the distributor, __________ ("_________"). At all other times during the term hereof, Employee shall render services on a nonexclusive, first-priority basis.

4. Compensation: Upon condition that Employee shall fully perform all services and obligations required to be performed by Employee hereunder and that Employee is not in default hereunder, and subject to Company's rights of suspension and/or termination on account of Employee's disability or default or an event of force majeure (as more particularly set forth in Exhibit "A" attached hereto), Company agrees to pay to Employee, as full and complete consideration for such services and for all rights transferred by Employee to Company hereunder, the following sums, at the following times:

(a) Fixed Compensation: The sum of ___________ Dollars ($_______) ("Fixed Compensation"), payable as follows:

(i) ____ percent (__%) thereof in equal weekly installments over the scheduled period for preproduction of the Picture;

(ii) ____ percent (__%) thereof in equal weekly installments over the scheduled period for principal photography of the Picture;

(iii) _____ percent (__%) thereof upon completion of dubbing and scoring of the Picture; and

(iv) ______ percent (__%) thereof upon complete delivery of the Picture, including television cover shots, to ___________.

(b) Contingent Compensation

(i) A contingent deferment ("Deferment") in the amount of ______________ Dollars ($_____), payable, if at all, out of the first sums that would otherwise constitute "net profits" of the Picture (as "net profits" are hereinafter defined). The Deferment shall be payable pro rata with all other contingent deferments payable out of the first sums that would otherwise constitute "net profits" of the Picture.

(ii) An amount equal to _____ percent (__%) of one hundred percent (100%) of the net profits of the Picture.

Employee acknowledges that Company has granted to _______ the right to distribute the Picture in any and all media throughout the universe, if accounted for and paid in accordance with _________'s standard definition of net profits. Company shall cause ___________ to pay all sums due to Employee. Company makes no representation that the Picture will generate any net profits, or any particular amount of net profits.

(c) Date of Payment: All payments of Fixed Compensation to Employee hereunder shall be made on Company's regular payday in the week following that week in which such payment shall have accrued.

(d) Agency Payment: All payments to Employee hereunder shall be made to Employee in case of ___________. Employee hereby authorizes Company to make all such payments as aforesaid.

5. Delivery; Length; Rating: Delivery of the Picture shall be in accordance with Company's customary delivery schedule, including the delivery of television cover shots as required to satisfy then prevailing network broadcast standards and practices. Employee shall deliver the Picture to _________, fully completed, no later than ____ (__) months following completion of principal photography of the Picture. The Picture, as delivered, shall (i) strictly adhere to the final approved shooting script (subject to such minor changes required by the exigencies of production); (ii) be no less than ______ (__) minutes in length; and (iii) qualify with the Motion Picture Association of America for a rating no more restrictive than "R."

6. Travel and Expenses: If Company shall require Employee to render services hereunder at a location more than fifty (50) miles outside Employee's principal residence ("Location"), then Company shall either provide Employee with, or reimburse Employee for (as Company shall determine), the cost of the following:

(a) Transportation: One (1) round-trip transportation, first-class, if available and if used, between Employee's principal residence and the Location.

(b) Expenses: Reasonable living expenses not to exceed the sum of _______ ($_____) per week, prorated on the basis of a seven (7) day week, commencing on the date of Employee's arrival at the Location and continuing until Company advises Employee that it no longer requires Employee's services at the Location.

7. Credit: Upon condition that Employee shall fully perform all of the services and obligations required to be performed by

Employee hereunder, and that Employee is not in default hereunder, Employee shall receive credit as a producer of the Picture, on screen, in the main titles (if other individuals are accorded credit in the main titles), and, subject to the customary exclusions and practices of Company, _________ and/or any third-party distributor(s) of the Picture, in all paid advertising under the control of Company.

All other matters with respect to Employee's credit shall be determined in Company's sole discretion. All references herein to the title of the Picture shall be deemed to mean the "regular" title unless such reference is specifically made to the "artwork" title. No casual or inadvertent failure to comply with the provisions of this paragraph or any failure by third parties to comply with their agreements with Company shall constitute a breach of this Agreement by Company.

8. <u>First Negotiation:</u> Upon condition that Employee shall fully perform all of the services and obligations required to be performed by Employee hereunder, that Employee is not in default hereunder, that Company has not engaged the services of any other producer in connection with the Picture, and that the final negative cost of the Picture was not in excess of one hundred percent (100%) of the final approved budgeted cost therefor, the following shall apply: If during the five (5) year period following the initial theatrical release of the Picture, (a) Company elects to produce a theatrical sequel or theatrical remake (as those terms are customarily defined in the motion picture industry) based upon the Picture, (b) Employee is still active as a producer in the motion picture industry, and (c) Employee is available as, when, and where required by Company, then Company shall notify Employee of such election and Employee shall be accorded the first opportunity to negotiate with Company with regard to producing the first such sequel or remake. If the foregoing conditions are met and Employee wishes to perform such producing services, Employee shall engage in good-faith negotiations for a period of ten (10) business days following said notice regarding the terms of Employee's engagement therefor, it being understood that, provided the budget for such sequel or remake equals or exceeds the final

approved budget for the Picture, Company shall offer Employee fixed compensation for producing such theatrical sequel or remake that is not less than the Fixed Compensation specified herein for Employee's producing services in connection with the Picture. If Company and Employee are unable to reach an agreement with respect to the terms of Employee's engagement for any such sequel or remake within said ten (10) business-day period, then Company shall have no further obligation to Employee in connection with any such sequels or remakes.

9. Grant of Rights: Employee hereby grants to Company all rights of every kind and nature in, to, and with respect to, the results and proceeds of Employee's services hereunder. Employee acknowledges that Company shall be the sole and exclusive owner of all rights in and to the Picture, including, without limitation, the copyright therein, and of all the results and proceeds of Employee's services hereunder and shall have the right to use, exploit, advertise, exhibit, and otherwise turn to account any or all of the foregoing in any manner and in any media, whether now known or hereafter devised, throughout the world, in perpetuity, in all languages, as Company, in its sole and unfettered discretion, shall determine. Any materials written or contributed by Employee are intended by Employee and Company to be a "work-made-for-hire" by Employee pursuant to Section 201 of Title 17 of the United States Code.

10. Name and Likeness: Employee hereby grants to Company the right to use Employee's name, likeness, and/or biography in connection with the production, exhibition, advertising, and other exploitation of the Picture and all subsidiary and ancillary rights therein, in any and all media, including, but not limited to, recordings (in any configuration) containing any material derived from the Picture, including, without limitation, all or any part of the soundtrack of the Picture, publications, merchandising, and commercial tie-ups; provided, however, that in no event shall Employee be depicted as using or endorsing any product, commodity, or service without Employee's prior consent.

11. Breach of Agreement: No act or omission of Company hereunder shall constitute an event of default or breach of this

Agreement unless Employee shall first notify Company in writing setting forth such alleged breach or default and Company shall not cure the same within thirty (30) days after receipt of such notice. In the event of any breach by Company of this Agreement, Employee shall be limited to Employee's remedy at law for damages, if any, and shall not have the right to terminate or rescind this Agreement or any rights granted herein or to enjoin or restrain in any way the production, distribution, advertising, or exploitation of the Picture, or any parts or elements thereof.

12. Standard Terms: All other terms and conditions of Employee's employment hereunder are set forth in the Standard Terms and Conditions attached hereto as Exhibit "A," which Standard Terms and Conditions are by this reference incorporated herein and made a part of this Agreement. NOTE: MOST OF THE BASIC BOILERPLATE PROVISIONS FROM THE ACTOR AGREEMENT IN APPENDIX N-5 (TO THE EXTENT NOT OTHERWISE ALREADY CONTAINED HEREIN OR OTHERWISE NOT APPLICABLE) MAY BE USED HEREIN.

IN WITNESS WHEREOF, the parties have hereunto set their hand as of the date and year first indicated above in ______, ___.

____

("Company")

By:____________________________

____

("Employee")

____

Appendix O

RELEASE AND COLLABORATION FORMS

Appendix O-1

RELEASE

For valuable consideration, the receipt of which I acknowledge, I irrevocably give my consent to and authorize ________ and anyone authorized by ___ (collectively "you") to record my audio and/or audiovisual performance(s) of the work entitled "_______" and to use such recordings and any and all biographical information, portraits, pictures, and likenesses of me and any reproductions thereof, in any media, throughout the universe, in perpetuity, with or without my name, for advertising purposes and for purposes of trade, including but not limited to the packaging and marketing of _________ and _________ in all forms, and for any other purposes. You will be the exclusive owner of all rights to my performances, which you may copyright in your name and use in any manner you choose in your sole discretion. I understand that I shall not be entitled to any additional compensation for my performances or any use thereof. I represent that I have the unrestricted power to grant the rights granted herein, and I agree to execute any further documents you may request to effectuate the terms of this Release, and to the extent I am not available to do so, I hereby grant you an irrevocable power of attorney to do so in my name.

Date:__________ Signature______________________________

Appendix O-2

COLLABORATION AGREEMENT

For good and valuable consideration, the receipt of which is hereby acknowledged, each of the undersigned hereby agree that the original work entitled "___________" ("_____________") was written by each of the undersigned in the following percentages: (Writer #1) _____%, (Writer #2) ______%. Without limiting the foregoing, the worldwide copyrights therein and all rights thereto shall be owned by each of the above Writers.

AGREED TO AND ACCEPTED:

(Writer #1)
Date:__________

(Writer #2)
Date:__________

Appendix P

COMPUTER SYSTEM CONFIGURATION
(As of Summer 2000)

Hardware	Full Tower Pentium III 333Mhz Workgroup System
	128MB RAM, 20GB internal Drive, 16MB ATI Video Accelerator 56K V.90 internal modem, Sound Blaster Sound Card and Speakers 10/100 Ethernet, Travan Tape Backup System, 10/100 Ethernet Switch Windows 98 Rev. B
	HP 4000NT Workgroup Printer
Software	Microsoft Office Professional 2000 TimeSlips Accounting WinPopup—Interoffice Communications
Internet	Earthlink Dialup Access Netscape Communicator Microsoft Outlook

Index

Selected Books From . . .
THE ABA LAW PRACTICE MANAGEMENT SECTION

Law Firm Partnership Guide: Strengthening Your Firm. Addresses what to do after your firm is up and running, including how to handle: change, financial problems, governance issues, compensating firm owners, and leadership.

Law Law Law on the Internet. Presents the most influential law-related Web sites. Features Web site reviews of the *National Law Journal's 250*, so you can save time surfing the Net and quickly find the information you need.

Law Office Policy and Procedures Manual, 4th Ed. A model for law office policies and procedures (includes diskette). Covers law office organization, management, personnel policies, financial management, technology, and communications systems.

Law Office Staff Manual for Solos and Small Firms. Use this manual as is or customize it using the book's diskette. Includes general office policies on confidentiality, employee compensation, sick leave, sexual harassment, billing, and more.

The Lawyer's Guide to Creating Web Pages. A practical guide that clearly explains HTML, covers how to design a Web site, and introduces Web-authoring tools.

The Lawyer's Guide to the Internet. A guide to what the Internet is (and isn't), how it applies to the legal profession, and the different ways it can—and should—be used.

The Lawyer's Guide to Marketing on the Internet. This book talks about the pluses and minuses of marketing on the Internet, as well as how to develop an Internet marketing plan.

The Lawyer's Quick Guide to E-Mail. Covers basic and intermediate topics, including setting up an e-mail program, sending messages, managing received messages, using mailing lists, security, and more.

The Lawyer's Quick Guide to Microsoft® Internet Explorer; The Lawyer's Quick Guide to Netscape® Navigator. These two guides de-mystify the most popular Internet browsers. Four quick and easy lessons include: Basic Navigation, Setting a Bookmark, Browsing with a Purpose, and Keeping What You Find.

The Lawyer's Quick Guide to Timeslips®. Filled with practical examples, this guide uses three short, interactive lessons to show to efficiently use Timeslips.

The Lawyer's Quick Guide to WordPerfect® 7.0/8.0 for Windows®. Covers multitasking, entering and editing text, formatting letters, creating briefs, and more. Includes a diskette with practice exercises and word templates.

Leaders' Digest: A Review of the Best Books on Leadership. This book will help you find the best books on leadership to help you achieve extraordinary and exceptional leadership skills.

Living with the Law: Strategies to Avoid Burnout and Create Balance. Examines ways to manage stress, make the practice of law more satisfying, and improve client service.

Marketing Success Stories. This collection of anecdotes provides an inside look at how successful lawyers market themselves, their practice specialties, their firms, and their profession.

Microsoft® Word for Windows® in One Hour for Lawyers. Uses four easy lessons to help you prepare, save, and edit a basic document in Word.

Practicing Law Without Clients: Making a Living as a Freelance Lawyer. Describes freelance legal researching, writing, and consulting opportunities that are available to lawyers.

Quicken® in One Hour for Lawyers. With quick, concise instructions, this book explains the basics of Quicken and how to use the program to detect and analyze financial problems.

Risk Management. Presents practical ways to asses your level of risk, improve client services, and avoid mistakes that can lead to costly malpractice claims, civil liability, or discipline. Includes Law Firm Quality/In Control (QUIC) Surveys on diskette and other tools to help you perform a self-audit.

Running a Law Practice on a Shoestring. Offers a crash course in successful entrepreneurship. Features money-saving tips on office space, computer equipment, travel, furniture, staffing, and more.

Successful Client Newsletters. Written for lawyers, editors, writers, and marketers, this book can help you to start a newsletter from scratch, redesign an existing one, or improve your current practices in design, production, and marketing.

Survival Guide for Road Warriors. A guide to using a notebook computer (laptop) and other technology to improve your productivity in your office, on the road, in the courtroom, or at home.

Telecommuting for Lawyers. Discover methods for implementing a successful telecommuting program that can lead to increased productivity, improved work product, higher revenues, lower overhead costs, and better communications. Addressing both law firms and telecommuters, this guide covers start-up, budgeting, setting policies, selecting participants, training, and technology.

Through the Client's Eyes. Includes an overview of client relations and sample letters, surveys, and self-assessment questions to gauge your client relations acumen.

Time Matters® in One Hour for Lawyers. Employs quick, easy lessons to show you how to: add contacts, cases, and notes to Time Matters; work with events and the calendar; and integrate your data into a case management system that suits your needs.

Wills, Trusts, and Technology. Reveals why you should automate your estates practice; identifies what should be automated; explains how to select the right software; and helps you get up and running with the software you select.

Win-Win Billing Strategies. Prepared by a blue-ribbon ABA task force of practicing lawyers, corporate counsel, and management consultants, this book explores what constitutes "value" and how to bill for it. You'll understand how to get fair compensation for your work and communicate and justify fees to cost-conscious clients.

Women Rainmakers' 101+ Best Marketing Tips. A collection of over 130 marketing from women rainmakers throughout the country. Features tips on image, networking, public relations, and advertising.

Year 2000 Problem and the Legal Profession. In clear, nontechnical terms, this book will help you identify, address, and meet the challenges that Y2K poses to the legal industry.

Order Form

Qty	Title	LPM Price	Regular Price	Total
______	ABA Guide to International Business Negotiations (5110331)	$ 74.95	$ 84.95	$________
______	ABA Guide to Lawyer Trust Accounts (5110374)	69.95	79.95	$________
______	ABA Guide to Legal Marketing (5110341)	69.95	79.95	$________
______	ABA Guide to Prof. Managers in the Law Office (5110373)	69.95	79.95	$________
______	Anatomy of a Law Firm Merger, Second Edition (5110434)	74.95	89.95	$________
______	Billing Innovations (5110366)	124.95	144.95	$________
______	Changing Jobs, 3rd Ed.	*please call for information*		$________
______	Compensation Plans for Lawyers, 3rd Ed. (5110452)	84.95	99.95	$________
______	Complete Guide to Marketing Your Law Practice (5110428)	74.95	89.95	$________
______	Complete Internet Handbook for Lawyers (5110413)	39.95	49.95	$________
______	Computerized Case Management Systems (5110409)	39.95	49.95	$________
______	Connecting with Your Client (5110378)	54.95	64.95	$________
______	Do-It-Yourself Public Relations (5110352)	69.95	79.95	$________
______	Easy Self Audits for the Busy Law Firm	*please call for information*		$________
______	Finding the Right Lawyer (5110339)	14.95	14.95	$________
______	Flying Solo, 2nd Ed. (5110328)	29.95	34.95	$________
______	Handling Personnel Issues in the Law Office (5110381)	59.95	69.95	$________
______	HotDocs® in One Hour for Lawyers (5110403)	29.95	34.95	$________
______	How to Build and Manage an Employment Law Practice (5110389)	44.95	54.95	$________
______	How to Build and Manage an Estates Law Practice	*please call for information*		$________
______	How to Build and Manage a Personal Injury Practice (5110386)	44.95	54.95	$________
______	How to Draft Bills Clients Rush to Pay (5110344)	39.95	49.95	$________
______	How to Start & Build a Law Practice, Millennium Fourth Edition (5110415)	47.95	54.95	$________
______	Internet Fact Finder for Lawyers (5110399)	34.95	39.95	$________
______	Law Firm Partnership Guide: Getting Started (5110363)	64.95	74.95	$________
______	Law Firm Partnership Guide: Strengthening Your Firm (5110391)	64.95	74.95	$________
______	Law Law Law on the Internet (5110400)	34.95	39.95	$________
______	Law Office Policy & Procedures Manual, 4th Ed. (5110441)	99.95	119.95	$________
______	Law Office Staff Manual for Solos & Small Firms (5110445)	59.95	69.95	$________
______	Lawyer's Guide to Creating Web Pages (5110383)	54.95	64.95	$________
______	Lawyer's Guide to the Internet (5110343)	24.95	29.95	$________
______	Lawyer's Guide to Marketing on the Internet (5110371)	54.95	64.95	$________
______	Lawyer's Quick Guide to E-Mail (5110406)	34.95	39.95	$________
______	Lawyer's Quick Guide to Microsoft Internet® Explorer (5110392)	24.95	29.95	$________
______	Lawyer's Quick Guide to Netscape® Navigator (5110384)	24.95	29.95	$________
______	Lawyer's Quick Guide to Timeslips® (5110405)	34.95	39.95	$________
______	Lawyer's Quick Guide to WordPerfect® 7.0/8.0 (5110395)	34.95	39.95	$________
______	Leaders' Digest (5110356)	49.95	59.95	$________
______	Living with the Law (5110379)	59.95	69.95	$________
______	Marketing Success Stories (5110382)	79.95	89.95	$________
______	Microsoft® Word for Windows® in One Hour for Lawyers (5110358)	19.95	29.95	$________
______	Practicing Law Without Clients (5110376)	49.95	59.95	$________
______	Quicken® in One Hour for Lawyers (5110380)	19.95	29.95	$________
______	Risk Management (5610123)	69.95	79.95	$________
______	Running a Law Practice on a Shoestring (5110387)	39.95	49.95	$________
______	Successful Client Newsletters (5110396)	39.95	44.95	$________
______	Survival Guide for Road Warriors (5110362)	24.95	29.95	$________
______	Telecommuting for Lawyers (5110401)	39.95	49.95	$________
______	Through the Client's Eyes (5110337)	69.95	79.95	$________
______	Time Matters® in One Hour for Lawyers (5110402)	29.95	34.95	$________
______	Wills, Trusts, and Technology (5430377)	74.95	84.95	$________
______	Win-Win Billing Strategies (5110304)	89.95	99.95	$________
______	Women Rainmakers' 101+ Best Marketing Tips (5110336)	14.95	19.95	$________
______	Year 2000 Problem and the Legal Profession (5110410)	24.95	29.95	$________

***Handling**
$10.00-$24.99....................$3.95
$25.00-$49.99....................$4.95
$50.00+$5.95

****Tax**
DC residents add 5.75%
IL residents add 8.75%
MD residents add 5%

Subtotal	$________
***Handling**	$________
****Tax**	$________
TOTAL	$________

PAYMENT

☐ Check enclosed (to the ABA) ☐ Bill Me
☐ Visa ☐ MasterCard ☐ American Express

Account Number ______ Exp. Date ______ Signature ______

Name ______ Firm ______
Address ______
City ______ State ______ Zip ______
Phone Number ______ E-Mail Address ______

Mail: ABA Publication Orders, P.O. Box 10892, Chicago, Illinois 60610-0892 ♦ Phone: (800) 285-2221 ♦ FAX: (312) 988-5568

E-Mail: abasvcctr@abanet.org ♦ Internet: http://www.abanet.org/lpm/catalo

Source Code: 22AEND499

THE SECTION OF LAW PRACTICE MANAGEMENT

CUSTOMER COMMENT FORM

ABA

Title of Book: ____________________

We've tried to make this publication as useful, accurate, and readable as possible. Please take 5 minutes to tell us if we succeeded. Your comments and suggestions will help us improve our publications. Thank you!

1. How did you acquire this publication:

- ☐ by mail order
- ☐ at a meeting/convention
- ☐ as a gift
- ☐ by phone order
- ☐ at a bookstore
- ☐ don't know
- ☐ other: (describe) ____________________

Please rate this publication as follows:

	Excellent	Good	Fair	Poor	Not Applicable
Readability: Was the book easy to read and understand?	☐	☐	☐	☐	☐
Examples/Cases: Were they helpful, practical? Were there enough?	☐	☐	☐	☐	☐
Content: Did the book meet your expectations? Did it cover the subject adequately?	☐	☐	☐	☐	☐
Organization and clarity: Was the sequence of text logical? Was it easy to find what you wanted to know?	☐	☐	☐	☐	☐
Illustrations/forms/checklists: Were they clear and useful? Were there enough?	☐	☐	☐	☐	☐
Physical attractiveness: What did you think of the appearance of the publication (typesetting, printing, etc.)?	☐	☐	☐	☐	☐

Would you recommend this book to another attorney/administrator? ☐ Yes ☐ No

How could this publication be improved? What else would you like to see in it?

____

Do you have other comments or suggestions? ____________________

Name ____________________

Firm/Company ____________________

Address ____________________

City/State/Zip ____________________

Phone ____________________

Firm Size: ____________ Area of specialization: ____________

We appreciate your time and help.

Fold

NO POSTAGE
NECESSARY
IF MAILED
IN THE
UNITED STATES

BUSINESS REPLY MAIL
FIRST CLASS PERMIT NO. 16471 CHICAGO, ILLINOIS

POSTAGE WILL BE PAID BY ADDRESSEE

AMERICAN BAR ASSOCIATION
PPM, 8th FLOOR
750 N. LAKE SHORE DRIVE
CHICAGO, ILLINOIS 60611-9851

Fold